Christ at the Crux

CHRIST AT THE CRUX

The Mediation of God and Creation
in Christological Perspective

PAUL CUMIN

☙PICKWICK *Publications* • Eugene, Oregon

CHRIST AT THE CRUX
The Mediation of God and Creation in Christological Perspective

Copyright © 2014 Paul Cumin. All rights reserved. Except for brief quotations in critical publications or reviews, no part of this book may be reproduced in any manner without prior written permission from the publisher. Write: Permissions. Wipf and Stock Publishers, 199 W. 8th Ave., Suite 3, Eugene, OR 97401.

Pickwick Publications
An Imprint of Wipf and Stock Publishers
199 W. 8th Ave., Suite 3
Eugene, OR 97401

www.wipfandstock.com

ISBN 13: 978-1-62032-595-7

Cataloguing-in-Publication Data

Cumin, Paul.

    Christ at the crux : the mediation of God and creation in christological perspective / by Paul Cumin.

    X + Y p. ; 23 cm. Includes bibliographical references.

    ISBN 13: 978-1-62032-595-7

    1. Jesus Christ—Mediation. 2. Mediation—Religious aspects—Christianity. I. Title.

BT255 .C86 2014

Manufactured in the U.S.A.

CONTENTS

Acknowledments | vii

Introduction: God for the Time Being—The Need for a Concept of Mediation | ix

1 Irenaeus and the Gnostic Option: Monism, Duality, and the "Two hands" of God (A Trinitarian Concept of Mediation) | 1

2 Cyril of Alexandria and the Nestorian Option: *Theotokos, Communicatio Idiomatum*, and the Single Subjectivity of Christ (A Soteriological Concept of Mediation) | 26

3 John Philoponus and the Miaphysite Option: *Creatio ex nihilo* and Substantiality after Chalcedon (A Cosmological Concept of Mediation) | 53

4 Martin Luther and the Problem of Distant Grace: Faith, Jesus, and the Immediacy of God (A "Theological" Concept of Mediation) | 71

5 John Calvin and the Problem of a *Logos Asarkos*: When Creation and Revelation Collide (An Ontological Concept of Mediation) | 96

6 Robert Jenson and the Spirit of It All: Christ as Space-time (A Dialectical Concept of Mediation) | 128

7 John Zizioulas and Being Free: Christ as Personal Paradigm (An Existential Concept of Mediation) | 151

8 Colin Gunton and the Integrity of Creation: Christ as a Particular Human (An Economic Concept of Mediation) | 169

Conclusion: God for the Time-being: The Need for a Christological Concept of Mediation | 197

Bibliography | 211

ACKNOWLEDGMENTS

I WOULD HAVE LIKED more help from Colin Gunton on this project, but he died halfway through its first draft. Even so, he inspired the whole, and if I can remain faithful with pulpit and pen for as long as he did, he will have inspired that too. Before him, James Houston, Stanley Grenz, John Franke, and Eugene Peterson were models to me of theological minds in service of the church. Murray Rae and Christoph Schwöbel adopted me and this project when I had very nearly lost my way. Some special thanks are due to Sandra Fach for her faithful friendship from the beginnings to the final editions. Along with her, Derek Brower, Lincoln Harvey, Chris and Hannah Roberts, Diarmuid ONeill, Douglas Knight, Rufus Burton, Brian Brock, Devin Henry, and Paul Dafydd Jones provided theological fellowship with momentum enough to sustain me still. I am indebted to the Research Institute in Systematic Theology at King's College, London, and especially to the patriarchs once within and near it: Steve Holmes, Michael Banner, John Webster, Alan Torrance, Thomas Weinandy, and Robert Jenson.

There were churches of support, too: Westminster Bible Chapel, Highgate International Church, and Pemberton Community Church each in turn sustained me. For their encouragment, generosity, and kindness, I thank Duncan and Carol Hay, Larry and Margaret Reimer, Bernie Wessling, Jenny Gunton, Frank and Katja Schlichtenbrede, and Moira Langston.

I gratefully acknowledge the various supports provided by The Calling Foundation, Goodenough College London, The German Academic Exchange Service (DAAD), the Ökumenisches Institut at the University of Heidelberg, and the staff and faculty of the Mennonite Brethren Biblical Seminary at Trinity Western University. The editorial staff of Wipf and Stock have been immensely helpful through an unexpectedly long process; in particular, I owe thanks to Dave Belcher, for his astute perseverance and excruciatingly careful attention to detail.

Earlier forms of the final three chapters have appeard, respectively, in *The Scottish Journal of Theology*, *The International Journal of Systematic Theology*, and *The Theology of Colin Gunton*, ed. Harvey (T. & T. Clark, 2010).

Readers will soon discover that among the weaknesses of this book is its ambitious scope. For all the other shortcomings I accept full responsibility, but for this one I would like to share onus with many of the people named above. They made Christian faith grand and mysterious at a time in my life, and maybe at a time in history, when every other pressure was to the contrary.

My wife, it seems, is a farmer. Yet in the dozen years behind this book she persevered in three different cities, in three different countries, all while becoming a mother three times over. And she did it with strength and style. I would dedicate this book to her but that would not suit; instead, I built her a barn (Mennonite-style, with Mike Fidork, Bert VanDeWetering, and many others). True, the barn is not quite finished, but then neither, really, is this.

Stl'atl'imx Territory, British Columbia, Spring, 2014

Introduction

GOD FOR THE TIME BEING
The Need for a Concept of Mediation

> Make yourself thoroughly, intuitively, master of the exceeding difficulties of admitting a one Ground of the Universe (which, however, *must* be admitted) and yet finding *room* for anything else.
>
> —S. T. Coleridge

How can theology say that God is other than the universe and also present within it in a way that compromises neither claim? Most modern thought has offered a simple reply: it cannot. Having tired of the cramped conditions afforded them by the Oversized Passenger in the adjacent seat, many today have simply returned their tickets and opted for an alternate train of thought. The complaint was widespread and plain: God takes up too much space. The existence of an all-powerful Creator is seen by many today to be so monolithic a belief that it displaces the possibility of contingency or an open future, and it leaves no room for even basic human freedom.

The distaste for divine transcendence has become so prevalent that it has even congealed into popular clichés. Now we are almost naturally repulsed by the idea of an oppressive Other or by the violence supposedly concomitant in totalizing metanarratives. And does not theology, by definition, involve precisely this kind of talk—large-scale stories about an all-powerful protagonist with the world and its inhabitants as only passive props in some larger plot?

How could theology possibly survive in such an intellectual climate?

If there is such a discipline alive anymore it is by virtue of at least one crucial development. The practice of constructive theology in the modern West was arguably refueled by the same anti-metaphysical reaction intended to burn it down.[1] Whereas the doctrine of God before the nineteenth century was almost entirely content with what is usually called deism, there has since then been a major recovery of the centrality of the doctrine of the Trinity. Beginning perhaps with Hegel and coming closer to mainstream orthodoxy through Karl Barth, theology about the Trinity is now thought by many to be no longer an awkward appendix to the doctrine of God but rather somehow its starting point.

The results have been immense. With what may seem like a rather straightforward dogmatic shuffle, there was opened the possibility to both accept and benefit from the late- or post-modern anti-metaphysical critique. At a time when the concept of God was widely believed to be either ontologically stifling or epistemologically redundant, modern theology has, for the most part, resisted the expected death-throe reflex. It now seems clear that the cut of the atheist critique marks not the end of God but the end of a certain kind of theology. Consequently, there is little talk anymore of a wholly transcendent God, simple in himself and timelessly unchanging. Instead, developments in Trinitarian theology have allowed the discovery—or indeed, rediscovery—of a way to have at the same time two things formerly presumed exclusive. Now there seems to be, in the words of Wolfhart Pannenberg, a "conceptual possibility for connecting the eternal self-identity of God with a becoming in time."[2] Pannenberg's observation raises the issue driving this book: the question about how the eternal Creator can be related to a temporal world in a way that compromises neither divine freedom nor the real integrity of creation.

From its earliest days, many within the church have struggled to confess Christ in a way that affirms and distinguishes his full deity and his full humanity. What we will discover in the course of this study is that various attempts to confess the relation of what would come to be called the "two natures" of Christ represent various attempts to answer

---

1. This and some of the claims made in the next paragraphs follow Pannenberg, "Problems of a Trinitarian Doctrine of God."

2. Ibid., 251.

the broader question about the relation of divine and contingent being. What follows is a study of the Christologies of eight thinkers for whom there is a link between theology about Christ and that about God's relation to the world. I will contrast each interlocutor's views with those of their broader theological context, and in so doing engage some of the most difficult aspects of the question about God's relation to everything other than him.

Although there may be other ways to grapple with this, I will use the concept of *mediation* to keep both poles of the issue together. At its most basic, all that is meant by "mediation" is exactly what the question demands; namely, a way of asking how God might be other than the world in a way that does not mean he is unrelated to it, and at the same time related to the world in a way that does not mean he is indistinguishable from it.

Once we have a grip on the question of mediation, we will need to enquire after some kind or kinds of media*tor*. At one level, the concept of mediation is already the claim that there is such a thing—a mediator—but how do we understand this? If this mediator is *between* the Creator and the creation, is he then neither of these? Or, as Christian theology would have it, is he somehow both? But how can that be possible? And, if the mediator is divine *and* human, is mediation something he does or something he *is*? What we will discover is that although there are well-worn routes through these questions, not all of the traditional paths arrive at their intended goals.

∼

It is the modern malaise to imagine we can neatly separate subject from object in our pursuit of knowledge. And even though the integrity of this study will depend on this distinction—I will indeed attempt to focus our attention on the way God and creation have their being as opposed to how we might come to know about this kind of relation—we will not get far without realizing that a separation of subject from object in theology is a capitulation to atheism: unless the Creator as our object somehow affects we creatures as subjects, whatever we are doing cannot possibly have any purchase on the way God and the world might actually exist.

This raises the question about the relation between "revelational" mediation and my more thorny and central concern about *ontological* mediation. Talk of the being of God and the world in any meaningful way requires some reason for thinking this kind of knowledge is possible in the first place. And although this is to get to the content of this study while only trying to describe its shape, I will here say at least this much: knowledge about God from within the world is possible only because this God as other than this world somehow makes it possible. The one making a theological claim about God must be enabled by God to make it meaningfully. And this idea is itself a version of my question: if God were not other than the world, there would be neither anyone to make knowledge of him possible nor anything to know other than ourselves. And conversely, if God were not somehow related to this world, there would be neither anyone here to help us know him, nor any reason to bother trying. In other words, knowledge of a mediatorial dynamic of God and the world depends for its possibility on its own actuality.

This need not be entirely convincing at this point in order to serve its purpose here of simply sketching the dilemma. The point is about the very close relation of revelation and ontology in this study, and the way that these pivot together on how it is that God is both distinct from and in relation to the creation.

Having set up the distinction between revelational and ontological mediation for the sake of describing our course, I can now say that the difference between the two is dubious at best. Since Barth, it has become almost a theological truism that God reveals *himself* and not just something *about* himself. Yet, as is becoming increasingly clear, too far in this direction and there is soon little if any difference between God's being and act. This is problematic on a number of fronts but perhaps most significant are the tensions it brings to a doctrine of creation. What does it mean to be a creature if the very creation of which you are a part is also the way the Creator meets his identity?

Consider three questions:

1. Would unmediated presence in God mean the realization or the annihilation of human being?
2. Is immediate knowledge of God the aim of theology or its opposite (that is, some form of sin)?

Those two questions may in fact be the same one asked differently, so a third to help sharpen the dilemma:

3. Is distinction from our Creator our existential problem or the premise of our existence?

We will find that answers to these apparently simple questions are themselves anything but. On the one hand, we will engage elements in the Christian tradition that suggest some kind of immediacy with God is our ultimate purpose, and the ontological or existential space between God and us now is due to our alienation from him. On the other hand, we will see that some in the Church have thought nearly the opposite, as if the mediation of God and world is itself the possibility of creatures, and therefore its undoing would be ours.

Even though I may have defined "mediation" well enough to begin this study, it remains to be seen whether this definition sets the terms of the dilemma or somehow describes its cause.

∼

I suspect that prior to my readers' interest in such large questions will be more preliminary ones about how this project aims to tackle them. Indeed, a journey across such broad terrain should not begin without a clear sense of how it could possibly be brought to completion. We do have a lot of ground to cover; eight different theologians—each of them sizeable enough—from at least three significantly different eras of church history. But the intention of this study is not as impossible as this scope might suggest.

It is the specific peril of the theologian to approach saints and their texts to ask questions in ways or about things they themselves would not have considered. In this respect, I am here attempting a specifically theological *voice*. The cohesion to all of this is not intended to arise out of its historical focus but instead around its *systematic* profile. This is neither a patristic study, nor a medieval-historical one, nor even one that will argue for a particular "reading" of certain contemporary theologians. It is rather one with a goal that is at once more historically modest and more theologically ambitious: I aim to analyze a particular dogmatic problem that has spanned three eras, and I aim to arrive at a consciously (post-/late-) modern Trinitarian suggestion. That said, and although I will at the end offer a small contribution to the theology I have chosen to follow, the value of this study lies more in its attention to the discussion itself than in whatever merit my own final suggestions may or may not have.

∼

There are two reasons for my choice of theologians. First, the eight I have chosen offer theological lines that broadly mark the bounds of a great deal of the Christian theological possibilities for understanding my question. These same lines could have been found in the theology of many other figures but these eight serve my purpose very well, maybe even best. That does, admittedly, risk overstating the significance of these eight—for there are certainly some conspicuous omissions—nevertheless, my intent is not to be historically exhaustive but systematically determined. And that leads to the second rationale for my choice: these eight figures were chosen from within a particular theological community. Like any academic discipline, theology often suffers from various pressures to feign objectivity, but unlike most other academic disciplines, the kind of theology in which I have been trained has as its internal structure a conscious posture of faith. This means, among other things, that I can admit plainly that I did not choose the eight "best" interlocutors for my purpose after somehow dispassionately surveying the entire tradition. Instead, I only say that these eight figures are either literal interlocutors within a particular academic community or are historical ones to whom those within my community often refer. My choice for them is thus similar to any others made in a theologian's life; it is shaped by my own biographical contingencies and so is simply offered as an attempt to speak from my particular place to anyone else, near or far, who cares to listen.

That said, I can now also point out that my chosen route does follow a deliberate structure. These eight will allow us to move through each of the three main *loci* of my central concern: God, creation, and whatever 'mediation' happens between them. With Irenaeus and Gunton we will look at all three of these together, but in the chapters between them we will find ourselves focused mainly on just one. With Cyril and Philoponus, it is the christological question that is forefront, and so we will be looking primarily at the nature of the creation in which the Son has become incarnate. With Luther and Calvin, the issue tends toward whatever is happening between God and the world. And in Jenson and Zizioulas, we will look mainly at the being of God on the "upper" end of the question. In this respect, and in the tone of the answers these eight will offer, this study forms a loose chiasm: Zizioulas and Jenson finding resonance with Cyril and Philoponus, Luther and Calvin establishing the watershed at the middle, and Irenaeus and Gunton corresponding to one another in their similar intentions and results.

We will begin early in the church's self-identification, with Irenaeus of Lyons and his opposition to *Knowledge Falsely So-Called*. The theology Irenaeus developed in response to Gnostic thought is an ideal start for many reasons not least of which is the way it offers a grand-scale view of the ontological demands of the Christian faith. With him we will see a remarkable sense of the triune nature of God, and in particular we will find that Irenaeus' situation led him to imagine God's work in the world to be mediated through the Father's "two hands," the Son and the Spirit.

After Irenaeus we will spend two chapters in the theological hotbed of Alexandria. Cyril and Philoponus are worthy subjects on their own credentials but they are even more important for us by virtue of their location on either side of the Council of Chalcedon. Both pastors dealt with the central questions about the two natures of Christ, and did so in a similar way. And they offer us a view of Christ and the salvation he achieved that will recur in our studies of Jenson and Zizioulas, albeit in different form. For these four, mediation is a concept either to be rejected or met with serious reservation: to describe something between God and world is for these theologians (generally speaking) to talk about the *problem* that Christ has overcome in his incarnation. In this respect, soteriology has the upper hand in its relation to theology about creation. With Cyril we will look at the theology developed by and in opposition to Nestorius, and consider the terms that brought these two to such a heated and longevous opposition. Then, with Philoponus, we will see how the roots of the rivalry between Cyril and Nestorius were set deep enough to remain with us today.

Next we will look at the two key Reformers, Martin Luther and John Calvin. These two came down on opposite sides of our dilemma; the former preferring to embrace a crucial degree of ontological ambiguity about the apparent contradictions in the christological confession, and the latter following through intellectually on his commitment to them. The contrast is especially fruitful for the way it opens up the respective problems in either direction. With Luther we will be forced to come to grips with the way theology about the christological mystery requires its own grammar, and we will need grapple with the way the new rules of this grammar bring old ideas about grace and substance into view. With Calvin, we have a mind not timid about the implications of its theo-logic, and so find with him an opportunity to see some of our most startling problems in their full relief.

After the Reformers, we will come to our own times and to three of the most constructive theologians among those behind the current renaissance in Trinitarian theology. John Zizioulas and Robert Jenson, the one an Orthodox thinker and the other a Lutheran, both offer ways of imagining the being of God much closer to that of creation than had formerly been thought possible. Their differences will be crucial, but more important will be the ways their respective theologies arrive at very similar conclusions, and so also at some similar difficulties.

Our final figure will be Colin Gunton. Despite the significant change in course we will find in Gunton's thought, he remains unique in our study as one especially concerned to find space for the creation to be itself while also holding onto the absolute distinction of God from it. His suggestions will require the drawing together of much of the ground we have covered in the seven previous chapters and will recall especially the terms established in the first by Irenaeus.

At the end we will find that the Christology we have covered has indeed been the way these eight theologians have wrestled with the question of God's relation to the world. And having seen the effects of their various systematic choices, and also their consequent variations on certain recurring problems, we will be ready to consider briefly some possible routes ahead.

Finally, an observation: the Church, almost instinctively, recurs to theology about Jesus—Christology—during times of crisis. And the three eras explored here are perhaps evidence enough. To question whether or not the modern church is in the midst of a crisis is almost a pleonasm; implicit anytime the words "modern" and "church" are found together is either irony or trouble. Consequently, there is much Christology to be done, and this is one contribution to the task.

1

IRENAEUS AND THE GNOSTIC OPTION

Monism, Duality, and the "Two Hands" of God
(A Trinitarian Concept of Mediation)

> For the only consistent position outside of Christianity is that of pantheism, the taking of oneself out of existence by way of recollection into the eternal, whereby all existential decisions become mere shadow-play beside what is eternally decided from behind.
>
> —Sören Kierkegaard

"[T]HAT GOD CREATES MEANS that there is other reality than God and that it is really other than he." So begins Robert Jenson's systematic development of the doctrine of creation.[1] Similarly, Eric Osborn has expressed near-consensus among scholars by identifying the primary characteristic of Gnostic[2] thought as "cosmic dualism" wherein "matter and spirit are

---

1. Jenson, *Systematic Theology*, 2:5.

2. Comments about "Gnosticism" or "the gnostics" will refer to the thought and thinkers responsible for rousing Irenaeus to write his "Refutation and Overthrowal of Knowledge Falsely So-called," (*Against Heresies*). The accuracy of Irenaeus' depiction of his opponents—albeit a valid and indeed theologically significant question— does not directly concern our intent. Moreover, the accuracy of the term "gnostic" as a

sharply opposed."³ The main task of this chapter will be to consider an element of the trend in which the former properly Christian duality has come to be neglected as guilty by association with the unholy latter—characteristically Gnostic—dualism. Irenaeus of Lyons should serve us well in this regard as he is unique in the tradition as one familiar with both key terms in the discussion. He is at once the one largely responsible for developing the ontology that has equipped Jenson for his observation, and the one who did so within the context of precisely the same Gnosticism to which Osborn is referring with his.

As a theologian whose thought has been characterized by one commentator as "relatively clear at the outlines and at the same time fuzzy in its details," Irenaeus may be particularly susceptible to the tendency for modern readers to peer down at him as if at their own reflection in the water at the bottom of a deep well.⁴ To complicate matters further the precise nature of second century Gnosticism is presently a subject of so much scholarly attention that one can hardly use the term at all without a lengthy explanation for the absence of inverted comas at either end of it.⁵ That said, and although Irenaeus is no longer regarded as an authority on the content and finer contours of Gnostic thought, he did, I will argue, analyze their theology with brilliant accuracy. Despite the immense variety and incredibly labyrinthine nature of Gnostic theology, Irenaeus saw in it repeated conceptual patterns and large-scale logical connections. Indeed, we might say he studied Gnostic theology *systematically*. If this is a fair claim—and if Richard Norris has correctly represented Irenaeus' dispute with the Gnostics as "perhaps the classical statement of Christian belief in terms of the problems and conceptions native to the rational

---

label for Irenaeus' interlocutors—a highly contested matter since the discovery of the library at Nag Hammadi and the subsequent eruption of scholarly activity on the subject—will be accepted as a matter of terminological convention. What follows is an attempt to engage theologically with the issues Irenaeus believed to be central to his case against those he perceived as a threat to the health of the Christian community. See n5 below for a counter-view of this possibility.

3. Osborn, *Irenaeus of Lyons*, 265. Cf. "The essential note of the Ptolemaean Gnosis, as Irenaeus presents it, is a thorough-going dualism. The Gnostic acknowledged not one world but two." Norris, *God and World*, 61.

4. Norris, "Transcendence and Freedom," 85.

5. Regarding the use of "Gnosticism," Williams suggests the term is too far gone to be useful anymore: "What is the worth of a category whose halfway responsible use has come to require more explanation and qualification than most scholars have time or energy for, thus encouraging the shortcut of misleading generalization?" Williams, *Rethinking "Gnosticism,"* 265.

theology of the Greeks"⁶—we have a sizeable, but highly significant task ahead of us.

One of the most important arguments to be made in this chapter is the one least likely to meet with widespread approval and for this reason ought to be said up-front: the Gnostics to which Irenaeus responded were not wrong about the gospel because they distinguished spirit from matter and God from world too sharply, but because they distinguished them insufficiently. Although Irenaeus did indeed take great pains to reunite all that was separated by the "dualizing" Gnostics, more importantly, he was able to see that the driving force behind the Gnostic impulse to divide was an ontology that was impotent to distinguish. Simply put, Gnostic thought is fundamentally monistic.

To support such a claim we will need to gain some perspective on Gnostic theology by climbing with Irenaeus above their "terminological fog"⁷ and trying to see larger movements in the course of their thought as a whole. What we will find is a recurring tendency to tell the cosmological story in terms of a fall and return to the One. Kurt Rudolph makes the crucial observation: "[Gnostic] dualism is carried along or, to put it more accurately, interwoven with a monistic idea which is . . . the basis for the identification of man and deity." Rudolph later refers to this "upward and downward" double movement in Gnostic thought as a "dualism on a monistic background."⁸ Hans Jonas offers a similar sketch:

> The Gnostic doctrines of the origin of the world, because of their central importance, are very richly developed, so that it is not easy to organize them systematically . . . Essentially it is always a question of the downward development from the highest being, already mentioned, which leads by ways usually described in very complicated fashion on the one hand to the

---

6. Norris, *God and World*, 78.

7. VanDenBroek, *Studies in Gnosticism*, 7. Cf. Irenaeus himself, "But since they differ so widely among themselves both as respect doctrine and tradition, and since those of them who are recognized as being most modern make it their effort daily to invent some new opinion, and to bring out what no one ever before thought of, it is a difficult matter to describe all their opinions" (*Against Heresies* 1.21.5). Subsequent references to Irenaeus' *Against Heresies* will be made thus and quoted from *Irenaeus* (ANF), or occasionally from Balthasar, *Scandal of the Incarnation*, or Grant, *Irenaeus*, in which cases the switch will be noted.

8. Rudolph, *Gnosis*, 58. Similarly, "Yet it is important to realize that all such dualism is driven by a monist conviction: that which truly exists is one and undivided." Farrow, "St Irenaeus," 335.

> creation of the world, but at the same time on the other hand to the embodiment of a divine and spiritual particle (which really makes possible the very creation itself, but is also a pledge of the later redemption).[9]

In the opening half of this chapter I will investigate briefly each of the two elements of this double movement in Gnostic thought. First in view will be themes that suggest everything comes from the One, and then those that suggest everything returns to the One. In the second half of the chapter we will see how Irenaeus responds, and come near its end to a consideration of his uniquely Trinitarian concept of christological mediation.

The Gnostic doctrine of creation—if this is what it should be called—is indeed a dizzying program. An initial observation will recur several times throughout this study: whatever else might be true of Gnostic theology about God and the world, it is almost entirely *vertical*. At the top of being there is an ontological singularity from which everything else is derived, and things descend from this one source directly or indirectly at more or less whimsical frequency. In one way or another, all of the characters in Gnostic myth have a common generic origin. One could almost randomly select a passage from Irenaeus' accounts of his opponents to illustrate the point,

> These Aeons having been produced for the glory of the Father, and wishing, by their own efforts, to effect this object, sent forth emanations by means of conjunction . . . In a like manner, the rest of the Aeons also, in a kind of a quiet way, had a wish to behold the Author of their being, and to contemplate that First Cause which had no beginning. But there rushed forth in advance of the rest that Aeon who was much the latest of them, and was the youngest of the Duodecad which sprang from Anthropos and Ecclesia, namely Sophia, and suffered passion apart from the embrace of her consort Theletos. (1.1.2 and 1.2.2)

With this we come to the element of Gnostic theology that functions as much like a presiding theme as is imaginable in such a diverse range of thought. The apparently endless stream of squabbling and copulating mediatorial "Aeons" in Gnostic myth is essentially a highly protracted theodicy. Richard Norris explains: "The myth of Achmoth and the story of the Demiurge are both attempts to explain the origin of evil without

---

9. Rudolph, *Gnosis*, 71.

imputing responsibility for it to the Supreme Father."[10] The problem of the reality of evil was the driving dilemma behind the convolution in Gnostic narrative. Their elaborate accounts of fracturing relations and digressing fragmentation among the members of the higher spiritual realms were effectively only sustained efforts to provide their benevolent source of being with an ontological alibi. For the Gnostic, whatever was to be said about the nature and reality of this world would be deferred to the priority of whatever was to be said about the impunity of the One for evil. In this respect Gnosticism foreshadows a trend we will see repeated in later chapters wherein theology about salvation *follows* theology about creation.

But if theodicy is what fuels Gnostic thought, it is not in itself the vehicle. Concern over the compatibility of a good God and an evil world is only ever given the pride of place in a theology where God and the world are imagined to be somehow ontological compatriots. That is to say, the problem of the reality of evil is especially normative for monistic theologies. Although he was far from immune to challenges over the problem of evil himself, Irenaeus' critique of the Valentinian attempt to explain the reality of evil as a kind of "vacuity" or "shadow" within the One gets us to the connection:

> But whence, let me ask, came this vacuity [of which they speak]? If it was indeed produced by Him who, according to them, is the Father and Author of all things, then it is both equal in honour and related to the rest of the Aeons, perchance even more ancient than they are. Moreover, if it proceeded from the same source [as they did], it must be similar in nature to Him who produced it, as well as to those along with whom it was produced. (2.4.1)[11]

Although Irenaeus never tired of pointing out the obvious logical difficulties with a monist theodicy, the point for our purpose is how Gnostic thought functioned quite naturally within its closed ontology. William Schoedel explains, "Irenaeus confronted a group of Valentinians willing to . . . imagine a realm of 'vacuity and shadow' or of 'defect' within the Father presumably because it was felt to be merely epiphenomenal to the reality of spirit."[12] Evil and its effects were only perceivable to the

---

10. Norris, *God and World*, 75.
11. Cf. *Against Heresies* 2.7.4.
12. Schoedel, "Gnostic Monism," 383. Cf. Irenaeus, *Against Heresies* 2.4.3.

Gnostic eye as passing "epiphenomena" against the larger canvas of divine goodness.

Hans Jonas has suggested that the Gnostic penchant for theodicy was compatible with their monist commitments because, "no original world of darkness or of matter is assumed to oppose the primal being, ... the dualism of existing reality is derived from an inner process within the one divinity itself."[13] In this respect, the matter/evil vs. spirit/goodness dualisms for which Gnostic thought are so well known are effectively just smoke and mirrors in front of the larger whole of the one divinity. By plotting the evil world and the one good God as two points on a single ontological continuum, the Gnostic mind became one of the most efficient myth-making machines in the history of western thought. Their efforts to established distance between God and the world required what seem to be intentionally befuddling narratives, but the dissimilitudes were relative, they could only ever be emphasized by what we might call *fictive distance*. Despite even their most creative flurries of narrative, Gnostic strategy depended entirely on compounded thematic complexity to provide the appearance of an ineffable separation between the One and the world. Beings from different points on the vertical continuum could be conceptually juxtaposed to form a false dualism, but beneath the façade all things were fundamentally connected and part of a larger whole. In later chapters we will find that a similar tendency to relocate christological duality to something perceivable "only in theory" also has an orthodox tradition. In common is the attempt to have a dualism in the front of the mind while knowing about and embracing a unity or oneness behind it.

Irenaeus, for one, did not find the rhetoric convincing:

> Iu! Iu! Pheu, Pheu!—for well may we utter these tragic exclamations at such a pitch of audacity in the coining of names as he [Valentinus] has displayed without a blush in devising a nomenclature for his system of falsehood . . . It is manifest also, that he himself is the one who has had sufficient audacity to coin these names; so that, unless *he* had appeared in the world, the truth would still have been destitute of a name . . . there exists a power which I term *Gourd*; and along with this Gourd there exists a power which again I term *Utter-Emptiness*. This Gourd and Emptiness, since they are one, produced (and yet did not simply produce, so as to be apart from themselves) a fruit, everywhere

---

13. Jonas, *Gnostic Religion*, 105. Cf. 174.

visible, eatable, and delicious, which fruit-language calls a *Cucumber*. Along with this Cucumber exists a power of the same essence, which again I call a *Melon*. These powers, the Gourd, Utter-Emptiness, the Cucumber, and the Melon, brought forth the remaining multitude of the delirious melons of Valentinus. (1.11.4)

Although not indicative of Irenaeus' more refined theological abilities, this less than subtle lampoon does serve to illustrate his rejection of Gnostic theological method. For him, any effort to honour the absolute freedom and sovereignty of the Creator by mythic cajolery or fictive distance was so categorically mistaken that, "simply to exhibit their sentiments, is to obtain a victory over them" (1.31.3).

∽

If Gnostic theology about creation recurs to themes in which everything comes from a single source, then Gnostic theology about salvation similarly recurs to themes in which everything returns to this source at the end. Irenaeus explains,

> He [Saturninus] declares, therefore, that this spark of life, after the death of a man, returns to those things which are of the same nature with itself, and the rest of the body is decomposed into its original elements. (1.24.1)

Although the details of the varying Gnostic systems differ widely, common among them is the belief that the final accomplishment of salvation occurs within a grand-scale eschatology of return. Robert Haardt comments, "The fundamental eschatological orientation in Gnosis lies in the element of dynamic movement . . . considered as an irreversible total process directed towards one end."[14] Another way of putting this would be to say that the Gnostics tended to understand salvation as the process by which one comes to realize—noetically, then ontically—one's own divinity. Eric Osborn explains,

> Resurrection is not an event for the body, say the Gnostics, but is the knowledge of the truth (2.31.2) . . . The Gnostics offered a real identity with God, with all the mystery of his being, an identity which precludes death and separation, which rejects the world and the body as ephemeral and irrelevant.[15]

---

14. Haardt, *Gnosis*, 9.
15. So Osborn, *Irenaeus*, 253. And cf. "I shall use the term Gnosticism to indicate

For the Gnostics, salvation is a "real identity with God," one which—and this is crucial for the direction of this study—"precludes . . . separation." Once again, we will return to similar themes in later chapters but for now we should notice that even though union with the divine is indeed the presiding paradigm in Gnostic soteriology, there is also more to it: alongside themes in which everything arrives together back at the original source of being, it is also true that some Gnostic eschatology included elements of final separation. There are the "spiritual ones" who will be saved, and there are "physical ones" who will fall off the bottom of being into nothingness. Irenaeus rightly traces both the implications and the heritage of this idea,

> Then again, as to the opinion that everything of necessity passes away to those things out of which they maintain it was also formed, and that God is the slave of this necessity, so that He cannot impart immortality to what is mortal, or bestow incorruption on what is corruptible, but every one passes into a substance similar in nature to itself, both those who are named Stoics from the portico (*stoa*), and indeed all that are ignorant of God, poets and historians alike, make the same affirmation. (2.14.4)

By contrast to the Stoic themes in Gnostic soteriology, Winrich Lohr can observe that for Irenaeus, "Salvation history has a higher goal than the final return of primary substances to their original positions."[16] And it is the mechanical tone of the Gnostic like-drawn-to-like eschatology that gets us to the point of the issue for Irenaeus. Lohr continues, "Irenaeus now argues that if the [spiritual ones] attained their final position because of the very substance of their souls, both the faith of the believer and the descent of the Saviour would be completely superfluous."[17] There are implications here for analyzing how Gnostics thought about the incarnation but the point for the moment is simply that their soteriology was functionally the same as Stoic determinism. Salvation cannot be open to the contingency and flux of time because time is itself a symptom

---

the ideas or coherent systems which are characterized by an absolutely negative view of the visible world and its creator and the assumption of a divine spark in man, his inner self, which had become enclosed within the material body as the result of a tragic event in the pre-cosmic world, from which it can only *escape to its divine origin* by means of the saving gnosis." VanDenBroek, *Studies in Gnosticism*, 7, emphasis added.

16. Lohr, "Gnostic Determinism," 386.

17. Ibid., 382.

of the need for salvation in the first place. As if in a mirror image of their heavily weighted eschatology, the deterministic themes in Gnostic thought further evacuated the present by overloading the past.

We return to our larger theme when we observe that determinism is the existential underbelly to a monistic ontology. Irenaeus repeatedly argues that wherever God is considered part of a larger whole, God's freedom is necessarily qualified by the conditions of the other beings with whom he shares this whole.[18] The Gnostics however, by trying to plot a perfectly beneficent God and the evil world of matter as two points on a single ontological line, had few if any other options for their soteriology. Irenaeus rejected Gnostic determinism because it displaced God as the free agent of salvation and made him instead "a slave to necessity."

Without a God who is freely willing the salvation of his creatures, Gnostic soteriology relied on theodicy and determinism to keep things moving. But there is at least one major problem with a Godless soteriology. When the Gnostic finally comes to consider his route back to the One, he finds it clogged with all the same mediatorial characters he originally cast to make sense of his theodicy and legislate his determinism. Irenaeus puts his finger on the irony:

> But if this be to make progress, [namely,] to find out another Father besides Him who was preached from the beginning; and again, besides him who is imagined to have been discovered in the second place, to find out a third other—then the progress of this man will consist in his also proceeding from a third to a fourth; and from this, again, to another and another: and thus he who thinks that he is always making progress of such a kind, will never rest in one God. For, being driven away from Him who truly is [God], and being turned backwards, he shall be for ever seeking, yet shall never find out God; but shall continually swim in an abyss without limits. (4.9.3.)

The chilling *reductio ad infinitum*—"continually swimming in an abyss without limits"—captures the heart of Irenaeus' critique. Where the *Aeons* are intended to distinguish the One from the world they connect the two as a matter of deterministic necessity, and where they are needed to bring the human into union with the One, there are constantly more of them popping up to remind him of the One's incompatibility with evil.

Thus Gnostic theology about mediation is exemplary for the way it is at odds with itself. Any effort to distinguish the One from the creation

18. See esp. *Against Heresies* 2.1

compromises the possibility of relation between the two, and any effort to relate the two compromises the possibility of their otherness. With this we have set the agenda for the rest of the chapter, and established a sizable mandate for Irenaeus.

⁓

Having looked at the shape of Gnostic theology about creation and salvation, we now turn to see what their foe had to say. On the first count we will see that in response to the Gnostic predilection for monistic cosmologies, Irenaeus repeatedly emphasized what later theology came to call an "ontological divide" between God and everything else.

> It is proper, then, that I should begin with the first and most important head, that is, God the Creator, who made the heaven and the earth, and all things that are therein (whom these men blasphemously style the fruit of a defect), and to demonstrate that there is nothing either above Him or after Him; nor that, influenced by any one, but of His own free will, He created all things, since He is the only God, the only Lord, the only Creator, the only Father, alone containing all things, and Himself commanding all things into existence. (2.1.1)

It is on the basis of passages like this that Richard Norris can identify "the central theme of [Irenaeus'] work: the thesis that God is one, and is himself the maker of everything that is."[19] Implicit in Norris' observation is a theologoumenon so decisive for Irenaeus' program that it is at least equally as central. To see it however, we need to take a step back. If the two most basic things to be said about God are that he is one and that he is the author of a creation other than himself, it follows that all things are not part of the same ontic lump. Rather everything is distinguishable into two basic categories: there is God and then there is whatever he has created. Irenaeus makes the claim himself,

> But the things established are distinct from him who has established them, and what have been made from him who has made them. For he is Himself uncreated, both without beginning and end, and lacking nothing. He is Himself sufficient for Himself; and still further, He grants to all others this very thing, existence; but the things which have been made by Him have received a beginning. But whatever things had a beginning, and

---

19. Norris, "Transcendence and Freedom," 88.

are liable to dissolution, and are subject to and stand in need of Him who made them, must necessarily in all respects have a different term [applied to them]. (3.8.3)

This is the bedrock to Irenaeus' doctrine of creation. Whatever else he will come to say, it will follow from this version of the "infinite qualitative difference" between God and everything else.

Irenaeus developed two formulae to support his belief in a basic ontological duality: the idea that God "contains all things but is himself not contained" and the claim that God "created all things out of nothing." I will start with the less familiar.

> Now the origin of all things is God. He was not created by anyone, but everything was created by him . . . calling into existence what did not exist. He contains all things, yet cannot Himself be contained . . . There is no other God above him and no other god beneath him.[20]

It is clear from the context here and from that of almost every other use of this "contains—yet cannot Himself be contained" formula that Irenaeus intends with it to affirm the absolute sovereignty of the Creator.[21] Although it is usually translated with derivatives of "contain"—as we have it here—William Schoedel has argued persuasively for "enclosing . . . not enclosed."[22] Indeed, insofar as the idea that God "encloses" all things reserves within it an element of divine volition, it is closer to Irenaeus' central concern for the absolute freedom of God. Accordingly, Schoedel has observed that for Irenaeus this "enclosing—not enclosed" formula presupposed "a God who transcends the cosmos and is not simply (as in Greek philosophy) a factor in the totality of things." Thus, despite its long history in other capacities, Irenaeus used the idea to "provide a context within which the infinite 'could be detached from the concept of the corporeal, with which it had been essentially united in Greek thought.'"[23]

20. *Dem* 4–5, in Balthasar, *Scandal of the Incarnation*.

21. See especially 2.1.1–5, 1.15.5, and 3.11.8, 4.19.3, 4.20.1; and compare 2.13.6, and 5.18.1.

22. The Latin verb *contineo*, or *circumcontineo*, in Irenaeus is likely based on the Greek περιεω or εμπεριεχω. See Reynders, *Lexique Camparé*, 1:87; 2:52, 68. Regarding its "philosophical" application, Schoedel, "Topological Theology," 93, notes, "Platonists, Aristotelians, Stoics, Epicureans, Pythagoreans, Philo, the Church Fathers—all make such a use of the term." Cf. Schoedel, "Enclosing, Not Enclosed."

23. Schoedel, "Enclosing, Not Enclosed," 76, quoting Ivor Leclerc, *Nature of Physical Existence*.

In this way, the "enclosing—not enclosed" formula is closely related to the concern about the possibility of mediation between a supreme God and a contingent creation. By saying that God encloses all things and is himself not enclosed by anything, Irenaeus insisted that there is no swath of intermediaries between God and the world. Yet Irenaeus is not, as some commentators would have him, simply espousing a Christianized form of panentheism.[24] As ever, the central issue for Irenaeus against the Gnostics is the ontological freedom of God, and for this reason the double movement of the formula is crucial. The point comes into focus when we note that the Gnostics also used the notion that God "contains" all things, but their version of the formula was significantly truncated. Schoedel explains, "No doubt Gnostics found it possible to speak of the Father as *containing* all because in their view nothing outside the Pleroma truly existed."[25]

The important second element of the formula—"and is himself not enclosed by anything"—gets to the intent of the idea for Irenaeus. Rowan Greer explains,

> To say that God is 'uncontained' is not simply to assert that there must be a single first principle; rather it is to proclaim the exaltation of God as Sovereign over all. . . . That God is uncontained in this sense implies that He is to be thought utterly distinct from everything else.[26]

For Irenaeus, there is that which is enclosed and then there is that which encloses, nothing more.

A raw cosmological duality of this sort might understandably lead one to wonder if Irenaeus had responded to Gnostic dualisms by simply replacing them with his own. But our course through Irenaeus' doctrine

---

24. Norris comes very close to the point: "Certainly one implication, as Irenaeus sees it, of the idea that God as *pleroma* 'contains everything' is that the idea of a cosmic hierarchy, and thus of intermediaries between a distinct God and the lower orders of creation, is superfluous." But in the end he reads Irenaeus without due regard for his own alternative to the gnostics' "mediatorial beings": "Irenaeus is dissatisfied with portrayals of the working of God which interpose mediatorial beings between him and the world of earthlings, because this too relativizes God, and fails to grasp him as what I have called 'the context'— perhaps one might better say 'the immediate context'— of all things . . . He [Irenaeus] wants above all to prove himself faithful to tradition; but he has become naturally suspicious of mediatorial beings" (Norris, "Transcendence and Freedom," 95, 99). And cf. Norris, *God and World*, esp. 72.

25. Schoedel, *Gnostic Monism*, 383, emphasis added.

26. Greer, "The Dog and the Mushrooms," 157.

of creation so far would suggest something else is afoot. The issue between Irenaeus and his Gnostic colleagues was establishing the ontological thinkability of divine otherness; accordingly Irenaeus saw a sizeable portion of his task to be the developing of a theology that affirms the distinction between the Creator and the creation. In the history of theology about creation there are few doctrines with as much significance for this task as the concept of *creatio ex nihilo*. The idea that God does not share eternity with anything and is free enough to call creation into being "out of nothing" is a fundamental pillar in Irenaeus' response to Gnostic monism.[27]

> Men cannot make anything out of nothing, but only out of already existing matter. God, however, is superior to men, because He calls into being the matter of his creation when previously it did not exist.[28]

By contrast to the extensive efforts of his Gnostic opponents to remove the One from the world by what I have called fictive distance, Irenaeus did his theology as if the distinction between the creation and the Creator was simply axiomatic. Irenaeus' suggestion that God called all things into being "out of nothing" refused any space to the Gnostic idea that an element of the human psyche, or a group of demi-gods, or indeed anything else, pre-existed this creation and ought therefore to be considered in some sense divine. By saying that everything arose from nothing at the command of God, Irenaeus made it impossible to imagine creation and Creator as somehow two parts of a single whole.

∼

The question about whether or not Irenaeus adopts a Platonic view of the "forms" as eternal models in the mind of God for the creation is not an easy one to answer. Irenaeus himself confesses to entertaining his opponents on this issue, "I have had very frequent discussions with them concerning forms of this kind" (2.17.9). The matter is complicated by the fact that where Irenaeus addresses the question of the forms it is not always clear whether he is representing the position of his opponents, or his own:

---

27. Although some attribute the development of this doctrine to Athenegoras or even Hermas, see May, *Creatio Ex Nihilo*, esp. 148ff.

28. *Against Heresies* 2.10.4, in Balthasar, *Scandal of the Incarnation*.

> Or is it really the case that, in regard to mere men, one will allow that they have of themselves invented what is useful for the purposes of life, but will not grant to that God who formed the world, that of Himself He created the forms of those things which have been made, and imparted to it its orderly arrangement? (2.7.5)

That might seem clear enough, but just a few lines later Irenaeus continues,

> But, again, how can these things [below] be images of those [above], since they are really contrary to them, and can in no respect have sympathy with them? . . . how can those things which are possessed of figure, and confined within certain limits, be the images of such as are destitute of figure and incomprehensible? (2.7.6)

Some read Irenaeus as himself defending what would have been at his time an orthodox Platonic view of the forms against the recent innovations of the Gnostics; E. P. Meijering is one:

> [I]n contemporary Middle Platonism the models were regarded as eternal thought of the Creator and were therefore not regarded as being superior to the Creator . . . When Irenaeus maintains against the Gnostics that there are no models of the world superior to the Creator, but that the Creator conceived in His mind a model of this world, he may therefore consciously oppose what he regards as a Gnostic transformation of Plato's theory of forms by the Middle Platonic interpretation of this theory.[29]

Meijering may be at least partially right (although his view has met strong criticism)[30] insofar as Irenaeus seems to make use of the theory of the forms when it serves his purpose of safeguarding the absolute freedom of the Creator. Yet it should be remembered that, for Irenaeus, the impetus and means for creation are solely God's own and he can in no way be restricted by anything before or alongside of him. If the forms played any role in Irenaeus' doctrine of creation it was of such a chastened version that calling them "forms" at all tends to compromise just how radical Irenaeus was.

> Still further, if these things [below] were made after the similitude of those [above], after the likeness of which again will those

---

29. Meijering, *God, Being, History*, 20.
30. See, e.g. May, *Creatio Ex Nihilo*, 168ff.

> then be made? For if the Creator of the world did not form these things directly from His own conception, but, like an architect of no ability, or a boy receiving his first lesson, copied them from archetypes furnished by others, then whence did their Bythus obtain the forms of that creation which He at first produced? It clearly follows that He must have received the model from some other one who is above Him, and that one, in turn, from another. And none the less [for these suppositions], the talk about images, as about gods, will extend to infinity, if we do not at once fix our mind on one Artificer, and on one God, who of Himself formed those things which have been created. (2.7.5)

For Irenaeus, the theory of co-eternal forms risks re-establishing the same vertical ontology to which he was so opposed. By making the connection between a divine creator and his creature a matter of necessity, the Gnostic use of the doctrine of the forms only reinforced the chain of mediatorial beings.

In any case, Irenaeus would have taken immediate departure of the theory at those points at which it infringes on the mediatorial roles of the Son and the Spirit. An idea to which we now turn.

∽

So far my relatively straightforward comparison of the Gnostic doctrine of creation with Irenaeus' alternative has brought us several times back to the question of the possibility for relation and otherness—what I have called "mediation"—between God and the world. Integral to the Gnostic idea that cosmic history is a fall and return within the One are the *Aeons* as mediatorial links; these are like ontological steps between the source of being, its distention in the world, and the final return of all into the One. As we have seen however, these beings are both the proprietors and ultimately the impediments to the Gnostic quest for union with the One. By contrast we have seen Irenaeus develop theology that affirms the distinction between the Creator and the creation. His use of the "enclosing—not enclosed" formula and his development of the concept of creation out of nothing make it clear that he simply took as granted the ontological difference between the Creator and the creature.

Yet setting up the Gnostics as closet monists and Irenaeus as a champion dualist is only half the task. Irenaeus was anything but a second century deist. He did not simply imagine the Creator and the creation in a kind of ontological face-off and consider his work finished. For Irenaeus, the Creator brings his creation into being by the mediating activity of the "two hands" of God:[31]

> It was not angels, then, who made or formed us. Angels could not make an image of God, nor could some 'power' remotely distant from the Father of all, nor could anyone except the true God. Nor did God need any of these to carry out what He had decided beforehand within Himself should be done. As if He did not have His hands! For the Word and Wisdom, the Son and the Spirit, were always with Him. Through Them and in Them He freely and spontaneously created all things.[32]

It is with this apparently simple image of God's "two hands" that we arrive at the crux of Irenaeus' doctrine of creation. Having already denied the reality of any semi-divine beings alongside the one Creator, Irenaeus reveals with this metaphor who it is he imagines to be doing the hard work of ontological mediation. And it is no one other than God himself. Where the Gnostics offered variously divine mediatorial beings between the One and the world, Irenaeus had God, "through" and "in" his own "two hands," the Son and the Spirit.

The contrast between Irenaeus' concept of mediation and the versions prevalent among the Gnostics comes into sharper relief when we see that for Irenaeus even man was created by the two "hands" of God.

> Now God shall be glorified in His handiwork, fitting it so as to be conformable to, and modeled after, His own Son. For by the hands of the Father, that is, by the Son and the Holy Spirit, man, and not [merely] a part of man, was made in the likeness of God. (5.6.1)

As we have seen, Gnostic cosmologies understood humanity to be in some way continuous with the divine, but Irenaeus made it clear that humans are first of all continuous with the rest of God's "handiwork." Humankind is a creature distinct from God, "modeled" by his "two hands," and only as such capable of authentic relation to him.

The most striking contrast between Irenaeus' "two-handed" concept of mediation and the monistic version of his Gnostic opponents is in the differing theological rationales that support them. In Gnostic cosmologies the appearance of the mediatorial beings between the One and the world occurs seemingly at random. For Irenaeus on the other hand, the

---

31. Cf. 4.Pref.4, 5.1.3, 5.5.1, 5.6.1, 5.28.4.
32. *Against Heresies* 4.20.1, in Balthasar, *Scandal of the Incarnation*.

mediatorial activity of the Son and the Spirit is the direct expression of God's own being and act. Whatever God does with his "two hands," he does himself.[33] Iain MacKenzie makes the point,

> The 'hands of God' are not mere instrumental appendages, as it were, for it is with these hands that the Father converses. They are divine and co-equal, inherent in the life of God.[34]

For Irenaeus, the work of the Son and the Spirit is Godself in action in the world. Moreover, the mediatorial activity of the Son and the Spirit is not something God needs for his own sake, as if he could only maintain his divine status by protecting himself behind an entourage of intermediaries, it is rather what happens when the Creator moves his creation to the end he freely intends.

That said, a quick and admittedly anachronistic summary might now be in order: In contrast to the Gnostic "vertical" ontologies in which the divine and the world were polar opposites on a single continuum, Irenaeus developed a "horizontal" ontology in which the sovereign Creator personally participates in the being of his creation. The question at this point, then, is about how Irenaeus imagined this could be possible. Three examples will need to suffice before moving, finally, to the central manifestation of this "horizontal" ontology in Irenaeus' Christology. The first two examples are more familiar and so offered only briefly.

To begin, there is Irenaeus' well-known concept of *anakephaleosis*, or recapitulation. In this theology, the life of Christ is like a summing-up of all that humanity was intended to be. Irenaeus' somewhat awkward insistence that Christ "sanctified every age" and so lived to be over fifty years old serves to illustrate his commitment to the uncompromised presence of the Creator in history, "He came to save all through means of Himself" (2.22.4). The duration of Christ's life is significant for Irenaeus. His concept of recapitulation is one that sees Christ living through every stage of humanity and thereby being the one who takes it forward to its intended end. We will return in a later chapter to an alternate concept of recapitulation where the idea takes on an element of *return* to an original

---

33. Even when the Spirit is occasionally referred to as the "finger of God," the point is the same: "And in the wilderness Moses received the Law from God, the ten Words on tables of stone, written with the finger of God (now the finger of God is that which is stretched forth from the Father in the Holy Spirit)" (*Dem.* 26).

34. MacKenzie, *Irenaeus's Demonstration*, 84, citing *Against Heresies* 2.28.2.

perfection, but Irenaeus' view is headed in the opposite direction: forward to a future perfection and consummation.

Second, one could also look to Irenaeus' particularly dynamic vision of the eschaton. For Irenaeus, the "new heaven and the new earth" is that time when the redeemed will "receive the Kingdom and make progress in it for ever."[35] Irenaeus even goes so far as to say that the eschaton is where "the new man shall remain, always holding fresh converse with God" (5.36.1).[36] There is a deliberate theological embrace of temporality in this. Where the Gnostics sought an escape from time, Irenaeus affirmed its goodness to the extent that for him even the eschaton will involve a kind of horizontal sequentiality.

A third example of how Irenaeus' ontology bisects vertical monism is the way in which he imagined particular creative roles for each of the three persons of the Trinity. A recurrent pattern of agentiality emerges in Irenaeus writing; he ascribes initiative and commanding to the Father, establishment and forming to the Son, and progression and nurturing to the Spirit:

> This is the order, this is the rhythm, this is the movement by which man, that created and organized being, is established in the image and likeness of God. The Father, in His good pleasure, commands, the Son works and fashions, the Spirit nourishes and gives increase, and slowly but surely man makes progress and attains perfection, that is to say, comes close to the Uncreated.[37]

Irenaeus seemed to consider this "commanding, fashioning, nourishing" pattern an ontological paradigm; as if it were the *way* God creates.[38] Again, in his *Demonstration of the Apostolic Preaching,* he comments, "The Father . . . [calls] into existence what did not exist . . . the Word "establishes," that is produces bodies and bestows permanence

---

35. 4.28.2, in Balthasar, *Scandal of the Incarnation*; cf. *Against Heresies* 4.11.2; 4.120.6. And see Boersma, "Irenaeus, Derrida, and Hospitality."

36. While Irenaeus does speak of a "passing" or "promotion" into God (*Against Heresies* 3.19.1; 3.20.2; 4.20.7; 4.33.4), this is clearly meant in relational terms— i.e. ones that *reinforce* the Creator-creature distinction. Whether one ought to see Irenaeus as a source for a doctrine of "deification" is of course a matter of ongoing debate. See Canlis, "Being Made Human," 434–54.

37. 4.38.3, in Balthasar, *Scandal of the Incarnation*.

38. Cf. *Against Heresies* 3.24.2; 4.20.5, 6; 5.5.1; and especially, "the Father planning everything well and giving His commands, the Son carrying these into execution and performing the work of creation, and the Spirit nourishing and increasing [what is made]" (5.38.3).

on what has come into existence, while the Spirit disposes and shapes the various powers."[39] Although I will need return briefly to this idea soon below, for now we need simply note that Irenaeus' notion of God's relation to the world is remarkably Trinitarian.[40] For Irenaeus, the work of God in creation is always the work of the Father, Son and Spirit.[41] And it is with this in view that we finally come to the central issue.

Gnostic christological speculation generally understood Jesus not simply as a docetic double in front of his spiritual divine counterpart—as is often presumed—but rather as the final downward expression of the same polymorphic ontological digression we charted in their cosmology. Irenaeus stereotypes his opponents accordingly:

> [U]nder the pretext of knowledge [they] understand that Jesus was one, and Christ another, and the Only-begotten another, from whom again is the Word, and the Saviour is another, whom these disciples of error allege to be a production of those who were made Aeons in a state of degeneracy. (3.16.8)

Although the composition of the historical Jesus in Gnostic thought was a phenomenological dualism of psychic and divine elements, this was a dualism that was itself only the observable spillover in front of an invisible spiritual stream of foundering divine beings behind Jesus. Alistair Logan explains, "[T]he Gnostic tendency, so characteristic of their mentality and mythology, was increasingly to split and multiply the redeemer figures to avoid any idea of a heavenly 'fall' or actual incarnation of the flesh."[42] Irenaeus, on the other hand, believed firmly in such an

---

39. *Dem.* 4–7. Cf. *Against Heresies* 3.10.3.

40. Although Irenaeus likely derived this pattern from Justin, the absence of Irenaeus' characteristically Trinitarian form in Justin's work is telling: "In his book against Marcion, Justin does well say: 'I would not have believed the Lord Himself, if He had announced any other than He who is our framer, maker, and nourisher'" (*Against Heresies* 4.6.2).

41. There can be no doubt that the triune persons are eternal for Irenaeus, contra Minns, *Irenaeus*, 52: "I think a case could be made from his arguments in Book II to the effect that he would, at the very least, not be disturbed by the notion that the Trinity did not exist as distinct persons before the creation of Adam." Yet, cf. Irenaeus himself: "I have also largely demonstrated, that the Word, namely the Son, was always with the Father; and that Wisdom also, which is the Spirit, was present with Him, anterior to all creation" (*Against Heresies* 3.20.3).

42. Logan, *Gnostic Truth*, 283.

"actual incarnation of the flesh," which concept was the thumping heart of his whole system of theology.[43] Trevor Hart comments,

> In stark contrast to some of the apologetic theologies of the early Alexandrian tradition in which the adoption of dualistic structures of thought made it difficult to do proper justice to the idea of an incarnation of the son of God, Irenaeus insists upon maintaining the integrity of the humanity and the deity of the Savior in the history of the person of Christ, for he realizes that it is precisely the *becoming* of God within this history that saves mankind.[44]

With Hart's observation, several of our previous lines converge: Irenaeus' insistence on what we will later call a christological "duality" in the being of Christ—"the integrity of the humanity and the deity of the Saviour"—was only sustainable by virtue of his view of a duality of God and the world. Furthermore, by imagining a real "*becoming* of God within history"—by embracing what we have called a "horizontal" ontology—Irenaeus achieved a theology with which it was possible to suggest that God has done the apparently impossible: He has remained the absolutely free Creator and has himself actually *become* one of his own creatures.[45] Irenaeus explains,

> There is therefore one God, who by the Word and Wisdom created and arranged all things. . . and who, as regards His greatness, is indeed unknown to all who have been made by Him . . . but as regards His love, he is always known through Him by whose means He ordained all things. Now this is His Word, our Lord Jesus Christ, who in the last times, was made a man among men, that He might join the end to the beginning, that is, man to God. (4.20.4)

Irenaeus has here put "[God's] love" at the center, and it is clear that he intended this in the most radical way imaginable,

---

43. Thus Meijering: "The heart of Irenaeus' religion is that in the Redeemer there appears the Creator and nobody else" (*God, Being, History*, 79).

44. Hart, "Irenaeus," 178.

45. Norris is not convinced: "[Irenaeus] tries to make of the Logos not a buffer between the ingenerate God and the generate world, but the presence within the world of the Godhead itself. The result of this attempt is, of course, a certain incoherence in his own position. His two ways of talking do not fit together very well" (*God and World*, 72). The "of course" in this is, of course, precisely the assumption which we are exploring in this study.

> [The heretics] err from the truth, because their doctrine is far removed from the true God. They are ignorant of the fact that His only-begotten Word, who has always been present to the human race, and who, by the Father's good pleasure, has been united and mingled with His own handiwork and made flesh, is our Lord Jesus Christ, who suffered for us . . . and so He recapitulated man to Himself; the invisible becoming visible, the incomprehensible becoming comprehensible, the impassible becoming passible, the Word becoming man.[46]

With this, a question that has until now hovered at the edges can no longer be postponed: How can the absolute and the contingent be both truly distinct and authentically related? Irenaeus says that in Christ we have the "invisible becoming visible, the incomprehensible becoming comprehensible, the impassible becoming passible, the Word becoming man." The absolute and the contingent are both in view here, and the word Irenaeus uses to describe the dynamic between them is *becoming*. Christ, who is the Creator, *became* a creature. But if, as we have seen, the cosmological duality of Creator and creation was ontological bedrock for Irenaeus, how can he claim that in Christ the Creator *became* a creature without collapsing this duality altogether? He had several carefully developed theological lines for sustaining the distinction between the Creator and creation—the "containing/not contained" idea, creation out of nothing, the "two-handedness" of God, etc.—did he have anything similar in his Christology? How can he speak of a "becoming" at the incarnation and still maintain the crucial distinction between the deity and humanity of Christ?

For many theologians this would be an unfair question. On the one hand, Chalcedonian concerns were simply not current for Irenaeus and, on the other, the duality of Christ's being—the upkeep of distinction between his so-called "two natures"—is often thought to be simply beyond one of the boundaries for theological speculation. But Irenaeus is unique in the tradition for many reasons, perhaps the most significant at this point is the way in which he is thoroughly Trinitarian. And so, finally, we will look at the possibilities Irenaeus' understanding of the Spirit might provide for the question of the nature of God's presence to the world in Christ.

It is generally agreed that Theophilus was the source from which Irenaeus borrowed his familiar Word-Wisdom typology. And aside from

---

46. *Against Heresies* 3.16.6, 7, in Balthasar, *Scandal of the Incarnation*.

concerns about Theophilus' biblical-theological coherence, his idea in Irenaeus' hands does mark an attempt to include the Spirit in the divine economy.[47] Theophilus himself was not able finally to identify the Wisdom of God and the Holy Spirit.[48] Nor, again unlike Irenaeus, was he able to adequately commandeer the language of "enclosing, not enclosed." Theophilus writes,

> The whole creation is enclosed by the spirit of God (just as fruit is enclosed by its skin), and the spirit which encloses is enclosed along with the creation by the hand of God.[49]

Even though the Spirit does feature here, it is a motionless, lifeless, and, we might say, spiritless Spirit; little more than a metaphysical "skin" in the single hand of God. With what was functionally an attempted binitarianism, Theophilus was left both to relate and distinguish God and world with just one hand.[50] Similarly, Justin Martyr, another contemporary, had little space for the Spirit. When he came to explain the incarnation, he used the term "Spirit" as a cipher for Logos:

> But the Spirit and the Power that is from God it is not allowable to regard as any other than the *Logos* . . . it was this Spirit that came upon the virgin."[51]

The effect of theologies like those of Theophilus and Justin was to make the Creator-creation relationship necessary—as a matter of *logos* or principle—and thereby to threaten the ontological difference between God and everything else. There is both an absence of the Spirit at the inception of this christological economy and, consequently, a theology of mediation borne entirely by the Word. This problem eventually pressed

---

47. "[T]he making of man he alone counted work of His own hands. Yea more, as though needing assistance, God is found saying, *Let us make* . . . But to none other did He say it, save to His own Word and His own Wisdom." *Ad Autol* 2.18; cf. 1.7; 2.10; and cf. Irenaeus, *Against Heresies* 2.30.9; 3.24.3; 4.7.4.

48. Thus Studer: "Theophilus of Antioch associated the two hands with Logos and Wisdom, whereas Irenaeus, in accordance with the baptismal faith, understands them as Son and Spirit" (*Trinity and Incarnation*, 39).

49. *Ad Autol*. 1.5; quoted by Schoedel, "Topological Theology," 97, 98.

50. Silvanus, likely writing around the middle of the third century, is indicative of the general loss of Irenaeus' insight on this point: "And it is the one hand of the Lord that has created all these things; for this hand of the Father is Christ, and it forms all" (*The Teachings of Silvanus* 115.3ff.; quoted in Schoedel, "Topological Theology," 98). The whole text with introduction is in Pearson, ed., *Nag Hammadi*, see esp. 115.2–5.

51. *Apol*. 1.3

toward a harder distinguishing of the Son from absolute deity, and it finally found its fullest expression in Arianism. For Justin at least, Christ was someone "other than the Maker of all."[52] But such a claim only leads to the Gnostic abyss, a swimming away from the possibility of a real relation between God and the creation. Thus Justin and Theophilus exemplify the same Gnostic attempts to explain God's presence to the world from within an essentially monist system. For both Irenaeus' Gnostic opponents and his Apologist colleagues, the problems began and returned to two apparently mutually exclusive pressures: If the mediator—or in Gnostic thought, the group of mediators—was primarily needed to *relate* the divine and the human, this seemed to lead to an immediate monism by a christological route. On the other hand, if the mediator(')s(') mandate was to *distinguish* the divine and the human, this seemed to render real relation impossible, ultimately separating God and world by a kind of stratified infinite regress, and thereby collapsing back into monism from the other direction.

Irenaeus himself connected the Gnostic propensity for ontological stratification with a weak pneumatology:

> [A]ll the doctrines of these men who have invented putative Ogdoads and Tetrads, and imagined subdivisions, have been proved falsehoods. These men do, in fact, set the Spirit aside altogether; they understand that Christ was one and Jesus another; and they teach that there was not one Christ but many. (3.17.4)

By making such a connection at least this much is clear: Irenaeus directly associated the Spirit with the mediating activity of Christ. I would like to say that Irenaeus regarded the Spirit as the one responsible for making sure the duality of humanity and deity in Christ did not dissolve into an infinite regress. But maybe that is to get too far ahead of ourselves; let us look a little closer.

The first thing to note is that Irenaeus clearly included the Spirit in his theology about the incarnation,

> These texts show that an impassible Christ did not come down into Jesus, but Jesus, since he was Christ, suffered for us, slept and rose again, descended and ascended (Eph 4:10), the Son of God become Son of man. This is what his name indicates, since the name "Christ" implies him who anoints, him who has

---

52. *Dial.* 56.4.

> been anointed, and the unction with which he is anointed. He who anoints is the Father; and the Son has been anointed in the Spirit, which is the unction.[53]

The Spirit for Irenaeus, is the dynamic, or *unction*, that makes the incarnation—"the Son of God become the Son of man"—possible. The critical point here is that unlike most of his contemporaries, Irenaeus believed it was not the Logos that "anointed" Jesus, but the Spirit. This is further illustrated in a unique passage from the *Demonstration* where Irenaeus distinguishes between the Spirit as the one who *sowed*, and the Son as the one who was *sown*, at the conception of Jesus:

> So then he who was proclaimed by the law through Moses, and by the prophets of the Most High and Almighty God, as Son of the Father of all; he from whom all things are, he who spake with Moses—he came into Judea, *sown from God by the Holy Spirit*, and born of the Virgin Mary.[54]

The poignancy of such a typically post-Nicene distinction serves to emphasize further the deliberately Trinitarian shape of Irenaeus' Christology. The possibilities available from Irenaeus come together in one more passage:

> Vain also are the Ebionites, who do not receive by faith into their soul the union of God and man, but who remain in the old leaven of [the natural] birth, and who do not choose to understand that the Holy Ghost came upon Mary, and the power of the Most High did overshadow her: wherefore also what was generated is a holy thing, and the Son of the Most High God the Father of all, who effected the incarnation of this being, and showed forth a new [kind of] generation. (5.1.3)

Irenaeus is asking after the "union of God and man in Christ." Who is the subject responsible for "effecting the incarnation of this being"? Is it the Son or is it the Spirit? Irenaeus, or at least the Irenaeus we have via his Latin translator, is not altogether clear here. This much is clear however, a little further on in the same passage Irenaeus suggests *both* of God's hands were involved in the creation of Jesus,

---

53. *Against Heresies* 3.18.3, in Grant, *Irenaeus*; cf. *Dem.* 40, 51 and 71.

54. *Dem.* 40; Regarding the translation of *sown*, see Robinson, "Doctrine of the Holy Spirit," 65.

> That is why, at the end, "not by the will of the flesh or the will of a man," but by the good pleasure of the Father, the *Hands* of God made the living Man [that is, Jesus Christ].[55]

With this we arrive at the critical contribution of Irenaean ontology: the Son alone does not mediate the Creator and creation. I suggest Irenaeus realized that restricting the christological equation to a brute one to one juxtaposition of the humanity and deity of Christ eventuated an unmediated ontological dualism at the very crux of reality. To merely stand the incarnate Son between the infinite and the finite and call the job done only passes the buck: if the creation cannot stand over against the Creator without the mediatorial initiative of God, it would seem that such is also the case for the humanity and deity of Christ. Although this is to anticipate concerns not relevant for Irenaeus, his "two-handed" concept of ontological mediation will offer some constructive possibilities for our study in later chapters.

Finally, although Irenaeus does not explicitly transpose his "commanding, fashioning, nourishing" pattern into the specifically christological categories I might like, perhaps it is fair to gloss him by implication to say that the Father was the one who initiated the mediation between the Creator and creation by "commanding" the creation of Jesus, and the Son was the one who "established" and "fashioned" that mediation by creating and becoming Jesus, and the Spirit is the one who "nourishes and gives increase" to that mediation by creating and mediating the being of the Jesus so created.

This of course raises at least as many problems as it seeks to resolve. But this is only chapter 1. For now, one thing seems certain enough: For Irenaeus God is not ambidextrous. In the face of intense pressures to the contrary, his functional distinguishing of the mediatorial roles of the Son and the Spirit served to vouchsafe a doctrine of creation that would not dissolve into monism. And so, in an area of theology that has often verged on the binitarian, Irenaeus has served us well by reminding us of the strong second hand of God. With such a reminder we turn now to later developments, and therewith to an era that, although having largely neglected Irenaeus' insights, is one that nonetheless has its own to offer.

---

55. *Against Heresies* 5.1.3, emphasis added; in Balthasar, *Scandal of the Incarnation*.

2

CYRIL OF ALEXANDRIA AND THE NESTORIAN OPTION

Theotokos, Communicatio Idiomatum, and the Single Subjectivity of Christ

(A Soteriological Concept of Mediation)

> For the Godhead and the manhood are two natures...
> but there are not two Sons or two Gods...
> For both natures are one by the combination,
> the Godhead made man or the manhood deified,
> or whatever be the right expression.
>
> —Gregory Nazianzen

During the build-up to the council of Chalcedon midway through the fifth century there were two beliefs that stood indisputable for all concerned: God does not change and Jesus is somehow both God and man. The impassibility of divinity was a belief so basic to philosophy that even the boldest heretics took it for granted, and the claim that Jesus was both divine and human was so basic to orthodoxy that only the boldest heretics dared question it. But the shadow of fourth-century Arianism still lingered. By managing to deny simultaneously both Christ's real humanity and his real deity, the Arian crisis left an otherwise theologically diverse church with a hangover of suspicion and defensiveness. The crucial point had been hard-won, *that* Christ is both man and God, but it was not yet clear *how* this was to be understood.

A quick sketch of the coming storm: at one end of the Church, near what was then its northeastern edge in Syria, were Christians thinking within an intellectual culture dominated largely by Aristotle. At the other, the southeastern end loosely revolving around the Egyptian See of Alexandria, were Christians breathing air permeated to a greater degree by neo-Platonism.[1] Albeit a simplification, the classic discrepancies between the Philosopher and his Teacher serve to frame the dilemma: the substantially-inclined "Antiochenes" from Syria tended to wrestle with the christological problem in terms of the compatibility of two disparate elements, humanity and divinity. By contrast, the more abstract "Alexandrians" tended to approach the same problem in terms of how a single entity could exist simultaneously as both human and divine. In Syria the question was grounded like Aristotle and so concerned the way the Logos assumed a specific human being. In Egypt the question was more ideological like Plato and so concerned the way the Logos assumed a general human nature. In short, the "Antiochenes" asked how God and man could be one, and the "Alexandrians" asked how this one could be both God and man.[2]

It was almost as though Christ stood on the 33rd Parallel, somewhere above the Mediterranean Sea, and from the North one looked across the water and saw the Son and man together, while from the South, another looked and saw the eternal Logos in the flesh. From one perspective, Christ was a duality, and to deny this was only possible if one or the other of his constitutive elements was eclipsed or ignored. From

---

1. See McGuckin, *Saint Cyril: Christological*, 209ff.

2. "Cyril, working with a 'katagogic' model, asking how does the Word become human without ceasing to be divine, Nestorius, working with an 'anagogic' model, asking how this man Jesus Christ is divine without compromising his humanity" (Russel, *Cyril of Alexandria*, 40). Thus, Nestorius himself writes against Cyril: "You start your account with the creator of the natures and not with the prosopon of union. It is not the Logos who has become two-fold, it is the one Lord Jesus Christ who is two-fold in his natures" (*Book of Heraclides* 225; in McGuckin, *Saint Cyril: Christological*, 156, 157n57).

the other perspective, Christ seemed the eternal Son he had always been, only now appearing in his newly acquired human form.[3]

At the time, differences in theological expression were considered a sure sign of the presence of error. And since all errors led to Arius, each side heard the other's theology with grave suspicion. In the Alexandrian ear, any squeamishness about the attribution of human traits to the incarnate Son smacked of adoptionism. If one could not say, for example, that God had a real human birth, then he obviously imagined the man born of Mary was someone other than the divine Son. And any talk of "conjunction" (*synapheia*) only confirmed the concern that Jesus was imagined to be merely inspired or adopted by God in some however special manner. In the Antiochene ear, anything less than some kind of ongoing duality meant Apollinarius was hovering nearby. Unless the humanity of Jesus stood squarely alongside the Logos, they believed it was bound to be fatally slighted, as if the Logos had simply replaced the human soul of Jesus. And regardless of how often the Antiochenes were told that the Logos assumed human flesh "united to a rational soul" the similar frequency of phrases like "one nature after the union" seemed to demand that something intrinsically human had been left out of the picture.

These tensions were only latent in midsummer 428 when a local but potent controversy broke out in the Imperial See of Constantinople.[4] Was it proper to say that Mary gave birth to God? If so, she is rightfully called *Theotokos*—God-bearer—if not, the popular title for Mary must be snuffed out. There was a new archbishop on the throne, Nestorius from Antioch, and the good pastor had sensed a troubling displacement of worship among his flock from Christ to his mother, so he came to a somewhat hasty conclusion: "That God passed from the Virgin *Christotokos* I am taught by the divine Scriptures, but that God was born from her I have not been taught anywhere."[5] This could be a lesson for pastors: Nestorius had learned his Classic logic but he had skimped on reading his predecessors. Not only was Mary's title *Theotokos* popular among the laity, it had a good genealogy of support among the Fathers.[6]

---

3. I have deliberately avoided the supposedly debunked *logos-sarx* vs. *logos-anthropos* stereotype of the issue, though it would provide a helpful element to this broad-stroke sketch. See Grillmeier, *Birth of Christology*, esp. 414ff.

4. The following account follows Russel, *Cyril of Alexandria*; Grillmeier, *Birth of Christology*; and Wickham, *Cyril of Alexandria*, "Introduction."

5. *Acta Conciliorum Oecumenicorum* 1.1.6, in Russel, *Cyril of Alexandria*, 34.

6. See Starowieyski, "Le Titre *Theotokos*," 236–42.

The history of the controversy is well documented so I will move quickly to the point. Through a somewhat bumbled Imperial Council in Ephesus in 431, and through what may have been a politically-induced formalization of it in the *Formula of Reunion* in 433, the two sides found a tentative, and temporary, peace. The theology at stake comes into clearest focus as it centres on the way it divided the church of the day over the title *Theotokos*.

Nestorius believed the title was an expression of ignorant piety, a product of theological muddle-headedness to be delivered from the Church by the clear-thinking. Language about God honoured him best when it was as precise as possible and calling Mary the *bearer-of-God* was insufficiently accurate since the one she bore was the Christ and not, strictly speaking,[7] the Godhead. Nestorius' attempt to peddle the title *Christotokos* as an alternative to the popular imprecision failed miserably, but he was quick to try again and differently. This time he agreed to accept the title *Theotokos* so long as it was accompanied by what was, in his opinion, its theologically necessary corollary, *Anthropotokos*, bearer-of-the-man. But this cumbersome option met a similarly short fate. Neither of Nestorius' alternatives to the *Theotokos* title found any support. But there is much more at play here than just a doomed attempt to harness hyperbole. For Nestorius the title was theologically inaccurate; Mary bore the Christ and Christ is both God *and* man.

On Nestorius' terms, Christ is "the common name of the two natures."[8] The name Christ is the adjectival sum of all the properties appropriate to the Son as both God *and* man. Human predicates—birth from a woman or dying on a cross, for example—could not properly be ascribed to the Logos *as Logos*. Yet if that were the entire content of the controversy the episode might have stayed untouched in the annals of Church history. But there is some crucial theology at stake here and Nestorius would sooner have impaled himself on it then let it go.

To repeat: for Nestorius Christ is not just God, he is God *and* man. The issue that had arisen can be put on that *and* like a fulcrum. For Cyril the Alexandrian Archbishop, Christ is God *as* man.

Nestorius argues:

---

7. This is a common qualification for Nestorius. See the comments at McGuckin, *Saint Cyril: Christological*, 28, and esp. 163n69.

8. Grillmeier, *Birth of Christology*, 454.

> Christ is indivisible in that he is Christ, but he is two-fold in that he is both God and Man . . . We do not acknowledge two Christs . . . but one and the same who has been seen in created and uncreated nature.[9]

The issue is about the relation of "created and uncreated nature," about how God relates to his world in Christ.

Cyril gets to the point when he says: "[Nestorius] not only disapproves of our custom of saying that the holy Virgin is *Theotokos* and that she has given birth to Emmanuel who is God, but in addition to this . . . he attempts to show us that [Christ] is a God-bearing man and not truly God."[10]

Is Christ God or is he the God-bearer? Either Christ *is* God relating to his world or he is *where* God relates to his world. Cyril's accusation is simple: Nestorius cannot call Mary *Theotokos* because he figures that is who Jesus is. On such a view, Christ is not God *per se*, since it is the eternal-Logos-united-to-the-human-nature-of-Christ who is "properly speaking" God. Although Cyril's way of casting his opponent is clearly skewed (Nestorius was no naïve adoptionist), the idea that it is not Mary but Christ who is the locus of God's entry into the world is indeed somewhere near the heart of the issue. I will come back to this broad perspective after a look at what Cyril has to offer but first, a rhymey question: What brought Nestorius to his notorious conclusions?

It was the scandal of Apollinarianism that set the agenda for Nestorius. Following Gregory Nazianzen, he attacked any theology that slighted the full human reality of Christ. And for him, leaving *Theotokos* unqualified meant leaving Christ un-humanized. There was, Courtesy of Apollinarius, a new demand for a human soul in Christ and Nestorius felt it incumbent upon thinking churchmen to find space for such a thing. To simplify: Nestorius preferred to find *room* in Christ for a complete humanity and the eternal Word. Cyril, on the other hand, preferred to imagine the *occasion* of the divine-human union in Christ. One mode of thought sought to find *space* for the incarnation, and the other *time* for it.

Aloys Grillmeier explains why Nestorius' search for christological space was especially challenging:

> Nestorius' particular difficulty arises from the fact that in interpreting Christ he is not dealing with two abstract natures, but

---

9. *Book of Heraclides* 280, in McGuckin, *Saint Cyril: Christological*, 165.
10. In Russel, *Cyril of Alexandria*, 141.

with an individual, concrete human nature and the Godhead which subsists in the Logos. Godhead and manhood in Christ are concrete realities.[11]

Nestorius found himself faced with a task that seemed to demand certain theological results; he needed to say that in Christ was both the eternal divine Son and a fully real human being. And because these were "concrete realities," he simply confessed them both:

> If he is truly God, we confess that he is truly God also in his nature and that he is complete, lacking nothing of the nature of the Father; and we confess that the man is truly man, complete in his nature, lacking nothing of the nature of men, neither in body nor in soul nor in knowledge; he has all this in our image, apart from sin.[12]

There are clearly "two" in this passage. There is the one who is "complete, lacking nothing of the nature of the Father" and there is "the man . . . lacking nothing of the nature of men." This *two-ness* was anathema to Cyril, and it formed the basis on which he accused Nestorius of a "two Sons" Christology. Nestorius was hard-pressed to defend his view:

> There is no division in the conjunction, or in the dignity, or in the sonship. There is no division in his being Christ, but there is division between the divinity and the humanity. Christ insofar as he is Christ is indivisible; the Son insofar as he is Son is indivisible; for we do not have two Christs or two Sons. Nor do we accept a first Christ and a second one, or two different Christs, or two different Sons. On the contrary, the Son himself is twofold, not in rank but in nature.[13]

Nestorius wants a "twofold" Christ, yes, but one that is undivided as such.[14] He was a Christologist keen to maintain the absolute difference between the Creator and the creation and on his terms confessing both of these together in the incarnate Son required a "division between the

---

11. Grillmeier, *Birth of Christology*, 458.
12. Russell, *Cyril of Alexandria*, 43.
13. Loofs, *Nestoriana*, 280–81, cited in Russel, *Cyril of Alexandria*, 148–49.
14. "Even before the incarnation the God-Logos was Son and God and together with the Father, but in the last times he took the form of a servant; but as already previously he was a Son both in name and in nature, he cannot be called a separate Son after taking this form, otherwise we would be decreeing two sons" (*Nestoriana* 275.1–5, in Grillmeier, *Birth of Christology*, 455).

divinity and the humanity."[15] Yet Nestorius' was not a simple doctrine of Christ. It was not merely a matter of setting the Logos and the human Jesus beside one another, confessing their unity, and leaving the rest in mystery. He clearly has some rubric for the unity of Christ: "There is no division in the conjunction (synapheia)."[16] But what does this mean? Here is the problem of only having Nestorius as he was quoted by his opponents. His concept of conjunction is either very complex or so politically misquoted that it is lost in muddled ambiguity. Even when Cyril allows us to hear Nestorius defend himself, more questions are raised than answered:

> You [Cyril] should not have accused me [Nestorius] and calumniated me as if I did not confess a single *prosopon* in two natures, or as if I set the natures apart in separation and division, as if they were separated in a spatial sense and distant from one another. For I have indeed called the "dweller" him who necessarily dwells in the nature. The dweller is he who dwells in him who serves him as a dwelling, and he has his *prosopon*, while he who serves him as a dwelling has the *prosopon* of him who dwells. So by the use of their *prosopa*, as though they were making use of their own properties in an authoritative way, the former is the latter and the latter is the former, the former and the latter abiding just as they are in their natures.[17]

The reason this passage has survived for us is the talk in it of a "dweller" and a "dwelling." Cyril latched onto this as a sure indication of the way Nestorius has two different subjects in view. Yet there is some constructive subtlety here, too, and it pivots on what Nestorius is doing with his use of the term *prosopon*. For Nestorius, any nature that is real has an

---

15. "As far as Nestorius was concerned, language about the incarnation had to retain a primary sense of the difference between deity and humanity: both that distance between God and his creatures, and that between the divine and the human aspects of Christ. Once language had established the respective differences, the Christian mind could appreciate the closeness of a God who, in the person of Jesus Christ, enters into association with humankind . . . it was a scheme that insisted on the full integrity of all the elements that comprised it: God and the creature were radically different . . . For Nestorius, the human life of Jesus was something that the Logos was in communion with, not one that dominated or subjugated him in any way" (McGuckin, "Introduction," in McGuckin, ed., *St Cyril of Alexandria: Unity*, 33–34).

16. "I did not say that the Son was one (person) and God the Word another; I said that God the Word was *by nature* one and the temple *by nature* another, one Son by conjunction" (*Nestoriana* 308.8–11, in Grillmeier, *Birth of Christology*, 455).

17. *Book of Heraclides* 2.1, 324–25; in Russel, *Cyril of Alexandria*, 43–44.

outward appearance, a prosopon,[18] so there were three *prosopa* to consider in the mystery of the incarnation: there was what we see when we recognize the eternal Logos, what we see when we recognize the man Jesus, and what we see when we recognize the union of these two together in the one Christ.[19]

> We do not speak of a union of prosopa but a union of natures, for in the union there is only one prosopon but in the natures there are two, such that the prosopon (of union) should be recognised in them both.[20]

So there are two *prosopa*, Jesus and Logos, and there is one *prosopon*, Christ. But of course, that is not especially clear. There is still the question of *how* and, unfortunately for anyone trying to be sympathetic to Nestorius, he compounds his problems by using the same term, *prosopon*, to describe this too.

> The union of prosopa took place in prosopon (at prosopic level), not in essence or nature. One must not think of an essence without a hypostasis as if the union had taken place in an essence, and that there was a prosopon of a single essence. The natures subsist in their prosopa, and in their own natures, and in the prosopon of union. As for the natural prosopon of each one, then one makes use of the other by virtue of the union. In this sense there is only one prosopon for the two natures.[21]

---

18. "*Prosopon* is a collective term for all that pertains to the characteristics of nature, inwardly and outwardly . . . Each nature realized in concrete existence has its natural *prosopon*" (Grillmeier, *Birth of Christology*, 461). See also: "For Nestorius, who in this respect was influenced by the manner of speaking common at that time, the main thing in his notion of *prosopon* according to the etymology of the word and to the earlier history of its meaning, was the *external undivided appearance* . . . the notion of *prosopon* in Nestorius grew upon another soil and, therefore, had a wider application than our term *person*" (Loofs, *Nestoriana*, quoted in Grillmeier, *Birth of Christology*, 459).

19. "An accurate scrutiny of the external visible signs and evidence concerning Christ, therefore, clearly tells the observer that there are two separate levels of reality in this figure; two prosopa (or prosopic sets of evidence) signaling to the intelligent exegete the fact that two different natures co-exist in this being . . . This experience our exegetical senses have of the one Christ must signify that Christ himself (that is 'he-who-combines-two-prosopic-realities') is in some sense a single prosopic reality, and this is the prosopon which is known to experience as, and commonly designated, 'Christ'" (McGuckin, *Saint Cyril: Christological*, 152).

20. *Book of Heraclides* 252, in ibid., 172.

21. *Book of Heraclides* 305, in ibid., 170, 171.

The crucial point here is Nestorius' claim that "one must not think of an essence without a hypostasis as if the union had taken place in essence." I will come back to the language of "hypostasis" with Cyril. The point here is that Nestorius could not imagine an "essential" union in Christ. For him the incarnation was a union of will, "one [the divine] makes use of the other by virtue of the union."[22] But his was not simply a cold voluntarism. On the contrary, at points it seems as if Nestorius puts God's love at the centre of his ontology: "He is the subject of the two natures which are separated in essence but united in love, and in one and the same prosopon."[23]

There is clearly a duality in Christ for Nestorius. On his terms, anything less than an ongoing duality in Christ required a denial of one or the other of the incarnate Son's constituent elements; either Christ would be some kind of Apollinarian pseudo-human, or else God would have changed into a man. Neither option was thinkable. For Nestorius, there was the untrammeled God and there was an authentic human, and it was only by confusing these two (or worse, by omitting one) that any serious theologian would possibly call a human virgin the bearer-of-God.

∼

Cyril championed the title *Theotokos* for Mary.[24] His position was a political convenience, albeit somewhat misguided since the laity rallied behind Cyril as a defender of the Virgin and not as a theologian making a claim about her son. But Cyril's defense of the title was also theological. By retaining *Theotokos* for the mother of Jesus, Cyril raised the two pillars at the base of his entire theological edifice. The first was his concept of the incarnational *economy,* and the second was what has since come to be called the *communicatio idomatum* (communicaion of attributes). As with any two elements of a systematic theology, these cannot properly be considered in isolation from one another and eventually effect every other part of the system. They are connected, and they both support Cyril's understanding of *Theotokos.* His concept of *economy* is an entry point:

22. "[O]ne discerns the central element of his [Nestorius's] thought to be an emphasis on the divine provenience and initiative whereby the Logos binds himself to the man Jesus in an unassailably intimate union, without destroying any of the free capacities of the human life he graces with his unlimited power and presence" (ibid., 161).

23. *Book of Heraclides* 81, in ibid., 162.

24. Summing up Cyril, Russel says, "In a single word it [*Theotokos*] encapsulates the entire plan of salvation" (*Cyril of Alexandria*, 44).

God's Word is, of course, undoubtedly impossible in his own nature and nobody is so mad as to imagine the all-transcending nature capable of suffering; but by very reason of the fact that he has become man making flesh from the holy Virgin his own, we adhere to the principles of the divine plan (*oikonomia*) and maintain that he, who as God transcends suffering, suffered humanly in his own flesh.[25]

By virtue of the special conditions within the incarnate economy the "undoubtedly impossible . . . suffered humanly in his own flesh." In a word, the "flesh" of the Son is what allows Cyril to attribute suffering to the impassible Word. He explains, "the flesh should be seen as the basis for the occurrence of the suffering whilst the Word is impassible."[26] The flesh of Christ is not *what* suffered, as if his humanity were some kind of Docetic insulation against change, rather the flesh of Christ is the special occasion—the "occurrence"—during which God can be said to suffer..[27] Cyril explains in *On the Unity of Christ*:

> [H]is was a matter of salvation for the whole world. And since on this account he wished to suffer, even though he was beyond the power of suffering in his nature as God, he wrapped himself in flesh that was capable of suffering, and reveals it as his very own, so that even the suffering might be said to be his because it was his own body which suffered and no one else's. Since the manner of the economy allows him blamelessly to choose both to suffer in the flesh, and not to suffer in the Godhead . . . then our proponents surely argue in vain[28]

The incarnate Son suffers in his flesh because he "wished to." The sufferings involved in the incarnation were his because of what the "economy

---

25. *On the Creed* 24, in Wickham, *Cyril of Alexandria*, 123, and cf. ibid., 125.

26. *Second Letter to Succensus* 2, in ibid., 87. "Both points, indeed, must be maintained of the one true Son: the absence of divine suffering and the attribution to him of human suffering because his flesh did suffer" (*Second Letter to Succensus* 4, in ibid., 91).

27. On this, see especially Cyril's comments in his *Letter to John of Antioch*, in McGuckin, *Saint Cyril: Christological*, 347; *On the Creed*, in Wickham, *Cyril of Alexandria*, 109; and see the commentary of Weinandy, "Cyril and the Mystery of the Incarnation," 49ff; and McGuckin, *Saint Cyril: Christological*, 201ff. And see also Gould, "Cyril of Alexandria," 247: "The human nature is, so to speak, an indispensable medium by which human attributes and experience are converted into divine, not a barrier by which they are kept separate."

28. Ibid., 118.

allows him blamelessly to choose." Or, as Cyril has said elsewhere, "he was in the crucified body claiming the sufferings of his flesh as his own impassibly."[29] The Son is clearly sovereign here. For Cyril the sufferings of Christ really belong to the eternal Logos because he "claimed" them; this Logos is Lord over his incarnate economy and so is the agent responsible for choosing his sufferings.[30] On first impression, there is an important similarity here with Nestorius. Both Fathers wanted a pride of place for the divine will in their Christology. But Cyril's emphasis is unique in at least one crucial way. Graham Gould makes the point: "[For Cyril,] [t]he divine Word is the only subject of action in the Incarnation."[31] The Son "tastes death" and comes "back to life again"[32] and is even responsible for the very inception of this economy: "he made his very own a body" and, "he issued from woman for us and for our salvation having personally united the humanity to himself."[33] There is a persuasive simplicity about Cyril's theology here but the parsimony comes with a cost. Maybe unintentionally, Ezra Gebremedhin uncovers the problem:

> The predominant tone of Cyril's theology of the Incarnation is that of a Logos who takes initiative in everything that the Incarnate Word undergoes. He who was *asarkos* now appears on earth as *sesarkomenos* Nevertheless, it is *He* who appears, moving as it were out of eternity and continuing *His* life as Incarnate among men.[34]

---

29. *Third Letter to Nestorius* 6, in Wickham, *Cyril of Alexandria*, 21. Chadwick comments that "the suffering of the flesh was redemptive because it was a flesh not separated from the Logos but indeed his *hidia sarx*. So he reaches his not very illuminating conclusion: the Logos suffered impassibly" ("Eucharist and Christology," 158–59). "He (the Son) suffered without suffering," *Scholia* 37, ET in Weinandy, "Cyril and the Mystery of the Incarnation," 50, where we hear a different perspective from Chadwick's: "To say, in accordance with Cyril, that 'the Impassible suffers' is not, then, to be incoherent, but to state the very heart of the incarnational mystery."

30. "As I have said, he made his very own a body capable of tasting death and capable of coming back to life again, so that he himself might remain impassible and yet be said to suffer in his own flesh" (McGuckin, ed., *St Cyril: Unity*, 127).

31. Gould, "Cyril of Alexandria and the Formula of Reunion," 241.

32. "[T]he resurrection has testified that he is greater than death and corruption. As God he is life and life-giver, and so he raised up his own temple" (McGuckin, ed., *St Cyril: Unity*, 118).

33. *To Nestorius* 2.4, in Wickham, *Cyril of Alexandria*, 7.

34. Gebremedhin, *Life-Giving Blessing*, 39.

This deserves a pause. There is without question a priority of the Son over his incarnate economy in Cyril's theology. On the one hand, this is simply a christological version of a basic theistic truism; if there is a God it tends to follow that this God is somehow superior to everything else. On the other hand, Cyril's use of the concept of economy does at times lead one to suspect that the life of Jesus is little more than a passing episode in an otherwise complete biography of the Logos.

Cyril:

> For he is not two different beings or two sons, or one and then another, or a first and a second, but clearly one both before the flesh and along with the flesh.[35]

> He remains what he was, that is God by nature. After taking on human existence . . . being made as we are in flesh from a woman, he remains one Son, not discarnate (*asarkos*) as of old, before the epoch of his becoming man, but clad, as it were, with our nature.[36]

Cyril's is what in modern lingo would be called a "Christology from above" and it is one with all the strength and glory of such a paradigm. Yet there is a price for such grandeur, and it has to do with the appearance here of this mysterious figure called the *logos asarkos*.

Although Nestorius could hardly be said to be overly concerned with the historical Jesus, his commitment to a human *prosopon* in Christ offers an important contrast. As I have already suggested, these two theologians stood across from one another by a division very similar to the one that once separated Aristotle and Plato. Nestorius sought *a* human in Christ while Cyril looked for *humanity*. The result in Cyril is the way the particularities and contingencies of Jesus' life tend to be peripheral to his Christology.[37] The one with whom we have to do is not the Nazarene but the *logos asarkos* behind him.

---

35. *Contra Nest.* 42, in Russel, *Cyril of Alexandria*, 149. Thus Gould, "Cyril of Alexandria," 241: "There remains one Son both before and after the Incarnation, the difference being that in the Incarnation he has taken on his own flesh, just as each of us has his own body." For a discussion on the popular patristic use of the body/soul:humanity/Logos model or analogy, see Weinandy, *Does God Suffer?*, 182ff.

36. *II Succ.* 4, in Wickham, *Cyril of Alexandria*, 87.

37. Meijering, having drawn parallels between Cyril's view of the Trinity and that of the triadic Principles of neo-Platonists, e.g., Plotinus, makes—perhaps too strongly—the point: "[W]e feel obliged to qualify Cyril's praise of the Platonists by pointing out the obvious fact they would still have differed from the Christians on

That is an admittedly anachronistic critique but I raise it here as a flag for what will recur more appropriately in later chapters.[38] Our present concern is with Cyril and with his: there is clearly a single subject in his Christology. It is a line of thought set mainly through his talk of the divine economy. And it is one that is extended even further through his theology about the communication of attributes.

∼

As with most (probably *all*) theological issues, the one between Cyril and Nestorius had a hermeneutical counterpart. Their questions about how an impassible God is present to his world in Christ found a grounding in ones about how to read different gospel passages. The nativity in which Mary is said to have borne God-with-us is a case in point, but there are many others: on some occasions Christ appears to be weak, hungry, or ignorant, and at others he can heal, forgive, and raise the dead. In his *Third Letter to Nestorius*, Cyril explains his way of dealing with such texts; he writes in terms of the various "statements" of Jesus, but the issue extends to the whole of Christ's life.

> As for our Saviour's statements in the Gospels, we do not divide them out to two subjects or persons. The one, unique Christ has no duality though he is seen as compounded in inseparable unity . . . We must take the right view and maintain that human as well as divine expressions are from one speaker . . . Accordingly all the sayings contained in the Gospels must be referred to a single person, to the one incarnate subject of the Word (*hypostasi mia te tou logou sesarkomene*).[39]

---

one important view: they would not have identified the second Principle with Jesus of Nazareth. Cyril obviously believes that it is enough to show that the Platonists could have believed in the possibility of the second Principle incarnating itself in *a* man; the fact that this man was Jesus of Nazareth is of secondary importance to him. This shows that Cyril's theological system did not start with Jesus of Nazareth, but with a preconceived philosophical-theological scheme into which he fitted Jesus of Nazareth" (*God, Being, History*, 126).

38. To be fair, Cyril did entertain the problem, albeit only in passing: "If anyone should say that Christ Jesus is before the ages he would not have departed from the truth, at least if it is true that there is One Son and Lord, the Word who is before the ages who underwent a birth from a woman according to the flesh in the last times of this age" (McGuckin, ed., *St Cyril: Unity*, 92).

39. *III Nest.* 8, in Wickham, *Cyril of Alexandria*, 23–25.

The Antiochene approach simply ascribed Christ's limitations to his human nature and his excellencies to his divine. But Cyril is clearly doing something different here. All the sayings of Christ are spoken by the "one incarnate *hypostasis* of the Word" and should in no way be doled out to the different subjects within a supposed "duality."

In 432, when he received the proposal for reconciliation with the Syrians from John of Antioch, their "two natures" hermeneutic was explicit within it.[40] Understandably, Cyril's reception of the *Formula* raised considerable concern among his followers. In his *Letter to Eulogius* Cyril defended his concession:

> So if we speak of a union we are affirming that it is a union of flesh, endowed with a mental life and reason, and the Word, and this is how those who say "two natures" understand it; yet, with the acknowledgement of union the united elements no longer stand apart from each other but from then on there is one Son, one nature of him, the Word incarnate. These truths the Easterns acknowledged, even if they were somewhat in the dark about phraseology.[41]

The mention of "one nature of him, the Word incarnate" is clearly Cyril's own formula and the fact that it comes in a passage intended to defend the Antiochene use of "*two* natures" only serves to suggest there is more in the dark here than just phraseology. The question about whether Cyril has developed his view or fudged it for the sake of peace with Constantinople need not occupy us, the central point has remained unchanged for Cyril.[42] For him there is still only a single subject to whom the various

---

40. "As for the terms used about the Lord in the Gospels and apostolic writings, we recognize that theologians treat some as shared because they refer to one person, some they refer separately to two natures, traditionally teaching the application of the divine terms to Christ's Godhead, the lowly to his manhood" (*Ep.* 39.5, in ibid., 222).

41. *To Eulogius*, in ibid., 65.

42. After the recovery from Ephesus, defending his acceptance of the *Formula*, Cyril charitably misrepresents the Antiochene brethren on this point to Acasius of Melitene: "The Antiochene brethren, on the other hand, taking the recognized elements of Christ at the level of only mere ideas, have mentioned a difference of natures, . . . they do declare there is one Son and Christ and Lord, and, since he is actually one in reality, that his person too is one; by no manner of means do they divide what are in union" (*To Acacius* 15, in ibid., 53). And compare the similar line offered to Successus: "So far, then, as the question of the manner of the Only-begotten's becoming man appears for purely mental consideration by the mind's eye, our view is that there are two united natures but one Christ, Son and Lord, the Word of God become man and incarnate" (*First Letter to Successus* 7, in ibid., 77).

saying of Christ ought be attributed. Putting this differently, there is a "communication of attributes," both human and divine, to the one *hypostasis* of the incarnate Son.[43]

> As the Word he is born divinely before all ages and times, but in these last times of this age the same one was born of a woman according to the flesh. To the same one we attribute both the divine and human characteristics, and we also say that to the same one belongs the birth and the suffering on the cross since he appropriated everything that belonged to his own flesh, while ever remaining impassible in the nature of the Godhead.[44]

For Cyril there is a bilateral attribution of characteristics (or communication of attributes) from the divine Son to his incarnate economy and from his own economic flesh to his identity as the divine Son. This is what made it so important for Cyril to affirm that God was indeed born of a woman. If one hesitated over such a claim then there was something impeding the free traffic of human attributes to the divine Son, and—just as importantly—reason to suspect attribution in the other direction was also somehow limited. For Cyril, this kind of traffic jam was what divided Christ into two subjects. This does not mean that Cyril did not distinguish between human and divine attributes; he clearly did.[45] When he came to comment on his contentious *12 Anathemas*, he explained:

---

43. Despite its historical significance, what Cyril meant with his famous use of the term "hypostasis" is simply not clear. (Indeed the temperature of the theological climate at the time suggests the ambiguity may not have been strictly unintentional.) Wickham suggests that Cyril used it as a mostly contentless negation of the Antiochene theology he opposed. See ibid., 4–5n6, and cf. ibid., 50–51n30. McGuckin, however, offers some purchase: "In the hands of Cyril the word is used in two senses, one in what might be called the standard 'physical' usage where it connotes the constituent elements of a thing, and the other in which it serves to delineate the notion of individual existent—or in other words individual subject" (*Saint Cyril: Christological*, 140); it is clearly the latter sense in use when Cyril says, as above, "there is one Son, one nature of him, the Word incarnate." See the following discussion (and at 209, 212ff.) where McGuckin unravels the complex terminological issue to such an extent that it almost appears the whole difference between the two archbishops could very likely have been avoided had the language been less vicious. That said, however, "The problem was not that Nestorius and Cyril were using different words for the same concepts, but rather they were using the same words for different concepts" (Weinandy, *Does God Suffer?*, 179n11). For further discussion on the terminological fog between Cyril and Nestorius see Russel, *Cyril of Alexandria*, 26, 40.

44. McGuckin, ed., *St Cyril: Unity*, 133.

45. "In no way does Cyril allow the natures to be distinguished as separate subjects of the various expressions, or even for various characteristics and experiences such as

> For this reason we apply all the sayings in the Gospels, the human ones as well as those befitting God, to one *prosopon*. We believe that Jesus Christ, that is the Word of God made man and made flesh, is but One Son. And so, even if he speaks in a human fashion, we relate these human things to the limitations of his manhood because, once again, that very human condition is his own. Yet, if he should discourse as God, believing him to be God made man, once again we attribute these sayings which are beyond the nature of man to one Christ and Son.[46]

Cyril recognized the sayings of Christ not as ones said by the human nature of Christ and others by his divine, but as things said by the one Christ *humanly* and others said by this same one *divinely*. And this recalls the space-time difference between Antioch and Alexandria. Whereas Nestorius and his colleagues located the different sayings "spatially" in the two natures of Christ, Cyril imagined a single subject saying different things at different times. So to the question: does Cyril have space in his theology for a christological duality? The answer must be a careful, "Yes, but not really" (at least not *real-ly* in an Aristotelian sense). For Cyril, the duality of humanity and divinity in Christ is something only imaginable in theory.

> The point is that man results from two natures—body and soul, I mean—and intellectual perception (*theoria*) recognizes the difference; but we unite them and then get one nature of man. So, recognizing the difference of natures is not dividing the one Christ into two.[47]

Even in 421, prior to his bout with Nestorius, Cyril was already insisting that it is "merely in thought" that the natures could be divided.[48]

---

suffering; to Cyril this is simply to make two Sons . . . A duality of the status of terms is accepted, a duality of reference is not" (Gould, "Cyril of Alexandria," 246, 247).

46. *Explanation of the Twelve Chapters* 14, in McGuckin, *Saint Cyril: Christological*, 287.

47. Wickham, *Cyril of Alexandria*, 64, 65. His footnote captures the issue: "The passage affirms a real distinction of natures for thought—and hence the disagreement, for in what respect is the duality *actual*?"

48. "We divide them, though, merely in thought accepting the difference as simply residing in the fine drawn insight or mental intuition; . . . the two are no more and the single living being is constituted complete by the pair of them" (*Ad Succ.* 2.5, in ibid., 93). Cf. n44 above.

And the idea was a repeated theme in his *Commentary on John* of 428.[49] Here is an element of Cyril's thought that stood more or less unaltered throughout his career. He was prepared to acknowledge a *theoretical* duality in Christ, but his theology about the communication of attributes and its demand for a single subject meant there could be no *real* duality in Christ *after* the union.[50]

> [W]e speak of two natures being united; but after the union, the duality (*diatome*) has been abolished and we believe the Son's nature to be one, since he is one Son, yet become man and incarnate.[51]

The point of all this comes into focus in a comment from Graham Gould: "Cyril's account of the two-nature formula relies on an explicit contrast of before and after the union. That the union was a union of two real different natures must be acknowledged, but after the union only the result, two united natures, is evident even to close scrutiny."[52] The bone of contention between Alexandria and Antioch was the *timing* of the incarnation. For Nestorius the incarnation was in some sense an on-going event, the conjunction of the human and divine natures being continuously maintained by the "dweller"-Word. But for Cyril the union of the human and divine in Christ was an instantaneous, even theoretically atemporal, event in the past of Mary's womb.[53] Cyril's most familiar

---

49. Chadwick, "Eucharist and Christology," 150. For discussion on the *Commentary*, see Welch, *Christology and Eucharist*, esp. 74ff.

50. "Cyril emphasizes unity as a present fact, a *result* which excludes duality of any kind" (Gould, "Cyril of Alexandria," 244).

51. *To Acacius* 12, in Wickham, *Cyril of Alexandria*, 49. And see also *II Prooem* 33, in Russel, *Cyril of Alexandria*, 142: "He is conceived of as one and only and every word befits him and everything will be said as from one person. For the incarnate nature of the Word is immediately conceived of as one after the union."

52. Gould, "Cyril of Alexandria," 240. "We say that there is one Son, and that he has one nature even when he is considered as having assumed flesh endowed with a rational soul . . . [the interlocutor asks:]Then does he not have two natures? that of God, and that of man? [Cyril replies:] Well, Godhead is one thing, and manhood is another thing, considered in the perspective of their respective and intrinsic beings, but in the case of Christ they came together in a mysterious and incomprehensible union without confusion or change. The manner of this union is entirely beyond conception" (McGuckin, ed., *St Cyril: Unity*, 77).

53. "[I]t cannot be too strongly emphasized that for him "after the union" has no temporal significance" (Sellers, *Two Ancient Christologies*, 99).

expression of this theology was in his repeated use of the Apollinarian phrase *one incarnate nature of the Word*:[54]

> We do not damage the concurrence into unity by declaring it was effected out of two natures; however, after the union we do not divide the natures from each other and do not sever the one and indivisible into two sons but say "one Son" and, as the fathers have put it, "one incarnate nature of the Word" (*mia physis to Theo Logou sesarkomene*).[55]

Excepting his rare but important gracious episodes, Cyril tended to restrict his understanding of *physis* (nature) to its meaning within his own semantic heritage. In Alexandria "nature" referred to an individual concrete entity; it was a concept almost equivalent to *hypostasis*. This allowed Cyril to rely on his *mia physis* formula as a final barrier against the obscene idea of "two Sons." John McGuckin explains: "What Cyril meant by this key phrase was to insist that the single individual reality of the Word of God, and no other, was the one who had now been incarnated: in other words, that the sole personal subject of the incarnation was the eternal Word, and that there was no human personal subject alongside God in the incarnate Lord."[56]

But Cyril's slogan never caught on in Syria, where the typical meaning of *physis* was significantly different. For Nestorius and the Antiochenes, "nature" referred to an identifiable assemblage of characteristics or attributes, something closer to the old use of *prosopon*; a "mask" or "role." For these theologians a single-natured Christ was a misnomer of catastrophic proportion. If Christ had only one nature then inevitably his humanity had been overpowered and subsumed by the "greater" nature of the divine Word.

Yet Cyril did at least somewhat appreciate his opponents' concern and even at the mature end of his career he continued to assure them

---

54. Due to the common patristic rhetorical practice of circulating writings by disfavoured authors under the names of more reputable ones, Cyril had received this phrase via what he thought was a work by Athanasius. Despite the irony, Cyril's use of the formula represents a significant development on Apollinarius' position. See Chadwick, *Church in Ancient Society*, 527ff. For a brief sketch of the lineage and reception of this Cyrilline trademark see also Wickham, *Cyril of Alexandria*, 62n3.

55. *First Letter to Successus* 7, in Wickham, *Cyril of Alexandria*, 75–77. This formula recurs throughout Cyril's writing, but it is especially central in his correspondence with Successus; see his *Second Letter to Successus* 2, in ibid., 87; *Second Letter to Successus* 5, in ibid., 93); and the further discussion in ibid., 49, 77.

56. McGuckin, *Saint Cyril: Christological*, 140.

that the humanity of Christ "was not soulless, as some have said, but rather is animated with a rational soul."[57] His repeated reference to the "one nature" of the Word was always closely qualified by the concept of incarnation, by which, Cyril explained, did not mean a mere "enfleshing" of divinity but "rather the *enmanment* of the Word."[58] He knew what the Antiochenes suspected him of, and he answered them accordingly: "The term union in no way causes the confusion of the things it refers to, but rather signifies the concurrence in one reality of those things which are understood to be united."[59]

This was not just semantic fidgetry, a practice Cyril often ascribed to Nestorius. The single nature of Christ and the consequent attribution of divine and human properties to the incarnate Word was the dynamic junction at the centre of Cyril's theology. The person of Christ is where it happened first: the free exchange of human weakness for divine life. And this was grounds for the element of Cyril's thought most influential in the worshipping lives of his supporting laity. More than anything else, it was Cyril's teaching on the Eucharist that translated his Christology into the currency of late Ancient church practice.

> When we perform in church the unbloody service, . . . we approach the sacramental gifts and are hallowed participants in the holy flesh and precious blood of Christ, saviour of all, by receiving not mere flesh (God forbid!) . . . but the personal, truly vitalizing flesh of God the Word himself. As God he is by nature Life and because he has become one with his own flesh he rendered it vitalizing.[60]

With this Cyril made the body of Christ "vitalizing" or life-giving (*zoeopion*).[61] Having worked so hard to remove any notion of duality in Christ after the union, Cyril had established a theology for explaining the Eucharist as a participation in the power and glory of the Godhead itself. This is the faith that instilled such zeal in his desert monks. Every Eucharist is a reincarnation of Christ and every communicant partakes of the very flesh of God. To divide the natures of Christ by, for example,

---

57. McGuckin, ed., *St Cyril: Unity*, 55.

58. Ibid., 57, 59.

59. Ibid., 73.

60. *Third Letter to Nestorius* 7, in Wickham, *Cyril of Alexandria*, 23. Cf. ibid., 81, and *Anathema* 11; see Chadwick, "Eucharist and Christology," 154n5, regarding the basis for this in Athanasius.

61. For discussion, see Gebremedhin, *Life-Giving Blessing*, 48ff.

denying the validity of the title God-bearer to Mary, would reduce the Eucharistic feast from an ontological union with God to an act of cannibalism.[62] Nestorius simply could not reply with anything approaching this scale of grandeur.

Cyril's potency here hung on the way his single-subject Christology led cleanly to an especially cogent soteriology and the way that both were logically nested in a similarly straightforward doctrine of creation. Ruth Siddals sketches the connection by grouping Cyril's understanding of the creation of man into three stages: the first is a calling into being out of nothingness, the second an "inserting" into humans of certain divine qualities—among them incorruptibility—and the third is humanity's fall where these qualities are lost and man's natural corruptibility reasserts itself.[63] This is the scenario that required a saviour in Cyril's theology.[64] Siddals comments, "What is needed is a new creation. The saving God must again 'insert' into man's nature his own . . . incorruptibility and holiness."[65] Thus Cyril:

> It is as if one took a glowing ember and thrust it into a large pile of straw in order to preserve the vital nucleus of the fire. In the same way our Lord Jesus Christ hides away life within us by means of his own flesh, and inserts immortality into us, like some vital nucleus that destroys every trace of corruption in us.[66]

Reception of the body of Christ in the Eucharist *is* salvation for Cyril:

> Those who do not receive the Son of God in the sacrament are thus completely excluded from the blessed life. Only so are we

---

62. See Chadwick, "Eucharist and Christology," 156.
63. Siddals, "Logic and Christology," 361ff.
64. On this, see also Young, "*Theotokos*," 55–74.
65. Siddals, "Logic and Christology," 363. Thus Chadwick can observe that, according to Cyril, "by partaking we receive the lifegiving and sanctifying power of Christ. The body of life which we receive is like a *sperma Zoeopoion* within us; the Logos thus implants himself within us . . . and makes us deathless and incorruptible . . . As we receive Christ's body, it is mingled with our bodies, and instills life into them" ("Eucharist and Christology," 153).
66. *Commentary on John* 6.54. See also his similar comments on John 6:35, 56, in Russel, *Cyril of Alexandria*, 117, 118.

intimately united to the Logos. For the Logos and his flesh are inseparable.[67]

And this Eucharistic theology is seamless with Cyril's Christology:

> This was why he appeared as we are and made his own a body subject to corruption according to the inherent system of its nature. In so far as he himself is life, for he was born from the life of the Father, he intended to implant his own benefit within it, that is life itself.[68]

Now the heavy conceptual work in Cyril's Christology has borne its soteriological payload: The enfleshed Word is a paradigm of divinization. Christ's divine nature pierced every fiber of his humanity and thereby deified it completely.[69] At the incarnation the Son overcame the corruptibility of human flesh and in the Eucharist he extends this possibility to others:

> It was not otherwise possible for man, being of a nature which perishes, to escape death, unless he recovered that ancient grace, and partook once more of God who holds all things together in their being and preserves them in life through the Son and Spirit. Therefore his Only-begotten Word has become a partaker of flesh and blood (Heb. 2:14), that is, he has become man, though being Life by nature, and begotten of the life that is by nature, that is of God the Father, so that, having united himself with the flesh which perishes according to the law of its own nature . . . he might restore it to his own Life and render it through himself partaker of God the Father.[70]

Here is an item of Cyril's theology under increasing scrutiny in current scholarship.[71] I will leave aside the debate about *how* central the idea of deification was for Cyril[72]—he clearly holds a variety of soteriological

---

67. Chadwick, "Eucharist and Christology," 154.

68. McGuckin, ed., *St Cyril: Unity*, 125; cf. ibid., 57.

69. "[A]s such the communicatio is shorthand for his whole doctrine of the incarnation itself as a transforming transaction whereby human nature is appropriated by God and deified in the process" (McGuckin, *Saint Cyril: Christological*, 192).

70. *Commentary on John* 14.20, in Weinandy, "Cyril and the Mystery of the Incarnation," 24.

71. See Keating, *Theosis*.

72. For the current state of play on the subject, see Keating, "Divinization in Cyril." McGuckin is one example of an otherwise very careful reader of Cyril who over-weights the concept: "The physical interchange that occurs when the believer

themes together[73]—and simply make the less ambitious claim: there is theology about deification in Cyril's thought.

> It follows, therefore, that He Who Is, The One Who Exists, is necessarily born of the flesh, taking all that is ours into himself so that all that is born of the flesh, that is us corruptible and perishing beings, might rest in him. In short, he took what was ours to be his very own so that we might have all that was his . . . he came down into our condition solely in order to lead us to his own divine state.[74]

The direct illusion to Irenaeus here—he took what was ours to be his very own so that we might have all that was his[75]—provides an occasion for an important contrast. Whereas Irenaeus' eschatological vision was one that saw God moving his creation from infancy in the garden through Christ and onward by the Spirit to its final completion at the end, Cyril clearly imagined an eschatology in which the goal was a return to a pre-fall condition. Cyril's own use of another Irenaean trademark further reinforces this difference:

> The Only-begotten became man in order to condemn sin in the flesh, kill death by his own death . . . For surely it was

---

communicates with his Lord in the Eucharistic mysteries is no less than a metamorphosis—healing and salvation are given. The believer is deified by the encounter, for the encounter brings him into life-giving proximity with the Logos, and this proximity . . . was the metaphysical root and sustenance of all being" (McGuckin, *Saint Cyril: Christological*, 188).

73. One more or less random example indicates Cyril's thought on the subject was anything but stereotypically "Eastern": "[H]e is truly the Son by nature who is beyond any yoke, and above all creation. It is in relation to him that we too have been fashioned as sons by adoption and grace" (McGuckin, ed., *St Cyril: Unity*, 82).

74. Ibid., 59, 63. Nestorius pejoratively calls Cyril's doctrine of *theopoiesis* "divinization" (*apotheosis*), a word deliberately reminiscent of similar themes in pagan theologies: "God the Word . . . has an unbroken conjunction with Christ and it is not possible for God the Word to do anything without the humanity. For the latter had been made to conform exactly to a perfect conjunction, not to an apotheosis, as our learned purveyors of novel doctrines maintain" (Loofs, *Nestoriana*, 275; cited in Russel, *Cyril of Alexandria*, 150, 155). Thus Cyril can retort: "Why do you mock the beauty of the truth and call the deification of the sacred flesh an apotheosis . . . ?" (cited in Russel, *Cyril of Alexandria*, 157).

75. Cyril's paraphrase takes Irenaeus in the direction most do, i.e., toward a doctrine of theosis, but Irenaeus' own formula allows for an alternative reading: "He became what we are in order that we might become what he is" could mean that the Son became a sin-cursed human in order that we might become truly free ones. We will return to this possibility in the chapter on Colin Gunton.

> well-planned that by this method the race that had fallen away should be recapitulated and brought back to its original state, that is to say, the human race.[76]

Whereas Irenaeus used the concept of recapitulation to describe the way Christ gathers up the backward creation and redirected it forward again, Cyril used it to suggest a going back to the way that "the human race" was in "its original state." The comparison with Irenaeus also offers a point of contrast. If salvation for Cyril was both a return and a deification then there is at least a schematic similarity between his theology of creation and the vertical fall-and-return monism of Ireneaus' opponents. That's not an altogether fair assessment of Cyril of course. A few more connections should improve the view.

~

Nestorius could not allow the notion that the Son took on a generic human nature as his counterparts in Alexandria would have liked. He preferred the idea that Jesus was "a man," indeed a *particular* man, and that this man was related—"conjunctively"—to the eternal Logos. Cyril on the other hand spoke of a "hypostatic union," which, despite the concept's lack of transparency, is maybe best understood when emphasis is placed on the second term in the phrase, *union*. Cyril himself draws the point of contrast:

> Deny substantial union (*kath' hypostasin*) as a crass impossibility and we fall into talk of two sons, for we shall be forced to assert a distinction between the particular man honoured with the title "Son" on the one hand, and the Word from God, natural possessor of both the name and the reality of sonship, on the other.[77]

For Cyril, the "distinction" between any "one hand . . . and the other" in Christ was itself a sign of wrong thinking. To simplify, Nestorius was a theologian concerned with the *otherness* of Creator and creation and Cyril was intent on their *relation*. In this respect, these two hold opposite ends of the dilemma at the crux of this study. Although both Cyril and Nestorius would have identified the same locus for God's mediating

---

76. *Commentary on John* 14.20, in Russel, *Cyril of Alexandria*, 19. See also: "[I]n him . . . the human race might be refashioned to what it was in the beginning" (McGuckin, ed., *St Cyril: Unity*, 88; cf. ibid., 55).

77. *Second Letter to Nestorius* 3, in Wickham, *Cyril of Alexandria*, 9.

activity—the single "prosopon" or "hypostasis" of Christ—each in their own way differed on what exactly was happening between God and the world at their junction in Christ.

Cyril's concept of this relation was one where salvation occurs as an exchange of creaturely mortality for divine incorruptibility. Mediation for him was about the "exchange" of one way of being for another. It was his need for a real exchange in Christ, and not merely some kind of close relation, that marked the point of contrast between his soteriology and that of Nestorius:

> [W]e [Cyril] affirm this: that the Word substantially (*kath' hypostasin*) united to himself flesh endowed with life and reason . . . uniting it substantially, not merely by way of divine favour or good will.[78]

This recalls the suggestion that Nestorius struggled to put love at the junction between the Creator and creation in Christ. John McGuckin explains, "[For Nestorius, and] contrary to the traditional cannons of Aristotelian logic, Grace (*charis*) could be posited in relation to God as a more fundamental category than nature (*physis*)."[79] The "natural" union of Cyril's Christ would not save creatures according to Nestorius because such a saviour could not have in fact become a creature: Cyril's "*kath' hypostasin*" union would either require the displacement of an element of Jesus' humanity (e.g., the Apollinarian soul) and thereby render him unhuman, or else require the blending of deity and humanity and thereby produce an also unhuman "third thing."[80] There was a Newtonian

---

78. *Second Letter to Nestorius* 3, in ibid., 5–7.

79. McGuckin, *Saint Cyril: Christological*, 169. This grace-nature question, one so large in Western theology, will occupy us throughout later chapters, and in our look at Luther in particular.

80. This is a 1+1=3 kind of logic whereby the first, pre-existent Logos, is somehow blended with the assumed second of his humanity to produce a third thing, the incarnate Christ. This is how Nestorius reads Cyril. In Cyril's *Letter to Acacius* he speaks of "the one God, Son, Christ and Lord who is *of* both [natures]" and "of which the one and only Son is understood [to come to be]" (*Book of Heracliedis*; ET, Driver and Hodgson, eds., *Bazaar of Heracleides*, 16; cited in Weinandy, *Does God Suffer?*, 177. Thus, Nestorius accused Cyril of theologizing a *tertium quid*: "You do not confess that he is God in *ousia* in that you have changed him into the *ousia* of the flesh, and he is no more a man naturally in that you have made him the *ousia* of God; and he is not God truly or God by nature, nor yet man truly or man by nature" (quoted in Gould, "Cyril of Alexandria," 240). Despite McGuckin's attempt to expunge Cyril of this common critique, the idea even appears in the defense itself: "God in his own being (the eternal and impassible Logos) cannot be impinged on by human events (historical

billiard-ball effect in Nestorius' Christology: the two natures of Christ could come into very close relation but could not become a single "ball" without either removing one or destroying them both.

Cyril's concern observed the same metaphysical tensions but took them to be the problem and not the terms for explaining its christological solution. Where Nestorius applied notions of substance as a framework for understanding the *relation between* the human and divine in Christ, Cyril took this same rubric as a way of emphasizing the *union of* Christ's natures. It was precisely the divine-human otherness Nestorius had enshrined at the centre of his Christology that Cyril understood as the problem overcome by the incarnation:

> When something does not arise from a nature, but instead is added on from outside, is there not always the possibility of losing it? . . . In that case it would be possible for the Son one day to fall from his sonship, since whatever is not stabilized by natural laws is not totally assured against loss.[81]

For Cyril, anything ontologically external to the being of the Son—anything related-to but not in-union-with—was not "stabilized" and so not "assured against loss." This was ontological bedrock for Cyril. Anything less than a union of natures was susceptible to change and therefore destructive of faith and piety.

Of the two fathers, Cyril was perhaps the more radical, effectively insisting that the incarnational union shattered logical constructs. But Nestorius was the more creative; his metaphysical fidelity pushing him to the awkward, and eventually condemned, views that it did. It is a case of soteriologies at odds. To Nestorius, Cyril's thought meant the transformation of the humanity of Christ into the divinity to such an extent that there were no longer grounds for a salvific solidarity with him. To Cyril, human solidarity with Christ was achieved precisely by and through the transformation, or 'remodeling,' of humanity into divinity:

> The passions of the flesh were aroused, not in order that they might gain control as with us, but that, having been aroused, they might be brought to naught [*katargethe*] by the power of

---

and passible). Similarly human nature, within its own terms, cannot exceed its own limitation. In the unique union of the two in the incarnation, a wholly new condition is created" (McGuckin, *Saint Cyril: Christological*, 200–201).

81. McGuckin, ed., *St Cyril: Unity*, 81.

the Logos dwelling in the flesh, the nature being remodeled into that which is better.[82]

Cyril and Nestorius would likely have agreed that there is a kind of ontological asymmetry between the human and the divine in Christ. But where Nestorius made every effort to sustain the tenuous balance, Cyril simply celebrated the subversion of the lesser by the "better." R. V. Sellers captures the problem:

> How, then, can Christ be in all points tempted like as we are if, as soon as temptation arises, the Logos steps in and uses His power to quash the human impulse? The Representative Man He certainly is, but He is hardly One whose manhood can be said to be individual if its faculty of self determination is never allowed free play.[83]

Nestorius' different approach to the christological problem had its own difficulties. Grillmeier identifies their roots:

> In the time of Nestorius, it is everywhere apparent that no adequate metaphysic of the substantial union of spiritual being had yet been evolved. More than all others, however, Nestorius saw the problem of finding such a substantial union which would leave intact the physis *qua* physis.[84]

Nestorius wanted a Christology that preserved the humanity of Christ from submersion in the being of God; he wanted space for the "physis *qua* physis." Cyril wanted nearly the opposite. For him the submersion was our salvation. In this respect Cyril advocated a soteriology that has made a reappearance in modern existentialist theologies. Now, as then, the aim is to find in Christ a kind of soteriological paradigm, a way to

---

82. *Commentary on John* 4, quoted in Sellers, *Two Ancient Christologies*, 105.

83. Ibid., 105.

84. Grillmeier, *Birth of* Christology, 463. Thus Turner: "The sole alternative is a union in prosopon or prosopic union . . . It is the only form of union suitable for complete natures. It is a voluntary union in both its possible senses. The common prosopon is constituted by a reciprocity or mutuality of the two natural prosopa. The initiative comes from the side of God and the contrast between the Assumer and the assumed is never far from his mind. Active verbs are freely used. The divinity 'makes use' of the prosopon of the humanity and vice versa. The humiliation (*antidosis*) is used to express this double interplay. The two natures may be complete; they are not hermetically sealed from each other, otherwise no Incarnation could have taken place. In the outcome Nestorius replaces Cyril's *communicatio idiomatum* by a far more extensive *communicatio prosopon*" ("Nestorius Reconsidered," 318).

bring other humans into union with God much like the humanity of Christ was at the incarnation. But all this emphasis on union did have its christological liabilities. For a start, it made the problem of a *logos asarkos* especially pronounced: if the Logos is the "single subject" of Jesus then whatever is the "single subject" of anyone else has not been assumed by the Son at the incarnation. To avoid calling this the "soul" of Jesus for the sake of sounding un-Appolinarian does little to avoid the same problem of leaving something unassumed and so unhealed. There may be modern routes around this problem—most notably perhaps through John Zizioulas' description of being-in-relation—but for Cyril and anyone else dealing with substantialist ontologies, the pinch seems unavoidable.[85] Such a concern has a more contextual corollary: it is the way Cyril's single subject seems also to be the single agent in the incarnate economy. If this single subject/agent is ultimately the unenfleshed eternal Son then a kind of Logos hegemony results. The created contingencies and particularities of the life of Christ (his teachings, his miracles, his death on the cross) and therewith those of creation as a whole, become theologically marginalized.

I would like to have both. I would like a physis-*qua*-physis-otherness *and* a real, "hypostatic" union. Next up is John Philoponus, and he would have said having both is not too much to ask.

---

85. See Macquarrie, *Christology*, 50ff.

3

JOHN PHILOPONUS AND THE MIAPHYSITE OPTION

Substantiality and *Creatio ex nihilo* after Chalcedon

(A Cosmological Concept of Mediation)

> True respect for the mystery [of the incarnation] can express itself, among other ways, just in the attempt to understand it fully.
>
> —Wolfhart Pannenberg

The council of Chalcedon marks the point in the Church's self-identification where metaphysical reflection on the Person of Christ was in sharpest focus. The divisions established between Antioch and Alexandria with Cyril and Nestorius had been resolved neither at Ephesus nor with their *Formula of Reunion*, but had only deepened, and Chalcedon was the Church's attempt finally to come to terms with the situation. The Alexandrian John Philoponus appears after the lukewarm reception of the creed. With Cyril on the other side, these two form chronological bookends around the development and reception of the creed in the town at the centre of the theology least amendable to it. Philoponus will require less ink here than Cyril since his Christology was very similar to his predecessor's. His key contributions sustain the tensions in Cyril's thought but are worthy of their own attention for the way they restructure the terms of the dilemma. His was a mind capable of such a task. Instead of looking for enough space in the cosmos for the incarnation, Philoponus looked for a cosmos with enough space for Christ.

Despite all the turmoil and complexity surrounding Chalcedon, the core of the quandary is simple: the single most hotly contested element of the creed was its use of *en* instead of *ek* for the preposition governing the relation between the single hypostasis of Christ and his two natures.[1] The crucial turn is almost too small to see: "Therefore, following the holy Fathers, we all with one accord teach men to acknowledge one and the same Son . . . recognized *in* two natures . . . coming together to form one person and subsistence."[2] The first thing to be said along with such a claim is that the post-Chalcedonian christological upheaval cannot be dismissed as a squabble over a couple letters of grammar. Much hung on those two letters. By choosing to say that the incarnate Son has his being "in" two natures and not "out of" or "from" two natures, many believed that the creed affirmed the dyophysite foundation of Antiochene Christology. The longstanding contention of theologians from Alexandria had been that the union accomplished in the incarnation was one that produced a single subject of Christ, one that might allow a theoretical observation of a duality, but only insofar as this was available for the mind in an atemporal past. So if the creed says that Christ somehow exists "in" two natures—and by implication that there is both a real and an ongoing duality to his being—it fails on the central point of all that miaphysite and "neo-Chalcedonian" theology considered (and still considers) most dear.[3] Recall the Cyril-Nestorius difference concerning the "timing" of the incarnation: is it a perpetual event or a past instant? Is Jesus in some sense a duality or is the incarnation of the Son an overcoming of precisely this Creator/creation divide? John Philoponus was a theologian who wanted it both ways, and his means to this end were unique. Philoponus was an intellectual up-to or beyond the calibre of Nestorius; he thought clearly within the rules of his intellectual climate and came to some alarmingly

---

1. For a characteristically lucid account of the theology hanging on this choice, see Chadwick, "Philoponus the Christian Theologian," 44ff.

2. ET in *Documents of the Christian Church*, eds. Bettenson and Maunder, 56; emphasis added.

3. We will return to this issue in chapter 6 when we look at the work of a modern and self-professed "neo-Chalcedonian," Robert Jenson.

creative conclusions. But, like Cyril, he was radical in his commitment to the priority of the incarnation; he would break the rules when he felt his faith required it.

~

Despite recent scholarly interest in Philoponus,[4] he remains an underappreciated theological figure. Many have recognized him for his paradigm-shifting scientific observations and for his unique and brave departures from the Aristotle commentary tradition but only a relative few have begun to see these advances in the context of his theological ingenuity.[5] Frans De Haas makes the critical observation, albeit cautiously, "Philoponus only felt secure enough to attempt to overthrow the doctrines of the main representatives of the ancient philosophical tradition (Plato, Aristotle, Plotinus, and Proclus) because he possessed a fixed point of reference outside that tradition."[6] The significance of this "fixed point of reference" becomes acute when near the end of his career Philoponus made a marked turn to christological concerns. Patristic scholars have widely divergent opinions about the biographical nature and cause of this "turning" in Philoponus's life but one account stands out:[7] I will here follow the reading of L. S. B. MacCoull. She argues that Philoponus's miaphysite commitments, far from politically duress-induced, were of the cultural soil in which all of his work was rooted:

---

4. Typified in the ongoing translation into English of much of Philoponus's extant work in the series edited by Sorabji, *The Ancient Commentators on Aristotle*.

5. For example, Sorabji, ed., *Philoponus and the Rejection of Aristotelian Science*. We will rely heavily on numerous articles in this work.

6. Haas, *John Philoponus's New Definition*, 294–95. He continues: "[T]hat might also explain why his Alexandrian successors all preferred Ammonius' doctrines" (295).

7. Verrycken, "Development," sees Philoponus consenting to a Christian conversion (from "Philoponus 1" to born-again "Philoponus 2") upon imperial proselytic pressure after the zealous new emperor Justinian closed the Academy at Athens in 529. This critique and earlier versions of it have been contested by many, notably, Grillmeir and Hainthaler, *Council of Chalcedon (451) to Gregory the Great*, 108ff.; and M. Shore in the introduction to her forthcoming translation of Philoponus's *Against Proclus on the Eternity of the World*. Macro and Lang side generally with Verrycken's reading, that "assuming Christian motives confuses the argument of Philoponus" ("Introduction," 14), contra Booth, "John Philoponus," esp. 408ff. who refers to the "turning" in Philoponus's life as an "Aristotelian conversion," that is, from the synthesis project to a dedication to Aristotle over Plato.

> Philoponus was aware of the issues preoccupying the wider Monophysite world of his time and this concern did indeed thoroughly permeate his work on philosophical texts. These assumptions I believe more truthfully reflect the realities of late antique society than does the sort of work that isolates "pure philosophy" from the world around it.[8]

Philoponus's theological insights should be read from within and not in spite of his ground-breaking philosophical science. And the place to begin is his *Arbiter,* a christological work most likely written between the closing of the Academy in Athens in 529 and the second council at Constantinople in 553.[9] Though the *Arbiter* is almost certainly Philoponus's attempt to sway the impending council toward Alexandrian interests, he did almost convincingly veil his intent in objectivity: "Truth is self-sufficient for its own advocacy with those who ardently regard it with the eye of the soul."[10] Henry Chadwick has paraphrased Philoponus's motive: "There is room, in this mutual misunderstanding exacerbated by misrepresentation, for a formula of peace and reconciliation."[11] The "formula" that Philoponus was finally able to offer his theologically torn world warrants a careful look. But first, a brief look at the groundwork he laid for it in his theoretical physics.

∼

Friedrich Gogarten has famously observed that the gospel "secularizes" a given culture before it takes hold within it; it strips the cosmos of any presumption of deity and thereby establishes the new terms in which it can be understood.[12] In this regard, Philoponus was a highly skilled *secularizer* of the late ancient world.[13] His radical disposal of the doctrine of

---

8. MacCoull, "A New Look," 49n10. See also Siorvanes, *Proclus*, 30: "With a deep concern for the truth-value of his Monophysite Christian religion, Philoponus rejected both Aristotelian and Platonic conceptions of the nature of the world. The universe is finite in time, having a beginning and an end according to the Bible, and is maintained by a power impressed by God."

9. Lang, *John Philoponus*. With scholarly citational discrepancies aside, references will be made by page number to Lang's translation here.

10. *Arbiter*, in Lang, *John Philoponus*, 173.

11. Chadwick, "Philoponus the Christian Theologian," 46.

12. Gogarten, *Der Mensch*, cited in Jenson, *Systematic Theology*, 2:113.

13. MacCoull observes that Philoponus's intention was "to deconstruct the old eternal universe in favor of one that had a beginning in a time which had itself begun; and to demythologize the far-off matter of the heavens in light of the one universal

the eternity of the stars and his similar rejection of the doctrine of the eternity of the world together plotted the basic parameters of the classic Christian cosmological polemic. His first line of attack was a defense and development of the doctrine of *creatio ex nihilo*.

Philoponus spoke within an Aristotle commentary tradition in which generated things (finite, created) required a prior substrate (metaphysical raw material). Against this he argued that God created the form and the thing itself simultaneously "out of nothing" and, furthermore, that this nothing—or "not-being"—could not be reified back into a substrate:

> For if something were generated out of complete not-being, they say, it would follow that not-being exists. For it has changed into being. Now if someone argues . . . that the things generated are generated out of not-being in the same way as a ship <is built> from timber—which means that not-being itself underlies the thing generated and changes into it—<then> it will truly follow that not-being exists. But I do not think that anyone is witless enough to understand generation out of not-being in this way; rather, anything generated is brought into being <only> insofar as it is generated without existing previously.[14]

This was all to say that the cosmos is contingent; it is not eternal since it has a beginning in the will of God. A straightforward enough point, perhaps. But at the time, it needed to be won the hard way. Philoponus's most celebrated effort here was his application of Aristotle's *reductio ad infinitum* to Aristotle's own cosmology. Philoponus argued that if the cosmos is uncreated than there must have existed an infinite number, an impossibility on Aristotle's own terms:

> If the cosmos were without beginning, history would be infinite, then the number of individuals which would have existed in that infinite time would also be infinite. Thus if the cosmos is without beginning then there must have existed an actually infinite number. But it is not possible for the infinite to actually exist . . . as we shall see fully, God willing, in what follows . . . [11.2] . . . imagine that the cosmos was without beginning, and that the number of individuals before Socrates, say, was infinite and then there was added to [this number of individuals] those who have

---

matter created and lived in by the Saviour" ("A New Look," 59).

14. *Simpl. in de Caelo* 136.18–26, in Philoponus, *Against Aristotle*, 87.

existed between Socrates and now. Then there would have been something larger than infinity, which is not possible.[15]

Part of Philoponus's broader argument is preserved within the reply to it by one of his opponents. In his *Against Philoponus on the Eternity of the Word,* Simplicius quotes Philoponus:

> If the capacity of each part is infinite, the whole . . . will possess either the same capacity as each of its parts or a larger one. Yet if it is larger there will be something larger than infinity, which is impossible; on the other alternative the same part will turn out to be both infinite and finite—infinite by hypothesis, finite insofar as it is exceeded by something. But it is in fact impossible that the capacity of the whole and the part be equal. For we clearly see everywhere that the whole possesses a larger capacity than each of its parts . . . And so, if the capacity of each of the parts is not infinite, it is finite. In consequence, the whole is finite as well, for it is impossible that something put together both in number and in capacity from finite parts be infinite in capacity. It remains, therefore, . . . that heaven as a whole as well of each of its parts is finite in capacity.[16]

True, this might not look like theology. But it needed to be done. Philoponus was establishing the space he needed for his Christology. Without this kind of groundwork, the cosmos was too metaphysically loaded, too clogged with superstition and stratificiation. In this respect Philoponus likely saw himself doing what Moses had done for the Egyptians. Chadwick comments, "Philoponus more than once insists that Moses never intended to provide a scientific cosmogony, but aimed to teach the knowledge of God to benighted Egyptians superstitiously worshipping the sun, moon and stars."[17] Consequently, Philoponus aimed to shatter his culture's philosophico-religious infatuation with astrology.[18]

---

15. Philoponus, *De Aeterntate Mundi* 9.14–16; 11.2–4 (translation mine).

16. *Simpl. in Phys.* 1335.30–41, in Simplicius, *Against Philoponus,* 126. The secondary literature on Philoponus is indispensable here, and my aim is not to duplicate its hard work but to observe Philoponus's basic cosmological beliefs then move beyond their complicated rhetoric to their relation to his Christology.

17. Chadwick, "Philoponus the Christian Theologian," 51. And cf. Philoponus, *De opificio mundi* 1.1; 4.17.

18. Chadwick observes that, for Philoponus, "the principal vindication of the truth of Christianity lies in its requiring the renunciation of astrology" (Chadwick, "Philoponus the Christian Theologian," 51). Cf. Scott, *Origen,* 164ff.

The second implication of Philoponus's commitment to the doctrine of *creatio ex nihilo* was his more controversial claim that the cosmos is ontologically homogeneous. The line of reasoning is relatively straightforward: if the universe had an absolute beginning from the will of a Creator than this universe can only be said to have being univocally, "For living being is animate and sensitive substance, in which commonly *and to the same degree* all living beings participate."[19] Against the Classic stratification of the universe in which the stars were considered eternal alongside the Neo-Platonic One, Philoponus argued that the stars are simply creatures along with everything else.[20] The difficulty of his argumentation is compounded by only being available from the also complex works of his less than sympathetic opponents, but his first line of thought is worth a quick look.

Philoponus suggested that Aristotle's ontological elevation of the stars' circular motion above the linear motion below them was groundless and arbitrary since both occurred naturally within the sublunary realm. Aristotle held that the superlunary spheres were in perpetual circular motion by virtue of their metaphysical superiority to the jumbled chaos apparent beneath them.[21] Philoponus however realized that the now counter-intuitive tone of such an idea arose out of a theological predilection for a world-soul or *nous*. He comments, "regarding the celestial (things) there is no longer any evidence that their circular movement is initiated by the intentions of their soul . . . nor do those souls influence the moving of these [earthly] things."[22] In short, Philoponus believed that bodies do not "have" motion, they are given it:[23] "the regular movements

19. *Arbiter*, in Lang, *John Philoponus*, 185; emphasis added.

20. For the history and theology behind this belief see Scott's comments regarding Philoponus: "The most intellectually rigorous criticisms were made by the sixth century Alexandrian Christian John Philoponus, who both denied the life of the stars and claimed (against Aristotle) that heavenly events were governed by the same physical principles as those on earth," (*Origen*, 166).

21. "Aristotle had erected an unnatural and apparently insurmountable ontological barrier between the sublunary and the superlunary regions" (Wildberg, *John Philoponus's Criticism*, 235).

22. Philoponus, *De opificio mundi* 6.2, 232, 7–15 (translation mine).

23. "After a long and complex discussion, Aristotle rejected the possibility of a void space existing in nature. Among his reasons for doing so was that he believed that all motion must be through a medium. If that were not so, Aristotle argued, the motion of bodies through space would all be instantaneous, since the velocity of motion is restricted only by the interference it meets by the density of the medium through which it is moving. In a void the resistance would be nil, and hence the velocity of motion

of the stars have been given to them by God, not by a soul . . . it is reckless to take something for granted which is neither made clear by argument nor borne out by the Holy Scripture."[24]

Philoponus also rejected the then popular Proclean gloss of Aristotle's *nous* which claimed that it was in fact mediatorial beings or "angels" who moved the stars:

> It is not impossible that God, who created all these things, imparted a motive force to the moon, the sun, and the other stars—just as the inclination to heavy and light bodies, and the movements due to the internal soul to all living beings—in order that the angels do not move them by force . . . how could the angels suffice for pulling bodies of such a number and size for so long by force?[25]

By installing God as the original and ongoing cause of this "motive force" Philoponus evacuated the cosmos of the determinations of the Aristotelian *nous* and homogenized it by eliminating the ontological stratifications of the Proclean mediatorial beings. Philoponus had worked very clear the ground and make his own as solid as possible: the stars are not eternal, the world is not eternal, and nothing exists more or less than anything else; only God is eternal, and being is not on a dimmer dial, but a simple on-or-off switch.

Philoponus's second move against the status quo of Neoplatonic Aristotelianism[26] came in his critique of the accepted doctrine concerning the fundamental substrate of matter. Aristotle's *aether* had long been held as the incorporeal bond and context of everything but Philoponus offered a three-dimensional concept of primary matter in its stead:

---

infinite. Philoponus took a different line on that issue (and on many others as well). He reasoned that the velocity of motion of any body through a medium is determined by the motive power of the moving body, which defines the maximum velocity. The density of the medium then *takes away* from the maximum velocity, so that when the density is nil (i.e. in a vacuum), the velocity will be a maximum, but non-infinite, figure" (Schmitt, "Philoponus's Commentary," 218).

24. *De opificio mundi* 6.2, 233, 10–17 (trans. Wildberg, *John Philoponus's Criticism*, 241). Cf. 6.2, 231, 2–233, 8.

25. *De opificio mundi* 1.112, 28, 20–29, 9 (trans. Wildberg, *John Philoponus's Criticism*, ,240). Cf. Chadwick, "Philoponus the Christian Theologian," 51.

26. "It should be taken for granted that the Aristotle received in the sixth century had first been adopted and meditated by Neoplatonists . . . It would be anachronistic to assume that Neoplatonists saw an opposition between Plato and Aristotle, as most moderns do" (Lang, *John Philoponus*, 160). Cf. Sorabji, "General Introduction," 8ff.

> If three-dimensionality is actually the substance of body, and it remains unchanged within the changes of bodies. . .then there is no case to show that incorporeal matter must underline it as its base. It alone is the first subject underneath all natural forms, furthermore, it is from it and from the substantial qualities together that real bodies come into being.[27]

The precise interpretation of this *three-dimensional . . . substantial-qualities-together* element of Philoponus's thought is a source of much scholarly controversy.[28] The divergence of views begins long before readers arrive at the concept proper. Those who see Philoponus as a philosopher with a dispassionate "interest in the problem itself"[29] tend to struggle for a coherent explanation for his oft-repeated and creative alternative to the tradition.[30] On the other hand, those who read Philoponus with intentional theological sympathy tend to see in the concept of three-dimensionality an oblique consistency at work. T. F. Torrance has observed that this move allowed Philoponus to conceive of the dimensions of space as mutually interrelated.[31] Though this had many implications for Philoponus's wider scientific community, there are two for our purposes: first, three-dimensionality allowed Philoponus to re-imagine spatial possibility. The trend in the Aristotle commentary tradition during Philoponus's day was to understand space as a container filled with either a substance or a void. Philoponus, by contrast, seems to have imagined space as a kind of dynamic potential, or a "seat of relations" in Torrance's words.[32] In effect, this "dynamic potential" view of space meant Philoponus could affirm the simultaneous co-presence of two "substances" or "natures" in the same place or body without compromise to their original integrity.[33]

Second, and consequently, Philoponus seems to have believed his concept of three-dimensionality allowed him to affirm the possibility of a substantial *mixture* (or, putting this in the terms we will soon come

---

27. Philoponus, *De Aeterntate Mundi Contra Proclum*, 424.23—425.14 (translation mine). And cf. 405.23–7; 428; and *Comm. in Phys.* 17.557.10—17.584.4.

28. Cf. Furley's comments in Philoponus, *Corollaries on Place and Void*, 117n29.

29. Haas, *John Philoponus's New Definition*, 284.

30. Contra ibid., who argues that Simplicius arrived quite naturally at similar philosophical convictions with apparently no "religious" commitments, (see, e.g., ibid., 292).

31. Torrance, *Transformation*, 261.

32. Torrance, *Space, Time and Incarnation*, 24.

33. See the next note and Sorabji, *Matter, Space and Motion*, 120ff.

to, a *composite* substance/nature).[34] Whereas his tradition understood substance as fundamental unchangeableness and space as whatever was between substances, Philoponus understood substance as fundamental unchangeableness and space as wherever substances might overlap. Crudely put, for his contemporaries space was about the *distance* between substances but for Philoponus space was about the *relation* between substances.

His innovations are irremediably complicated but one point of difference can be put simply: instead of a two-part train of thought where space tended to be informed by substance logic, Philoponus had a three-part train where both space and substance were informed by his Christo-logic.

~

Even from within the bounds of his dedicated miaphysitism, Philoponus's concept of three-dimensional extension allowed him to speak of a genuine "composition" in Christ. Commenting on Chalcedon's *without confusion* clause, Philoponus laboured to create the intellectual possibility of a substantial "overlapping" in space. He spoke of "the simples" (natural attributes) being "preserved" in Christ:

> For if "without confusion" must introduce a duality in Christ, and duality [must introduce] division, as we have shown . . . then it is impossible for any things whatever to be joined in an undivided union unless they have experienced confusion . . . [But] should those who say that there is one nature from two say that it is simple and not composite, I think perhaps there would be a reason justifying the [concern]. But as it is, there being one composite and the simples being preserved in this composite, the [concern] is completely absurd. For if it were necessary for one of those which have come into union to perish, then the remainder would not be composite but simple. If, however, it is not simple, but composite, it will all be one in virtue of the composition.[35]

The critical move at the crux of Philoponus's Christology was his particular route between boldly dyadic statements like this and his

---

34. We should note here that their common Alexandrian mileu meant Philoponus shared Cyril's semantic tendency to treat nature and substance (or "hypostasis") as near synonyms. See the discussion above at 48, 51ff.

35. *Arbiter*, in Lang, *John Philoponus*, 207.

unwavering devotion to a single composite nature of Christ. All the work in his theoretical physics is beginning to pay. Philoponus's willingness to exceed typical Alexandrian christological boundaries was a natural feature of his libertarian career as a whole; his theology developed symbiotically alongside his relational cosmology. He confidently mingles his insights,

> To be three-dimensionally extended and perceptible belongs specifically to the nature of each [of Christ's "properties"] . . . i.e. *the encounter of one thing with another, or countercheck of one thing upon another.*[36]

For Philoponus the compositional *encounter* in Christ in no way required a compromise of a nature's property, since each "belongs to it exclusively, . . . resistance can also pertain to composites."[37] With the space made possible by his concept of three-dimensionality and the resultant possibility of a real "composition," Philoponus was prepared to extend what may have been the most "substantial" olive branch of the era:

> If, therefore, they say that there is a single composite nature which exists in two simples, as we say that there is a single whole in many parts: someone will allow this locution, because of a consensus on things which are commonly recognized, even if the locution itself is imprecise. For in the case of composites, all the more if they result in mutual composition, we are accustomed to use [the phrase] "out of them" rather than "in them" . . . Still, as I have said, if they acknowledge his totality, (i.e. [his] one nature) as composite, for Christ is composite, we

---

36. Ibid., 208; emphasis added. And cf. McKeena, "The 7th Chapter of the Arbiter": "I believe that Philoponus understood the infinity of the void as filled with a structure the extension of which was not the same as matter or energy in its particular place. It may be understood in theory as that dimension of the cosmos in which the universal and the singular are composes [*sic*, composites] of one another without logical contradiction . . . Do not concepts like these help us to understand the dynamic definition he sought for *nature* when he wrote his argument for the divine and human *nature*s of the *person* of Jesus Christ?

37. *Arbiter*, in Lang, *John Philoponus*, 208. And cf., "[I]n Christ also the properties of each of the natures from which he has been constituted are preserved, and that there is one composite nature and hypostasis of the whole." p.210. Cf. also, "there being one composite and the simples being preserved" (ibid., 207). This diplomatic tone was soon to change. After the second council of Constantinople, in his *Four Themata against Chalcedon* (in Michael the Syrian's *History* 8.13), Philoponus felt emboldened to criticize diophysite Christology more bluntly.

> shall permit them to say that he is "in" those two natures out of which he is, even if they use the locution improperly, as we have shown.³⁸

Philoponus went even further than this. He was so comfortable with a duality of "properties" in the single composite nature of Christ that he could define these properties as "the distinctive characteristics of each nature, which appear in them as belonging to them specifically."³⁹

Recall Nestorius' billiard-ball problem. Philoponus thinks he has a solution: he thinks he has found space for a mixture that would not mean the destruction of the two original elements. We could also recall Cyril's Apollinarian indiscretions. Again, Philoponus's new notions of space and composition seem to make it possible to imagine enough room in Christ for both a human soul and an eternal Logos. That said however, and despite the space Philoponus had won for an albeit carefully qualified duality to the being of Christ, it was the single subject of Christ, the one agent in the incarnate economy, that was the object of theological reflection for Philoponus:

> Concerning our Lord Christ, however, the omnipotent divinity extended to every effect, and hence no natural movement, either of the soul or of the body, simply occurred merely according to the principle of its nature, but it was governed by the divinity united to it, in such a manner as seemed good [to the divinity].⁴⁰

As with Cyril, the Logos, or, in Philoponus's words, "the divinity" was the agent under consideration. Yet Philoponus advanced the Cyrillene demand for a single incarnate subject by actually locating the medium for the transmission of the divine will to the life of Christ. For Philoponus, the *soul* of Christ is the incarnational intersection of divinity and humanity. He continues:

> [The divinity] transmitted the divine will to the body voluntarily through the mediation of the soul . . . each operation must be predicated of the completed whole; originating from the divinity as from the principal cause it is completed through the mediation of the soul in the divine body united to it.⁴¹

---

38. *Arbiter*, in Lang, *John Philoponus*, 214, 15.
39. Ibid., 208.
40. Ibid., 176; cf. ibid., 175.
41. Ibid., 176; cf. ibid., 175.

For Philoponus, Christ's soul was the locus of the mediation between the Creator and the creation at the incarnation. The rationale behind such a claim arose from his common belief in the way the human soul was both "linked" to the mortal, changing body, and at the same time was itself unchangeable and immortal. As such, the soul was for Philoponus an ideal forward edge to the human nature of Christ.

> It has been generally acknowledged by all of us who proclaim the things of Christ that in Christ the divine nature has persisted whole without change, i.e. the divinity of the Logos will be just as it was both before and after the union with the human nature. Since even the rational soul, *qua* being capable of suffering, namely in its operation, suffers in some respects and is changed by its natural link with the body and by the affection [arising] through it, however, *qua* being incapable of suffering in the intelligible content of substance, it remains no less impassible and immortal, even if it is linked with the passible and changeable body.[42]

In this respect, Philoponus appears to be one step forward and one step back from Cyril's position. Whereas Cyril had his concept of economy for maintaining the sufferings of Christ's flesh as the Word's very own, Philoponus—while sounding less Apollinarian than Cyril by having a constructive role for the soul of Christ in his theology—seems to have used the soul as an ontological barrier against the suggestion that the divine actually suffered.

Like Cyril, Philoponus advocated a communication of divine and human attributes in Christ (thus, "each operation must be predicated of the completed whole," cited above), but the concept is less normative for the later Alexandrian. For Philoponus, the theological function of the *communicatio idiomatum* was carried more by the *mediatorial function* of Christ's soul. Despite the development there remains a significant problem: both theologians share a desire to press an impersonal concept (*communicatio*) or an inanimate thing (Christ's soul[43]) into mediatorial agency at the centre of the Mediator's being. The crux is borne not by God (or the incarnate Christ) *per se*, but by the human soul of Jesus. Thus Grillmeier and Hainthaler:

---

42. Ibid., 213.

43. It is clear in Philoponus's theology about the human soul of Christ in this respect that it is indeed an impersonal thing or locus; the motivating power behind all of Christ's acts being provided solely by "the divinity," i.e., the Logos.

> The union in Christ is (presumably) conceived as one that is called forth by the natures of *ousiai* themselves, not by something that adheres to them; we have not encountered any statement in Philoponus as to whether it was by a creative act of God.[44]

~

What emerges under Philoponus's arbitration is a remarkably singular theological field: for all the political froth, the Chalcedonians and the miaphysites were incredibly close in principle. Indeed, as is often the case in theological discourse, the ideas at the extremities of this debate bent inward to the extent that intense opponents found themselves closer to one another than they were to the orthodox centre.[45] And similarly, with Philoponus it was becoming clear that more creative opponents found themselves in functional agreement in all but their terminology. That said, however, it was by virtue of the opposing tensions within Philoponus's theology that he found himself pulled in both directions at once and eventually suspended by them above the impossible middle ground between the Chalcedonians and the miaphysites. The sheer uniqueness of this awkward position means he functions as an ideal interlocutor for a constructive critique of the Christology developed from both sides of the theological hotbed surrounding the council. The first thing to observe with Philoponus-the-arbiter is the common ground between Alexandria and Antioch. Most significantly, both parties—Philoponus's own creative theologoumena included—functioned within the bounds of a fundamentally substantialist ontology. It is clear in this regard that Philoponus did not altogether grasp the radicality of fully rejecting Aristotelian cosmology. Throughout his career he maintained substance as the basic ontic rubric. Even for the fundamental distinction between Creator and creation, Philoponus had substance at the base of his theology: "*created* and *uncreated* are not indicative of substances, but of that which is recognized as belonging to substance."[46]

44. Grillmeir and Hainthaler, *Chalcedon to Gregory the Great*, 144.

45. Thus Prestige can observe, "the doctrine of the two Sons undercuts the Gospel: on that point Apollinaris and Nestorius, the extreme representatives of rival theological methods, are entirely one . . . Apollinaris . . . fastened on the indispensability of divine action . . . Nestorius . . . clung to the necessity of a full human experience" (*Fathers and Heretics*, 132).

46. *Arbiter*, in Lang, *John Philoponus*, 199. This intractable substantialism drove

On this field, the christological objective was to develop an equation that would add the immutable Logos to a complete human nature and produce a single subject in a way that would not compromise either of the original elements. But when substance is of ultimate priority, it is difficult if not impossible to develop a theology that is not at its base a kind of *ontism*—a way of understanding reality that establishes a primal rubric for being in advance of any concept of an incarnate Creator. In the late Antique era this meant the only available means for relating the immanent and the transcendent were variations on the fundamentally unalterable theme of metaphysical mechanism. Theology about the being of Jesus was reduced to the practice of observing and describing the fated machinations of an *ipso facto* impersonal system. The result in Philoponus's day was the way both parties tended to approach the search for an effective christological equation within terms reminiscent of a Stoic default to cosmological necessity. Christologically, this meant that the conundrum of relating God to the world in the historical Jesus was driven by a search for an efficient conceptual device to describe what was effectively an automatic coincidence of divinity and humanity.

Even after such a quick sketch of the christological possibilities and problems opened by Philoponus, it is clear that there also opened an impassable chasm in the very midst of Chalcedonian orthodoxy: the incarnation seemed to demand a substantial impossibility. There was simply no way of preserving the otherness of the Creator should his crossing of the ontological divide between the substance of his being and the substance of his creation be taken seriously. On these terms the Son might somehow have "invaded" humanity but could in no way have substantially *become* a human. Faced with such a dilemma the differing schools of theology could only deepen their divisions.

At the miaphysite end stakes were placed in the single-subjectivity of the Logos to the extent that christological efforts tended to err via a Word-flesh asymmetry. By effectively hybridizing the union, a "third thing" evolved "out of" the divine and human composite to install a Logos hegemony and so an inevitable compromise of Christ's real humanity. At the dyophysite end stakes were placed in the full humanity of Christ to the extent that Christology here tended to err via a Word-man dualism.

---

his nominalist refusal to distinguish between nature and hypostasis and likely thereby eventuated his descent into virtual tritheism. See Martin, "Jean Philopon." It perhaps could be argued that Philoponus's thought at this point epitomized a consistently Western logic applied to its own doctrine of the Trinity.

By apparently only juxtaposing the Logos with the humanity of Jesus, "two Sons" eventually emerged "in" place of the single-subjectivity of Christ.

At this point we should recall the distinction drawn earlier between the possibilities within a universe oriented around a Logos that is Jesus "out of" two natures and one where this Jesus is "in" his two natures. Once again the *timing* of the incarnation is pivotal. The coming together of deity and humanity in Christ either "happened" so that there is "one (composite) nature after the union," or it rather somehow *is* happening. The latter route at least allows for an ongoing christological duality while the former is characterized by the denial of just this. Yet the problem remains; neither the dynamism implicit in the Chalcedonian decree nor the miaphysite version developed most creatively by Philoponus could finally sustain itself. As we have seen with Irenaeus, an "ongoing duality"—be it theoretical[47] or actual—cannot on its own avoid dissolution into dual*ism*. Even Philoponus's efforts to reconstruct a more cooperative universe could not finally offer appropriate ontological space to a truly humanized Creator. Nestorius and Eutyches, on this account, are not really the reckless heretics history has painted; they are simply the figures unfortunate enough to have taken mechanistic Christology to its two logical conclusions.

With such a broad stroke we come to the end of our treatment of patristic notions of the mediation of God and creation in Christ. But before we move to the next significant era in our study, a few concluding general observations.

∼

At the root of the common commitment to substantialist ontological categories in late antique Christology was a subtle subtextual devotion to Parmenidean stability. The tendency tracked in Cyril repeated itself

---

47. Like his predecessor, Philoponus tended to claim that one could distinguish the two natures of Christ only by mental abstraction or *theoria*. This kind of onto-epistemic rift ran through almost every theological system of the day, and was the compromise made at the Fifth Ecumenical Council in Constantinople (canon 8). Yet it should be noted that it is one thing to say that knowledge of the being of Christ is in a certain way beyond the bounds of human understanding, and it is an entirely different thing to suggest that his being is so ineffably unified as to transcend our restricted theological perceptions of a duality. This second maneuver maintains the first's patina of piety yet is in fact an attempt to establish compulsory epistemic humility as a barrier around its presupposed monophysitism.

in Alexandria with Philoponus: Hellenic heritage bequeathed a tradition to these Fathers in which existential security was ultimately an effect of one's belief in the static unity of the cosmos. And here "static" is the binding term. Philoponus's ontological homogenization of creation achieved space for God in his world but his fidelity to substantialism meant God's participation in this creation could not be conceived in the kind of relation-and-otherness that the notably more Trinitarian theology of Irenaeus seemed to anticipate. The result was a theologically arbitrary yet deeply ingrained preference for being over becoming, for the theological priority of divine impassibility over some kind of mediated God-world dynamic. The mediatorial role of Christ as such was understood to be a function undertaken by virtue of his status as a possessor of perfectly stable divine being. This mediatorial status was essentially an ontic *position*, it was what located Christ between the otherwise metaphysically polarized Creator and creation.

With this as a paradigm, theology about reconciliation tended to displace any theology about ontological mediation on its own terms. Soteriology drove theology about creation such that the being of Christ was likened to an ontological funneling device. His redemptive "being" became functionally indistinguishable from that of a passive mediatorial *aeon* with a particular ontologically necessary "act": lesser lower beings get gathered up into the supreme higher being of God. In this way the incarnation was either about becoming enfleshed, or it was not really about a *becoming* at all. In either case, God's movement to humanity was something of an unfortunate necessity predicated entirely by the problem of evil. This tendency to develop the doctrine of creation *from* the doctrine of redemption effectively conflated the two. The clock of salvation history was wound back so tightly that theodicy and soteriology were compressed into a metaphysical singularity: ontological distinction and relational distance were indistinguishable and so treated as one and the same problem.

For the miaphysites—Philoponus included—atonement tended to be understood as a product of that theoretical past instant when the two "natures" of Christ were instantaneously melded into one. To put this to a point: neo-Chalcedonian Christology presumed that the Christian *kerygma* was not finally about Christ's recapitulative lifestyle and redemptive death but something more like an allegory of how humanity-in-general might come to pass into the divine life through the mechanical association of Jesus' human nature with the deity of the Son. This however is an inversion of the presumption that it is distinction from the Creator that is the problem and not the nature of one's relation to him; as if human creaturehood is better off transcended—indeed *deified*—than it is consummated.

For the diophysites the perpetual duality of Jesus' being was carefully upheld, and so a systematic rubric for this distinction of mediation and redemption was in place, but in an ironic mirroring of their opponents' weaknesses their conceptual distinguishing at this point was won in a way that compromised the possibility of relation. By only establishing the otherness of the divine and human in Christ, there was no medium, nor indeed any Mediator, to effect a real relation. The diametric departure of these two schools on this serves as a reminder that the appropriate mediation of the two natures of Jesus is not simply a trivial ontological abstraction but is the start and finish of the closed loop on which all the rest of Christian theology is spun.

Although it is clear that both the sixth-century Chalcedonians and their miaphysite colleagues were prepared to think about the real humanity and divinity of Christ within the resources afforded them by the demands of their counciliar authorities, each party similarly restricted itself to mining these resources with the pick and axe of Neo-Platonism and Aristotelian substance categories. The result was a sustained divergence between two increasingly entrenched camps due to restrictions inherent to the tools of their discourse, rather than the content of their theology on its own terms. The sheer longevity of this dilemma is testament to the remarkable scope of Christian theology exploitable from within Neo-Platonic and Aristotelian commitments but its stubborn resilience is further testament to the immense significance of those elements of Christian theology only available beyond them.

For a start into those resources we should look to the theology of Martin Luther.

4

MARTIN LUTHER AND THE PROBLEM OF DISTANT GRACE

Faith, Jesus, and the Immediacy of God
(A "Theological" Concept of Mediation)

> When a human being is united with God, he or she becomes a participant
> not only in the human but also in the divine nature of Christ...
> a kind of "communication of attributes" occurs:
> the attributes of the essence of God...
> are communicated to the Christian.
>
> —Tuomo Mannermaa

To appreciate Luther's ontological innovations, one first needs to understand Augustine's influence on medieval notions of grace.[1] Robert Jenson explains that for theology in the Augustinian tradition there was on the one hand,

---

1. It needs to be emphasized, since it is so often forgotten in modern theological discussion, that the issue about to be identified has to do with the *influence* of Augustine on a particular kind of theology and not necessarily with what Augustine himself may have thought. On this, compare the scholars in the notes immediately below with the opinions of, e.g., Barnes, "De Regnon Reconsidered," and see, too, the recent related works by Sarah Coakley.

> God, conceived as a supernatural entity who acts causally on us; and on the other hand there are the results among us of this causality. . . . God and the objects of God's causality are then both interpreted accordingly: they are "substances," fundamentally self-sustaining and self-contained entities, who "act" over against each other, the result of which action is in us a *habitus*, an acquired disposition to behave and react in ways obedient to the will of God.[2]

In this model, grace is twofold: there is an "acquired disposition," a kind of "habit" given to creatures to do things that correspond to the will of their Creator and then there is the giving of this gift in the first place. The crucial point here is that this twofold nature of grace corresponds to two distinct entities, what Jenson provocatively calls "substances," acting more or less causally on one another. Jenson's observation rests on a soteriological model, perhaps arising out of Augustine but in any case receiving much momentum from Aquinas, in which "created habits of grace" functioned almost like an intermediate state or meeting point between sinful humanity and the perfections of divine life.[3] These "habits" were like a bridgehead, a point from which the process of ascent to God—salvation—could begin.

This sketch is especially poignant for the way it illustrates an essentially dualistic theological structure. Broadly viewed there is once again a single continuum with creatures at one end and the Creator at the other. Such indeed was the theological field on which much of spirituality was played. God did his part by providing Christ as a model for a life of obedient devotion, and Christians did their part with varying degrees of success by imitating this Christ and thereby achieving some of the "Father's good pleasure" that was enjoyed by Jesus.

The system functioned well enough but problems began to arise when the Church tried to solidify this practice into doctrine. Over time the result was the always dangerous move of dissembling a great theologian's ideas to pick and choose which ones to keep and which to condemn.[4] As Christoph Schwöbel explains, the three Augustinian dogma

---

2. Jenson, "Pneumatological Soteriology," 126, citing E. Kahler, *Die Religion*, 1639–40.

3. The received influence of Augustine and Aquinas will occupy us again, and with some more detail, in the following chapter on Calvin.

4. Beginning with the Synod of Orange in 529, where Augustine's concept of grace was formally upheld, but his notion of the Fall rejected, views latter confirmed by papal decree in 531.

the Church accepted were: "the understanding of original sin as the radical inability of fallen human nature to will and to do the good unaided, the emphasis on the necessity of grace for willing the good and the stress on the continuing dependence on divine grace after justifying grace has been received."[5] With this much of Augustine at least this much is clear: humans *need* God. But how is one to be helped? Schwöbel continues: "What is not approved or is even explicitly rejected is Augustine's emphasis on the irretrievable loss of free will, the view of the irresistibility of grace and his view of predestination excluding, as it were, the salvific significance of human merit."[6]

In this way the concept of grace as a given habit was separated from the absolute *givenness* of this gift and the behavioral results of the habit, "righteousness," came to be understood as somehow arising out of two instead of just one original agent.[7] With this the problem was set: how could the lesser of these two agents sufficiently cooperate with the greater. In short, the issue at the boiling point when Luther arrived on the scene was that of how the absolutely free and all-powerful Creator could possibly be morally compatible with sinful contingent agents who were at least partially responsible for this compatibility. And this brings us to the crux of Luther's historic development: for Luther the central issue was not about compatibility with a God somehow very distant from his creation but rather about the immediate presence of this God right at hand. Saving faith for Luther was no longer the moral or epistemic exercise it had become in much medieval theology. Salvation as he saw it was a "union" with Christ:[8]

> By these words [I Corinthians 1.30] [Paul] has shown very well the power of this name, the salvation and union of Christ and

5. Schwöbel, "Triune God of Grace," 52–53.

6. Ibid. For the theological reception of Augustine, see Mühlenberg, "Dogma Und Lehre Im Abenland," cited by Schwöbel, "Triune God of Grace," 445–76.

7. "Thus 'righteousness' in its theological as opposed to its moral sense cannot be understood as one of the virtues which men can acquire as a habit by doing right, for if it could be understood in this sense nobody ever could be called righteous because no man is able to do what is right, i.e. please God" (Dalferth, "Visible and Invisible," 21).

8. The standard secondary literature has much to say about the roots and details of Luther's shift from a typical Nominalist critique of *via antiqua* syntheses through his own break with the *via moderna* to his mature view of faith as itself both the start and normative shape of theology. See esp. Brecht, *Martin Luther*, 33ff.; and Dalferth, "Visible and the Invisible," 15–44; and regarding the disintegration of the *via antiqua* in late medieval thought, see Gilson, *History*, 499ff.

our incorporation in him, all of which are incompatible with the ideas of those dreamers in sophistry who make Christ our justice and wisdom by considering him as the object or cause of our justice and who entirely overlook that union which exists through faith in him; and it is about this that Paul is speaking. For faith in Christ makes him live, move and act in me in the same way as healing ointment acts on a sick body, and we are made one flesh and one body with Christ through the close and wonderful change from our sin to his justice. Just as the holy sacrament of the altar represents him to us when the bread and wine are changed into Christ's flesh and blood. (WA 5:311.6–17)

Luther is here juxtaposing his own view of faith with that of "those dreamers'" who make Christ merely the "object or cause" of salvation. Such a view is simply "incompatible" with Luther's own, wherein the salvation of the believer involves a "union," an "incorporation,," or a being "made one flesh and body with Christ." The contrast is indeed sharp: on the one hand is a faith that somehow acquires justice from Christ as from an external "object or cause" (or "substance" in Jenson's sketch) and on the other is a "faith" that is such a perfect "incorporation in" Christ that Luther says it is like the union between Christ and his body and blood in the celebration of the Lord's Supper. Yves Congar makes the point when he says that, for Luther, "faith applies the mystery of Christ to us: not as an act thanks to which, or on the basis of which, Christ acts upon us from without but as the extension of the unique reality of this mystery to us."[9]

In short, Luther found himself heir to a convergence of theological systems in which divine and contingent acts were stretched across a kind of ontological fulcrum where freedoms at one end seemed to compromise those at the other. Luther's historical mandate was to reject the ways his received traditions attempted to balance this tension by distinguishing God from the faithful believer as if the two parties were somehow distantly opposed. For Luther, in Congar's terms, God does not simply act upon us "from without," but rather extends the christological mystery *to us*.

∼

There are certain doctrines that make only rare and passing appearances in the pulpit but soteriology is not among them. And of the theologians to preach their theology Luther is surely high-ranking among them. Put

9. Congar, "Considerations and Reflections," 378.

together, these claims bring us to Luther's sermons for an investigation into his theology about salvation. Beyond that, a focus on Luther's sermons on John can be justified if not by a sheer necessity of scale then by David Yeago's observation: "[S]ince Luther's lectures on Galatians, on which the famous *Commentary* is based, began about six weeks later, on July 3, 1531, the John 6 Sermons can be read as the commentary's christological prolegomenon."[10]

Written sufficiently after the colloquy at Marburg to have allowed once young and viscous opinions about the Eucharist to now be solidified into dogmatic conviction, Luther's sermons on John 6 come at a prime time for some of the Reformer's sharpest theology.[11] I will focus on his series on John 6:26–71, delivered during the Winter and early Spring of 1530–1531.[12] Sermons generally allow for less precision on items requiring careful nuance, and Luther does have a penchant for homiletic hyperbole. In the next section on his *Disputations*, I will try to bring to closer analysis questions raised by his preaching.

To start, a passage that places Luther squarely within the christological tensions established around the *Theotokos* controversy in Ephesus and later affirmed at Chalcedon:

> In Him I believe; and I believe, therefore, in the Son of God without severing Him from the Son born of Mary. My faith adheres not only to the Son of God or to his divinity but also to Him who is called Mary's Son; for they are identical [*derselbige*]. I am determined to know nothing of a Son of God who is not also Mary's Son who suffered, the God enveloped [*eingemischelt*] in humanity who is one Person. I dare not separate the one from the other and say that the humanity is of no use, but only the divinity . . . If he is not the Man born of Mary, I will have none of him. (*WA* 33:154, 155; *LW* 23:101, 102)

Despite perhaps the (Appolinarian) slip in the bit about "God enveloped in humanity," Luther is here deliberately aligning himself with a Christology that observes the full integrity of both the humanity and divinity of

---

10. Yeago, "Bread of Life," 258. The following analysis relies, at least initially, on this important work.

11. That Luther himself struggled with his opinion of the eucharist, at points being tempted to something more like what would be Zwingli's, is clear from a number of his letters from, for example, 1524; see Althaus, *Theology of Martin Luther*, 376ff.

12. Luther, "Auslegung"; ET, Luther, "Sermons," cited hereafter as *WA* 33 and *LW* 23.

Christ. Front and centre is Luther's concern to "not separate" the divine Son "from the son born of Mary" since the two "are the same one." He may even be on the defense against opponents who would claim that for him the humanity of Christ "is of no use."

The humanity of Christ as that in which the Son of God "is enveloped" is clearly of utmost importance in this passage. There is simply no way around it to God. Yet if this is, as it were, *where* the humanity of the incarnate Son is—between us and God—it could still be asked *what*, if anything, this humanity *does*. Or, as Luther himself has it here, what exactly is the "use" of the humanity of Christ?

> But listen to what Christ says here: "I am the bread of life." He reminds us that God is the source and wellspring of life, and that no one can give life but God. You might think: "'Well, how can You, the human Christ, be the Fountain of life here on earth and dispense the bread of life unless You are God?'" Yes indeed, He is just that; and apart from Christ you will not find God in heaven, in hell, or in the sea. Even if you were to go to heaven right now, you would nonetheless not come to God if you had not previously come to the Person of Christ, who is God and man. Now if the Father is in Christ, why search for him elsewhere? . . . You must trust that Christ is the Fountainhead of life, and that God has poured all His gifts, His will, and eternal life into Christ and has directed man to Him. There we are to find all. If you take hold of Him, you have all; you have taken hold of the entire Godhead. (*WA* 33:81–82; *LW* 23:55–56)

In this passage Luther has a strong grip on the integrity of the union between humanity and deity in Christ. Luther draws his congregation's attention to the fact that this obviously human Christ[13]—the one making apparently ludicrous claims about himself being the "source and

---

13. Much of these sermons are occupied with the deity of Christ, but this is not because Luther was unconcerned about his humanity. As Yeago points out, the polemic explains the orientation: "It is the claim of this human being to be the *bread of life* that must be accounted for" ("Bread of Life," 68n9). Indeed, as Luther himself confesses, an overemphasis on the deity of Christ "was the doctrine of many teachers, and formerly I myself was a doctor who excluded Christ's humanity, supposing that it was proper to separate His divinity and His humanity . . . But one must approach and hold to the divinity of Christ without overlooking His humanity . . . Otherwise, in the name of all devils, we tumble from the ladder that leads to Christ. Therefore beware of that!" (*WA* 33:155; *LW* 23:102). It was precisely a leaving behind of the humanity that Luther charged Zwingli—in his principle of *alleosis*—of advocating. (see *LW* 23:101n80). On this, see Cross, "Alloiosis," especially 120.

wellspring of life"—is just that: God himself. And then Luther seizes the opportunity to make the corollary claim just as strongly: this human Christ is God such that he is in no way incidental to the identity of this God. Even if it were possible to jaunt off to heaven right now, Luther suggests it would be impossible for anyone to find God without first coming "to the person of Christ, who is God and human being." Aside from the polemic undertones about ubiquity (if God is not "in heaven, in hell or the sea" apart from Christ, then clearly Christ must somehow be in all these places), Luther aims to emphasize the extent of the union in Christ. So completely is this man God that God will not be accessible to us in any other way. It's this talk about God's accessibility that signals the second important feature of this passage.

Across much of Luther's work he refers to the humanity of Christ as the place where God has become tangible, present, accessible or otherwise available to sinful humanity.[14] In this passage hearers are told to "take hold" of Christ since in so doing they "take hold" of "the entire Godhead." Leaving aside (for the moment) the shift here from the reality of "the Father in Christ" to having "the entire Godhead" in him, a second passage highlights the "graspability" of God in Christ:

> [Christ] says, "'I am the bread and food from heaven; he who eats of Me shall live.'" No one can gainsay that He is speaking of Himself. And since He is speaking of Himself, that is, of His Person, it is for us to take hold of and apprehend the Person of Christ without wavering and not to stray onto other paths, as though thereby we might escape death and be saved. No, we must cleave and adhere to Him [*sondern sollen an dem hangen und hasten*]. (*WA* 33:176; *LW* 23:114–15)

Christ "Himself, that is . . . His Person" is paramount here. No alternate set of "other paths," neither *antiqua* nor *moderna*—neither imitative morality nor any middle terms—can bring the believer safely past death to salvation. Luther insists that the only God is only available in this man's suffering flesh. Simply put, this is where faith can "cleave and cling to Christ":

> Do not give way to wild speculations; it is not advisable to discourse on this subject with too much subtlety. The maxim

---

14. "God will, and may, be found only through and in this humanity" (*WA* 10.1.1 and 208.24; *LW* 23:155 and *LW* 23:189n8. And see: "Whoever wants to reflect or speculate in a salutary way about God, let him set everything aside for the humanity of Christ" (*WABr* 1.145, 50.52; quoted in Lohse, *Martin Luther's Theology*, 224).

> should be: Do not let your thought take flight, flutter, and climb. Simply cleave and cling to Christ . . . do not stray beyond, even though your eyes do not see and your reason does not comprehend. Look here, my dear man, this cannot be understood by reason; otherwise why should we be asked to believe? (*WA* 33:80; *LW* 23:55)

With this I should say that Luther is not merely re-packaging some kind of Augustinian (or otherwise) Neoplatonism.[15] Two points here: first, Luther was no naïve dualist. If anyone deserved such a tag it was one of Luther's most notorious opponents, Zwingli. With his dependence on Aristotelian logic—like "spirit has an effect only on spirit"—Zwingli felt he had a clincher with his favorite proof-text, John 6:63, "the flesh profits nothing."[16] In contrast, with Zwingli (and with a radically different view of what "spiritual" meant—more on this below), Luther repeatedly appealed to the flesh of Christ as precisely the place where God was available. He advocated what could be called an "economic" Christology "from below":

> The Holy Spirit insists that we never teach, know of, think of, hear, or accept any other god than this God, whose flesh and

---

15. There is a longstanding tradition behind such an accusation. Thus, Congar piles it on: "The opposition between the visible and invisible, which Luther followed till he fell victim to it, no doubt has its roots in his Augustinianism. Many categories of Luther's thought call to mind Platonism and even Alexandrianism and would even be possible to draw certain parallels between him and Origen," (from his reply to Wolfhart Pannenberg following Congar, "Considerations and Reflections," 405). Yet, contrast Vogelsang's more sympathetic reading: "The point of departure and the aim of Augustine's Christology is the non-historical (*geschichtslos*) *verbum aeterna*, which does not participate in the act of becoming historical and has always remained the basically Neoplatonic foundation of Augustine's theology. The *verbum incarnatum*, the humiliated Christ, are for him only the means whereby access is obtained to the contemplation of the *verbum aeternum*. Luther completely restructures this speculation on the *verbum* from within. At the heart of his theology is the Word of the gospel, as is the word from the cross. It is this clear, bright *Word* whose rays can shine on the preexistence and on eschatology. But the other way round would be quite impossible" (Vogelsang, *Die Anfänge von Luthers Christologie*, 165; ET cited in Lienhard, *Luther: Witness to Jesus Christ*, 85n88, where: "Traces of Neoplatonic terminology can certainly be found in Luther's writings . . . But this does not mean he followed Neoplatonism fundamentally. What is fundamental to Luther is that the inaccessible God is—hidden certainly—but real, in the humanity of Christ. That is where God would be found, not in speculation or ecstasy."

16. Thus, Zwingli felt justified in asking, "What is the sense of the bodily eating of Christ?" See Althaus, *Theology of Martin Luther*, 397.

blood we imprint and hold in our hearts if we want to be saved. We must not let ourselves be taught a god who sits in his throne room up in heaven, one who is to be sought only in the Godhead. If we do, we find ourselves misled. But if you want to escape death and be saved, admit no other God than the Son of Man. (*WA* 33:201; *LW* 23:129)[17]

A second defense of Luther against the charge of Neoplatonism requires a fuller picture of his Christology. As Yeago has observed, "Christological conviction is *constitutive* of what Luther means by faith, in such a way that no full and proper articulation of his doctrine of faith can avoid also articulating his Christology."[18] Following Yeago's cue, a classic illustration provides a grip on Luther's Christology:

> Take a different illustration. Unheated iron is, of course, still iron. But when fire and heat are added, and it glows, I can say: This iron no longer has the qualities of iron; it is like fire. To be sure, it is iron, but it is diffused to such an extent with fire that when you see or touch it, you cannot call it iron but feel only the fire . . . On the other hand, the fire will not accomplish these same things without, and apart from, the iron, where the fire burns and bores. Thus the divine power is present bodily in the humanity of Christ and does what God naturally does, or does what the fire in the iron does. Only flesh and blood are visible. But faith sees a Man, sees flesh and blood which is like a fiery iron; for it is permeated with the Divine. (*WA* 33:191; *LW* 23:123–24)[19]

Whereas for the unspecified observer "only flesh and blood are visible," the one who looks in faith "sees a Man [*einen solchen Menschen*], sees flesh and blood which is like a fiery iron." On the analogy, the first sees only the iron where the second, in seeing the iron is immediately aware by faith

---

17. Thus: "Therefore do not listen to those who say that the flesh avails nothing. For it is on the flesh of Christ from the Virgin's womb that your eyes must be fixed, so that you may take courage and say: 'I have known nothing of God, neither in heaven nor on earth, apart from the flesh, sleeping in the Virgin's womb.' . . . For otherwise God is in all ways incomprehensible, it is only in the flesh of Christ that he can be grasped" (*WA* 25.106.33—107.11).

18. Yeago, "Bread of Life," 261.

19. In the text we will look at next, Luther explicitly rejects the image of fire and iron for representing the two natures of Christ. One reason for Yeago's plea for recognition of a "Cyrillene" doctrine of theosis in Luther, if plausible in these texts, is at least not fully reflective of Luther's more mature view. Cf. *WA* 39:2.95 (thesis 43).

that this iron is fiery hot.[20] Operative here is Luther's deep conviction that theology about the person of Christ is and must be soteriological. The one with faith is aware of the fiery nature of the iron because she has experienced the saving heat. It is not simply a case in which the faithful one (or seeer) has an extra capacity to see something that is "invisible" to someone without this added ability; rather the one who looks on Christ in faith can see that this crucified man is in fact the divine Son because by this faith—by "union" with him—she has known him as her savior.

And it is this grey line between Christology and soteriology that provides an entry into the element of Luther's theology that has been especially popular in recent scholarship.[21] Whereas the observer without faith sees simple, normal flesh and blood, the one who looks with faith sees a flesh and blood that "is permeated with the Divine [*den es ist durchgöttert*]." In Yeago's attempt to draw connections between this idea in Luther and a particular reading of Cyril's concept of "vivification," he translates this "for [Christ's flesh and blood] have been entirely deified."[22] This is perhaps a venturesome rendering, but it raises the issue well.[23] A second passage brings the question into better focus:

> This flesh is not merely empty flesh; it is a flesh permeated with God [*sondern ein durchgöttert Fleisch*]. Whoever encounters this flesh encounters God. (*WA* 33:194; *LW* 23:125–26)

There is a deliberate God-believer immediacy in this and other similar passages. Luther makes every effort to emphasize the absolute presence

---

20. That Luther is here dealing with an appropriation of the presence of Christ "by faith" and not, for example, the literal eating of the eucharist is clear: "Earlier He explained the term 'to eat,' namely, that it denotes to believe in Him, that he who adheres to His flesh and blood by faith is eating and drinking it, and that it is this faith, this eating and drinking, or this food and drink, that affords eternal life" (*WA* 33:194; *LW* 23:125). Luther is, however, not entirely consistent on this; he has also applied this "eating" directly to the taking of the eucharist; see *WA* 23:205o1e and *LW* 23.122n93.

21. The primary text in this school is Mannermaa, *Christ Present in Faith*. See also Sammeli Juntunen, "Luther and Metaphysics. "

22. Yeago, "Bread of Life," 273. And Yeago does the same at *WA* 33:194 on ibid., 267.

23. We will return to an observation made by Mozley: "Cyril's distinction between the proper nature of the Word and the body which the Word has made his own vanishes in Luther's exposition" (*Impassibility of God*, 212). See also Ngien, "Chalcedonian Christology," esp. 66ff.

and availability of God *in* the flesh of this crucified man.[24] Encountering it is to encounter God.

Much more could be said here about this "immediacy," but for now there is at least one more important note to hear from these sermons. A listener could ask, "'If the flesh of Christ is deified by virtue of its union with his deity, what effect does the union of the believer with Christ have on this believer?'" Recalling Origen's analogy above, if the iron becomes fiery when "fire or heat enter into it" what happens to the faithful hand that "grasps" this hot iron? In other words, if we have just looked at the way in which Luther's soteriology controls his Christology, we now ask about how his Christology affects his soteriology. Luther explains by preaching as Christ in the first person:

> If you touch My flesh, you are not touching simple flesh and blood; you are eating and drinking flesh and blood which makes you divine [*sondern issest und trinkest Fleisch und Blut, das Göttert*] [N.B. the American edition here omits: *das ist: es gibt die art und kraft der Gottheit*], that is, which give the mode and power of the Godhead. (*WA* 33:188; *LW* 23:122)

Here Luther explains that being made "divine" is equivalent to being given "the mode and power of the Godhead." He clarifies:

> It does not make you flesh and blood, but it has the nature and strength of God [*sondern es hat die art und kraft, so Gott hat*] ... This flesh does not have the qualities of flesh ... But it will imbibe you with godlike power [*sondern wird dich durchgöttern,*] that is[25] [*das ist*], with godlike virtues and works. It will wipe out your sin; it will deliver you from the devil and from death; it will free you from all wretchedness. (*WA* 33:188; *LW* 23:122)

Here Luther says that eating the flesh of Christ—which, on this occasion at least, means to be participating in Christ by faith—is to be "imbibed with godlike power" and this, moreover, is to receive "godlike virtues

---

24. Although the christological implications would be immense, we do not have the space here to explore the way Luther spoke likewise about things which are not the flesh of Christ. Leaving aside the eucharistic elements, Luther referred to the preached gospel, the believer's heart, baptism and the church all as various *loci* of God's presence. We will deal with this when we come to similar theology in John Zizioulas (see chapter 7).

25. Aside from the phrase-length lacuna, the Philadelphia translation has also twice left "*das ist*" untranslated in this passage. The combined effect of these omissions is some unnecessary ambiguity where Luther is clearly trying to explain his intent.

and works," to "wipe out sin," "deliver from the devil and death" and to be "free from wretchedness." These are all concepts that will strike the reader—even if only slightly familiar with Luther—as sounding remarkably similar to how he describes the results of justification.[26] Unlike the passages we have just looked at, Luther is here deliberately bringing his theology about the mediation of humanity and deity in the person of Christ to bear on theology about the salvation of the believer.[27] The line has been fairly straight from standard christological confessions, to questions about the status and function of Christ's humanity, to the implications these together have for soteriology. And whatever disagreements scholars may have over Luther, the idea that justification is by faith—and as such is a gift and not due to anything on the part of the individual Christian—is surely a point of consensus. Aside from whether or not there is a doctrine of theosis here, there is the less contentious point: whatever is happening, it is the result of *gift*. Touching Christ's flesh, says Luther, gives "the mode and power of the godhead," *that is*, it gives the kind of power that will "wipe out sin and deliver from death" and so on. This brings the line back round to opening one about grace.

Quoting Henri Strohl, Marc Lienhard offers a reminder of the critical contrast: "For Augustine, grace was a created gift and became a quality infused in human beings. 'For Luther, on the contrary, grace is none other than God himself.'"[28] But what does it mean to have "God himself"? To drag this passage into the twenty-first century: Does a gift like this transform the recipient into the giver? Does "deification" in Luther's theology mean the "power"—the attributes specific to triune life—become the believer's and thereby make the believer divine? Or does it rather mean the believer somehow gains the effects of the divine life—is affected *by* divine power—without becoming the one that lives it? Continuing the passage quoted above Luther says:

---

26. See the discussion cited at n21 above.

27. The divide among Luther scholars on the issues we are here exploring can be tracked along Melanchthon's so-called dictum, "to know Christ is to know his benefits" (*Loci theologici* [1521], *CR* 21:85). Yeago and the like see Luther "inverting" it, while others, more "traditional" in their reading, see him upholding it; see, for example, Althaus, *Martin Luther's Theology*, 201ff. We will recover this discussion when we come to one of Luther's most creative modern exponents in chapter 6. Cf. Congar, "Considerations and Reflections," 374n5.

28. H. Strohl, *Luther Jusqu'en*, 181, cited in Lienhard, *Witness to Jesus Christ*, 24.

> [The flesh of Christ] will free you from all wretchedness. If water were separated from sugar, then sugar would remain sugar, and water would remain water and would taste like water. Each would retain its substance and essence. But when the two constituents are boiled, cooked, and mixed [*vermenget*], then water no longer tastes like water; but it is sugary and as sweet as honey. This also holds true here. (*WA* 33:189; *LW* 23:122)

With this we have come from some careful courting of Chalcedonian tension to at least one rhetorical flourish where Luther seems to have overstepped the straight and narrow: the analogues in view in this text are clearly the flesh and divinity of Christ, and Luther suggests that the special power of Christ's flesh is due to the fact that it is, recalling the phrase above, "not just simple flesh." The explanation he offers for such a claim pivots on the fact that the flesh of Christ has been "mixed" with his divinity and therefore no longer retains its original "substance and essence." And it is the deep ontological tone of that combination—"substance and essence" [*wesen und substanz*]—that means there is likely more in view here than the "mixing" of Luther's famous "happy exchange." The exchange here is about the status of Christ's human nature, on where Christ is on the map of ontological possibilities, so to speak, and not about a swap of the status of his humanity (righteous) for that of the believer's (sinful).

Here is where the relationship of Christology and soteriology in Luther's theology may have become a beacon on the rocks. The distinction in the person of Christ between a divine and a human "nature" was established at Chalcedon to preserve, on the one hand, a soteriology that admits—in the words of Gregory Nazianzus—"the unassumed is the unhealed" and, on the other hand, a way of doing Christology in which the ontological uniqueness of the Creator is preserved lest the whole thing collapse into Arianism. When the boundary between this soteriology and this Christology becomes as permeable as it seems to have become in these sermons from Luther, there is a risk that the two will unravel each other. Here we return to questions raised during the previous two chapters in Alexandria. Did the hypostatic union alter the humanity of Christ to the extent that his is no longer like ours? Do the benefits of Christ for the believer involve this same kind of "mixing" and changing, from the substance and essence of simple flesh to the power and virtues of divine living? We are clearly in need of more precision from Luther, and he has plenty to offer, but to get it, we need to switch genres.

Luther's *Disputations* give us all the clarity we could want and more. The first item for consideration is already familiar ground; it is Luther's use of the *communicatio idiomatum*. The question with Luther is whether or not there is attributive traffic between the two natures of Christ, whether divine attributes can be predicated of humanity and *vice versa*. To choose the most well-known example: does it follow from God's omnipresence that the body of Jesus is also everywhere? If omnipresence is an attribute of divinity and finite location is one of humanity does the Church's faith require that Jesus exists in both of these ways at the same time? Or, is it correct to think of the deity and humanity of Christ as somehow being "mixed"?

I have deliberately not gone into the eucharistic controversy and so the question about the ubiquity of Christ's body is not of direct interest here. The main concern is how Luther understood the nature of God's relation to the world. That this is a christological question would have been a pleonasm for Luther (all questions would have been in some respect christo-logical for him). Nevertheless Luther replies to the question plain enough:

> 32. Argument: He who makes something cannot be the same as the thing which he makes. Christ is the creator. Therefore he cannot be a creature.
>
> Response: We join the Creator and the creature in the unity of the person. (WA 39:2.120)[29]

This brings the question to a point: what is the nature of this "joining"? How did Luther understand the relation of the humanity and divinity of Christ?

Much of his *Disputation Concerning the Divinity and Humanity of Christ* is occupied with asserting a particular use of language[30] so it would be very difficult to translate his theology in it from its particular agenda

---

29. For this Disputation we will rely mainly on the translation by Christopher Brown for Project Wittenberg, Luther, *Disputation on the Divinity and Humanity of Christ (1540)*, and occasionally on my own or that of Tolpingrud, "Luther's Disputation de Divinitate," in which case the change will be noted. Parenthetical references will also be made to Luther, "Die Disputation," with WA 39:2. The heading for this section of the disputation reads, "Nos coniungimus creatorem et creaturam in unitate personae."

30. Regarding which, see esp. White, *Luther as Nominalist*.

and style.[31] Nevertheless, this Disputation represents some of Luther's sharpest thinking about the relation of God and creation in Christ and as such is as transparent as he can make it. His main aim is clear:

> May you preserve this article in its simplicity, that in Christ there is a divine and a human nature, and these two natures in one person, so that they are joined together like no other thing, and yet so that the humanity is not divinity, nor the divinity humanity, because that distinction in no way hinders but rather confirms the union! (*WA* 39:2.97)

There is already a marked contrast here with the Christology in his sermons on John. Here Luther is adamant about a distinction with which a decade earlier he was much more casual. Here he goes so far as to say that this very distinction *confirms* [*confirmet*] the union of humanity and divinity in Christ. But the contrast is not as bleak as it might first appear. This distinction is not a raw duality of humanity and divinity but one that, in its *confirmation* of their union, allows a communication of attributes between them:[32]

> Because of the undivided union and the unity of the two natures there is a communication of attributes, so that, what is attributed to one nature is attributed to the other as well, because they are one person. (*WA* 39:2.98)

Following and advancing from his nominalist predecessors, Luther is suggesting that because of the union "what is attributed to one nature is attributed to the other as well."[33] The communication of attributes is *mutual*, so to speak, *between* the natures.

The point becomes clearer when Luther uses split attribution to distinguish the two natures of Christ:

> Question: It is asked, whether this proposition is true: The Son of God, the creator of heaven and earth, the eternal Word, cries out from the Cross and is man?

---

31. Regarding the genre of the medieval disputation, see Drews, *Die Disputationen*, xvii–xviii; and Helmer, *Trinity and Martin Luther*, esp.ch. 1.

32. On this, see Steiger, "Communicatio Idiomatum," and cf. Ngien, "Chalcedonian Christology."

33. Cf. the response at Argument 17 (*WA* 39:2.111): "But that unity of the two natures in one person is the greatest possible, so that they are equally predicated, and communicate their properties to the person, as if he were solely God or solely man."

> Response: This is true, because what the man cries out, God also cries out, and to crucify the Lord of glory is impossible according to the divinity, but it is possible according to the humanity; but because of the unity of the person, this being crucified is attributed to the divinity as well. (*W* 39:2.131)[34]

In this respect Luther follows Cyril: some things the one Christ says *humanly* and others *divinely*.[35] For Luther, the Son of God exists *as* a man, and now that this is true, this same man exists *as* a member of the divine Trinity. While there are indeed semantics at play[36] these subtleties signal real referents.[37] Luther explains:

> Even though he was not man born of the Virgin Mary before the world, nonetheless he was the Son of God, who is now man. Thus, for example, when I see a king in purple and crowned on his throne, I say, "This king was born of a woman, naked and without a crown." How can this be, and yet he sits on a great throne crowned and clothed in purple? But these things he put on after he was made king, and yet nonetheless he is one and the same person; and so too here in Christ God and man are joined in one person and must not be distinguished. But it is true that Christ created the world before he was made man, and yet such a strict unity exists that it is impossible to say different things [of divinity and the humanity]. Therefore whatever I say of Christ as man, I also say rightly of God, that he suffered, was crucified. (*WA* 39:2.101)

The first observation must be that Luther is advocating his version of Cyril's "single subject" Christology. But a second observation is unique to him: there are two logical fallacies that Luther advises we avoid. The first one involves reference to a general and inference about a specific or *vice versa*. In this case two apparently similar statements produce opposite

---

34. Also: "[W]e say that Christ is a creature according to his humanity, and the creator according to his divinity" (*WA* 39:2.99).

35. White, *Luther as Nominalist*, 249.

36. For Ockham's view of the communication of attributes one need come first to grips with his theory of terms. See Loux, ed., *William of Ockham's Summa Logicae*, esp. 1:100–104, 135–41.

37. Contra White, *Luther as Nominalist*, 287ff. White himself says that Luther's use of "natures" indicates "*the way* in which this one entity [the Logos] makes itself manifest" and yet his own thesis about the "non-compositional" nature of Luther's arguments here seems based on an *a priori* equation of ontology and substance such that the "way" something exists is strictly accidental and thus merely "semantic." But such is the boundary between semantics and ontics that Luther is here bold across.

results. For example: "This purple-dressed-crown-wearing throne sitter was born naked of a woman, without a crown" is false but "this particular man was born just like the rest of us" is true. In the first statement the referent is "king" and a king cannot be born naked, etc. In the second statement the referent is a particular individual in time, one who at the moment happens to be royally dressed but since he is identified as a particular man can be said to have been born like any other. White explains: "As with the king, so too with Christ. Here we have *one* person; and this person is both God and man, so that, although one might *identify* the person under a description pertaining to the man Jesus, it is nevertheless true that this person has got up to things like creating the world, which *as* the man Jesus, it did not do."[38] With this approach Luther was able to respond to a classic question about the relation of the incarnate Son to created temporality:

> Argument: Christ was not man before the creation of the world. Therefore it is not rightly said that the man Christ created the world. Or thus: When the world was created, Christ did not create it as a man [*tamquam homo*]. Therefore it is not rightly said that a man created the world.
>
> Response: There is the communication of attributes; and moreover [this is] a philosophical argument. This stands: The natures are distinct, but after that communication, there is a union, that is, there is one person, not two persons. But that person is God and man, one and the same person, who was before the creation of the world; even though he was not man born of the Virgin Mary before the world, nonetheless he was the Son of God, who is now man. (*WA* 39:2.100,1)

This marks a return to what I have called the "timing" of the incarnation; "after that communication, there is a union." A passage plucked for some further clarity here from his *Treatise on the Last Words of David* even further sharpens Luther's point:

> According to the second, the temporal, human birth Christ was also given the eternal dominion of God, yet temporally and not from eternity. For the human nature of Christ was not from eternity as his divine nature was. It is computed that Jesus, Mary's Son, is 1543 years old this year. But from the moment when deity and humanity were united in one person, the man, Mary's son, is and is called almighty, eternal God, who

---

38. Ibid., 242.

> has eternal dominion, who has created all things and preserves them through the communication of attributes because he is one person with the Godhead and is also very God. (*LW* 15:293ff.)³⁹

Given what has happened to the eternal Son, his having been made man, it can now be said that this very man (by which is meant the person of the eternal Son) existed prior to the world and is almighty, eternal God.

There is a second fallacy especially tempting in christological discussion. This is one in which two references to the same thing are made, one with restrictions and the other without, but these two kinds of reference are mixed up: one cannot infer from a statement with specific restrictions directly to one without these restrictions. Luther's example is a classic:⁴⁰

> 51. If [anyone] is not pleased by this or does not understand it, that Christ according as he is a man is a creature [*Christus secundum quod home est creatura*], the grammarian consoles him.
>
> 52. Let him who has learned to discuss the same matter in various ways be commanded to speak as simply as possible.
>
> 53. As the Ethiopian is white according to [*secundum*] his teeth, the grammarian could speak otherwise thus: The Ethiopian is white with respect to his teeth [*albus dentibus*], or "white of tooth" [*alborum dentium*]. (*WA* 39:2.96)

Following this Luther demonstrates with numerous examples in both cases that it is okay to say "the Ethiopian has white teeth" and "Christ's humanity is a creature" in many different ways yet, so long as the meaning is correct, all the various forms of expression are acceptable. The point is that the same thing can be seen and described differently from different perspectives but the thing so seen remains one thing despite differences among the resultant descriptions.

> Thus, since there is nothing else intended by these forms of speaking . . . one should condemn the perverters of logic who, corresponding to grammatically different forms of speaking, dream up different propositions about the same thing. (*WA* 39:2.96)⁴¹

---

39. From Wyatt, *Jesus Christ and Creation*, 33–34.
40. This illustration has a long history in the tradition and likely originates with Aristotle; see White, *Luther as Nominalist*, 243n32.
41. Translation is in White, *Luther as Nominalist*, 245.

For Luther, there is something inconvertible at the hub of orthodox Christology, a "same thing" that can be described differently but in any case cannot be let go. The ontological result of all this logical semantic is a Christology in which the "single subject" of the human acts of Christ is clearly the divine Word:

> We concede to the Fathers, after their fashion, that Christ is called a creature; but because among the untrained "creature" always signifies something separated from the Creator, this is not well done. But when we call Christ a creature, we understand the divine person which assumed [*assumpsit*] human nature. Nor is the creature in Christ the subject [*suppositum*], not even according to philosophy, but something assumed [*assumpta*]. Christ being a creature is not separated from God. Therefore he is not a creature in the old sense of the word. (WA 39.2.118)[42]

For Luther there is clearly only one *suppositum* in view—the Son, the "divine person" of the Trinity.[43] And given that this subject has "assumed" a human nature, it can now be said that "according to the humanity" this divine Son is a creature. But with this is raised another issue: having said that the divine Son "assumed" human nature, there are some important implications here for my earlier claim that Luther had indeed distanced himself from his nominalist upbringing. The text that brings the issue into clearest focus is Luther's from his theses 46–48:

> 46. But none have spoken more foolishly [*insulsius*] than the Nominalists [*Moderni*], as they are called, who of all men wish to seem to speak more subtly and properly.
>
> 47. These say that the human nature was sustained or "'supposited'" [*sustentari seu suppositari*] by the divine nature, or by a divine supposite.

---

42. "A creature, in the old use of language, is that which the creator has created and distinguished from himself, but this meaning has no place in Christ the creature" (WA 39:2.105).

43. Contra Congar, "Considerations and Reflections," 384ff., who suggests the single identity of Christ for Luther arises up out of or *from* the union of divine and human natures at the incarnation. Although Congar has clearly not given ample weight to the Christology Luther is developing in texts like the *Disputation* here, his observation nonetheless serves both to recall the dilemma faced by Philoponus and to anticipate the one posed by Jenson. Which would be better in the Creed: a single person *in* two natures or one *from* them? Contrast Congar's reading on this with Wyatt, *Jesus Christ and Creation*, 54n81.

> 48. This is said monstrously and nearly forces God as it were to carry or bear the humanity. (*WA* 39:2.95)

Luther has his finger on the problem with this so-called "modern" Christology: it suggests a relation between the humanity of Christ and the second person of the Trinity that is somehow incidental to the identity of the divine Son. Reinhard Schwarz gets us to the point:

> Luther criticized the Ockhamist interpretation of the hypostatic union; that God by the supposit [*suppositalen*] so to speak carries or transports the human nature. Luther means: [In] the way which one carries something—something other than what is in one's person—so have the Ockhamists understood how God took on humanity in Christ, without totally allowing the human nature to participate [*teilhaben*] in his personal being.[44]

Now the important connection: this talk about a relation between the divine and human natures of Christ as if one is "carrying" the other, as if to exclude the human nature from "participating" in Christ's personal being, is a christological version of the medieval grace scenario sketched above. In both cases there is a kind of "thing:thing" juxtaposition; something like Nestorius' pre-quantum billiard-ball-atoms bouncing into one another with no interpenetration or "real" relation. Heiko Oberman captures the christological dilemma that Luther would have faced in late medieval nominalism by asking:

> Whether perhaps the concrete presence of one of the two natures is the pivot and point of departure while the other nature only appears in the form of predication . . . We must be on our guard against a mere verbal subservience to the subsistence theory: in this case the unity of the two natures is captured only in the *communicatio idiomatum*, with the result that the mutual predication camouflages an essentially Nestorian Christology.[45]

Oberman's warning about "mere verbial subservience" strikes at the root of Luther's christological heritage. The question here is of whether Luther's departure from his nominalist/"Nestorian" heritage[46] led him to

---

44. Schwarz, "Gott Ist Mensch," 301–2. For this issue in the broader context of Luther's whole theology, see Lohse, *Martin Luther's Theology*, 228ff.

45. Oberman, *Harvest of Medieval Theology*, 263.

46. The problem with a Nestorian Christology as it came to expression in medieval nominalism was its soteriological pay-load; now the doctrine was "explanatory enhancement" (McGrath, *Life of John Calvin*, 161; cf. note 23) for something that was

take refuge in the other extreme. Although this is by no means a new suggestion for how to understand Luther's Christology, the idea has come to an especially sharp point in some relatively recent scholarship by Yves Congar. Congar suggests that the one in the seat of the divine economy in Luther's theology is essentially "God" and that Christ is simply the way this God looks when he does saving things among creatures.[47] According to Congar, Luther's "God" is "in, with and under" the incarnation but has not genuinely become a human in any meaningful sense:[48] "Fundamentally, if one interprets the word 'saviour' as meaning the active cause of salvation, it cannot be said that Jesus Christ is really our saviour: it is 'God' who saves us."[49]

On Congar's reading Luther neither sees the humanity of Christ in any sense actually internal to the being of God nor acknowledges the God so conceived as anything other than God *simpliciter*—an abstract *monotheos* hovering through creation. And this recalls the earlier observation of Luther's sermonic claim to have "the entire Godhead" in hand when one "takes hold of Christ." Indeed it is precisely this kind of scenario that usually raises the specter of Eutyches. If God and world simply stand over against one another in this kind of ontological competition then the co-existence of the two in the person of Christ can only be imaginable at the expense of one or the other. And since creation is contingent on the divine, it is Christ's creaturehood that typically pays most for the ontological compromise.

With this we return to the image considered under the heading of Luther's supposed opposition to medieval notions of grace: God and creation as competing "substances" where grace is either an acquired disposition for the good or the original giving of this capacity by God. Both forms of grace trace their origin back to the same substance-agent and

---

essentially true of all humans. That is, Christology was not hard against soteriology as we are seeing in Luther; rather it functioned as a sub-category of anthropology.

47. And see Congar, "Considerations and Reflections," 384 and n39: "This humanity is not that aspect of Christ which he has in common with men but the outward form in which the Godhead becomes perceptible to men." Huck, "Die Entwicklung," 127, cited in ibid.

48. Congar, "Considerations and Reflections," 385.

49. Ibid., 392. So Congar can reach his well-known conclusion: "In a word, Luther espouses a Christology of the *Alleinwirksamkeit Gottes*" (ibid., 402). And, more to the point of our own concerns: "All this is because his system of thought is dualistic while his religious affirmation in monistic," (ibid., 401). And, on the following page: "Luther is a monist in his affirmation of salvation as an act of God."

since this Giver is not himself the grace he gives, the gap between him and the recipient remains and indeed must remain for the giving to continue. So here we return to the question with a christological handle on its centre. If grace is something like the neo-Augustinian version that was common prior to Luther then deity and humanity exist at either ends of a continuum on which freedoms at one end are exercised at the expense of those on the other. In this kind of ontology Christ is somehow both ends of the continuum joined in the middle so that too much of a grip on God in Christ inevitably means the human end of the arrangement has sprung loose. On the other hand, if Luther really has completely re-wired the Western notion of grace then it's only theology that is Nestorian in its doctrine of creation that reads Luther as Monophysite in his doctrine of Christ. If the ontological terms for understanding salvation are presupposedly dualistic then any immediacy of God in Christ is just that, *im*-mediate. But if with Luther we begin from the radical condescension of God in Christ then the theological structure of mediation finds it shape from the other direction and soteriology must *follow* Christology. In short, the terms on which Luther appears "monophysite" are written according to an out-moded grammar.

If this is the case, Luther must have in mind some kind of *new* grammar. In his *The Disputation Concerning the Passage: "The Word was Made Flesh." (John 1:14)*, Luther explains:[50]

> 40. We would act more correctly if we left dialectic and philosophy in their own area and learned to speak in a new language in the realm of faith apart from every sphere . . .
>
> 42. In articles of faith, the disposition [*affectus*] of faith is to be exercised, not the philosophical intellect. Only then will we truly know what this means: "The Word was made flesh." (*WA* 39:2.5; *LW* 38:243)

The so-called "new language" Luther is attempting to apply in these *Disputations* becomes more explicit in his christological application of his characteristic "visible/invisible" dialectic:

---

50. Luther, "Die Disputation De Sententia"; ET: Luther, "Disputation concerning," cited here as *WA* 39:2.3ff., and *LW* 38:239ff.

> Argument 18: God is not at all visible. Christ is visible. Therefore, Christ is not God.
>
> Response: These are syllogisms which are valid in logic, but not in theology. For Christ is visible and invisible in accordance with the properties of his natures. But in the concrete person of Christ there is unity. Therefore, Christ is visible and invisible. The man Christ is one person because the Virgin is the mother of the Son of God who suffered and was crucified. How? Because the two natures in him are inseparable. (WA 39:2.23; LW 38:256)[51]

If it could be said that Luther was simply repeating a Neoplatonic cosmology with his "visible and invisible" concept then this would be the worst kind of Gnostic Christology. But recall that for Luther "invisible" is precisely accessible in the visible for those who can see what God is doing by faith. *Faith* is the lynchpin here. If by faith Luther simply meant we can see past the material to a secret, spiritual realm of hidden ideas and gods then we have nothing here but the opponents Irenaeus faced. But with even a moderately sympathetic reading Luther seems to mean something radically different when he says "faith": this could be the moving and re-moving of the medieval boundaries between epistemology and ontology. "Faith" for Luther was not one style among several for approaching God with our minds, it was rather the saving reality of this God right at hand. And when this God is present—precisely as the subject-enabling object of faith—established linguistic norms, while still continuing to function, must bend and bow to the grammar of a "new language." The subjects considered may at times be cloudy and incomprehensible but the language is one that comes with its own tutor. Luther explains:

> 6. Argument: Everything that is born begins to be, or everything that is born has a beginning. Christ was born. Therefore he began to be. He is a creature, and not from eternity.
>
> Response: I concede this, with a distinction. In philosophy this is true, but not in theology. The Son is born eternal from eternity; this is something incomprehensible. [But] this belongs to theology. For the Holy Spirit has prescribed models for us; let us walk in that cloud.

---

51. The result here, as we shall see, is a genuine advance, and yet one that maintains some classic difficulties: "Christ has a twofold nature, and according to one of the two he was born outside of time, in opposition to time, and before the circumstances of time" (WA 39:2.24; LW 38:257).

In the response to the next argument Luther clarifies:

> The Holy Spirit has his own grammar. Grammar is useful everywhere, but when the subject is greater than can be comprehended by the rules of grammar and philosophy, it must be left behind . . . Our eloquence must be restrained, and we must remain content with the patterns prescribed by the Holy Spirit. (*WA* 39:2.104)[52]

The Holy Spirit has his own "grammar" and "patterns" of speech. God himself makes it possible to speak the "new language" and thereby grasp in faith what would otherwise be invisible to reason and philosophy. And finally, it can be said that it is not the limitation of human sight that defines what is invisible, but this same Spirit:

> Everything that comes from the Holy Spirit is spirit, spiritual, and an object of the Spirit, in reality and whether it is physical or material, outward or visible; similarly, everything which comes from the natural power of the flesh, without Spirit is flesh and fleshly no matter how inward and invisible it may be. (*WA* 23:203; *LW* 37:99)[53]

Thus what we have come to at the end of our analysis is a central place for the Spirit in Luther's theology. It is only by the enabling of this Spirit that the believer can see in faith what to her would otherwise be invisible. In this respect the Spirit has an active role to play in the "mediation" of the visible and the invisible. And yet, despite the otherwise overlapped relation between Luther's Christology and his soteriology, what here is a profound insight about the place of the Spirit in theology about salvation seems not to have any observable effect in Luther's theology about the person of Christ. One consequence is commonly noticed: Luther's doctrine of redemption is too much bigger than his of creation. What has not been observed, however, is that this may well be due to a dogmatic list; a lopsided doctrine of God in which it is the Father, Son and Spirit who cooperate to save a creature but it is mainly just the Father and Son who have anything to do with God's saving presence in the creation. In redemption the three of the Triune life are active, but in Christology it is

---

52. The classic study here is Prenter, *Spiritus Creator*; see also Lienhard, "La Doctrine Du Saint-Esprit"; and Carlson, "Luther and the Doctrine of the Holy Spirit," 135–146.

53. Quoted in Althaus, *Martin Luther's Theology*, 395–96.

the Son of the Father and the communication of attributes, with little or no place for of the Spirit.

Yet there are much more positive things to be said, too: Luther's alternative to substantialist-dualist ways of understanding God's relation to the world is what can only be called, perhaps despite himself, "Trinitarian." The question that remains at the end of this chapter, however, is whether or not Luther's Trinitarian ontology must centre around a concept of *theosis* or if, on the other hand, there might be something more akin to the line he was crossing between ontology and epistemology. With that possibility raised one wonders if the trend in much modern Luther scholarship in which Luther's solutions to the West's theological problems are understood as essentially Eastern does in fact—with no slight to Eastern achievements—underestimate what Luther was up to. In any case, Luther has sharpened and deepened enough questions to lead us to Calvin, and beyond him to several on the constructive edge of modern Trinitarian theology.

5

JOHN CALVIN AND THE PROBLEM OF A *LOGOS ASARKOS*

When Creation and Revelation Collide
(An Ontological Concept of Mediation)

> Calvin is a cataract, a primeval forest, a demonic power . . .
> I lack completely the means, the suction cups, even to assimilate this phenomenon, not to speak of presenting it adequately.
>
> —Karl Barth

Good theology always involves tension and John Calvin made some very good theology. F. L. Battles: "[E]very fundamental notion of [Calvin's] thought is defined as a field of tension—a true middle between false extremes."¹ Similarly, Wilhelm Niesel has said that the apparently contradictory emphases in Calvin are held by and resolved around the Chalcedonian model of the hypostatic union.² This chapter is about these

---

1. Battles, "Calculus Fidei," 85, 107, cited in Wyatt, *Jesus Christ and Creation*, x.

2. "[T]he form of Calvin's theology was shaped by the axis on which it revolves. Jesus Christ controls not only the content but also the form of [Calvin's] thought . . . The thought of Calvin in many other doctrinal matters is guided by this [Chalcedonian] attempt to apprehend and describe the Person of Jesus Christ" (Niesel, *Theology of John Calvin*, 247).

tensions; it's an attempt to engage Calvin's thought in order to feel their respective pulls. This will require wrestling with several so-called "false extremes," but it will hopefully lead to a better understanding of the Christology that Niesel has suggested can hold it all together.

The issue came to a head, as theology often does, in the heat of a particular controversy. Christological questions divided the Polish Reformation in the early second half of the sixteenth century. One party's leader was an Italian Reformer and Hebrew scholar named Francesco Stancaro.[3] Stancaro was brash even on Reformation standards. He was the sort of theologian who seemed to either revel in controversy or at least be so dogmatically zealous that he fostered degrees of dissent and confusion at every major stage in his career. The view to earn him a place in Calvin's busy sights was how he understood Christ to be Mediator, and how especially this view came to effect the young Protestant church in Poland.

The story begins in 1552 when Calvin received a collegial letter from Francis Dryander in which he was briefly informed that "some old Italian, Stancaro, was creating confusion by maintaining that Christ was mediator only in his human nature."[4] As a concept of no little importance to Calvin's own thinking, and due moreover to Calvin's widely accepted theological authority, the Reformer's opinion on Christ as Mediator was entreated by the "Polish Brethren" for assistance in quelling a schism in their young project. Calvin let this first request go unanswered, but then, in 1559, after Stancaro had been forced from various chairs as Professor of Hebrew into a season of peripatetic wandering around Transylvania, Hungary and Poland, Calvin received another letter. This time from Peter Statorius, complaining that Stancaro was

> renewing the heresy of Nestorius, only giving it a new name. He teaches that the human nature of Christ is the only mediator between God and men and that the divine nature has nothing to do with it.[5]

---

3. For the following account we will follow the work of Tylenda. His excellent work has all the necessary bibliographic information for readers interested in more detail on Stancaro and the Italian Reformation. See Tylenda, "Christ the Mediator," and idem, "The Controversy on Christ the Mediator." References to Calvin's letters to the Polish Brothers will be made to the standard texts in *Responsum ad fratres polonos*, CR 9:337–42; 349–58, and will be quoted from the English translations provided at the end of Tylenda's two articles by page number as *First Reply* and *Second Reply*.

4. CR 14:404, quoted in Tylenda, "First Reply," 9.

5. CR 18:600–603, col. 601, quoted in ibid., 9.

Stancaro was to be officially condemned at the Synod of Pinczów in August of that year, and Calvin's first response to the Polish brothers was likely intended to heal the rift caused thereby, but for reasons unknown, Calvin's letter was not published and the divisions continued and deepened. Calvin was then asked for a second response and despite his growing distaste for controversy he obliged by publishing his first reply himself and sending a second in which he repeated and expanded his original position. Doubtless the desire of the Polish church leaders was to set Calvin's views within an anticipated consensus achieved across those also solicited from other Reformation leaders and to therewith so overwhelm their resident schismatist as to inspire a self-induced exile. But in the next year (1560) when Polish Protestants finally assembled to rid their country of "Stancarism" the defendants cried foul, claiming the letters from Zurich and Geneva were fakes.[6] Then a certain nobleman intervened and, after much uproar, a four month truce was established between the opposing groups. The hiatus was a busy period, both parties setting to acquire the endorsements of their southern experts. Stancaro himself wrote to Calvin, in even somewhat friendly terms, warning him that "Arianism" was being broadcast in Poland under the auspices of Calvin's approval and demanding that Calvin take immediate and decisive action:

> This heresy and madness, not to say blasphemy, they affirm and proclaim in public and in private to be your teaching, and that you are one with them in this doctrine . . . We ask you not to be reluctant to write your opinion to us; either you approve the faith of those Arians, or you approve our faith on the Trinity and mediator. There is no middle ground![7]

One can only wince at the irony. The absence of "middle ground" that Stancaro claimed ought force Calvin onto his own resembles almost exactly the dimensions of the theological issue between them. For Stancaro's part, as Stephen Edmondson explains,

> [T]he divine nature, because it is shared equally and fully by the three person of the Trinity, cannot mediate or stand between God and humanity—to say that the Son mediates between the

---

6. Tylenda suggests the possibility that forgeries being circulated in Lesser Poland under Calvin's name may even bear some weight; see Tylenda, "Second Reply," 143, and the editors' comments at *OC* 9:xxxvi.

7. Ibid., 136, 137.

Father and humanity in his divinity would imply that he was subordinate to the Father in his divinity, and this would be the Arian heresy.[8]

As far as Stancaro was concerned to say that Christ in his divine nature is on some kind of "middle ground" between God and humanity would make him less than God the Father and thus succumb to the ancient logic of Arius. As Edmondson goes on to explain, for Stancaro, "to be a Mediator is to be one who is *between* two parties."[9] And it is this idea of Christ somehow being "between" the Father and creation that hardened into the core of the dilemma. Stancaro's position was simple enough: Christ is indeed "the mediator between God and man"—as his favorite prooftext insisted—but it is only insofar as he is "the *Man* Christ Jesus."[10] For Stancaro, Christ can be said to be between the Father and creatures, yes, but since Christ in his divinity is *homoousion* with the Father, he can only stand *between* him and creation by way of something other than their common divinity. Stancaro considered himself an orthodox Trinitarian and—with some foreshadowing of similar attitudes in modern theology—he also managed to consider his opponents to be either tritheists or Arians or somehow both at once. What is of especial interest for the purposes of this study are the reasons and ways he came to connect so closely theology about Christ as Mediator and theology about God as Trinity. For Stancaro, what was said about Christ bore directly on what was believed about the being of God, and *vice versa*.

Contrary to what his opponents, Calvin included, never tired of suggesting, Stancaro's theology did not crop up out of his own imagination. His thinking about Christ as Mediator was a classic case of ideas at the forward edge of an old paradigm. He represented a particular tradition, and he did it in a way and at a time that meant he felt the brunt of a push for something new. So, before coming to Calvin's own theology, a brief digression here to see Stancaro's in its broader context.

8. Edmondson, *Calvin's Christology*, 14. Thus Tylenda on Stancaro: "Christ was not the mediator between God and men with respect to his divinity, for this would attribute to him a divinity inferior to that of the Father. A mediator is one who intercedes and prays for us, and since intercession and prayer are signs of inferiority in reference to the one who is addressed, Stancaro concluded that Christ was mediator only as man" ("First Reply," 5).

9. Edmondson, *Calvin's Christology*, 17, emphasis added.

10. According to Tylenda, 1 Timothy 2:5 is the only verse Stancaro cites for support of his position in his letter to Calvin of February 25, 1561; see Tylenda, "Second Reply," 138n29.

For theologians writing before the Arian crisis theology about mediation took shape around an understanding of the divine economy in which the Son was clearly in a middle position.[11] Knowledge of God and recreation in his image was centered on and achieved through the incarnate Christ. The pattern was Father <–> Son <–> Humanity, with the Son unhesitatingly between God and creation. But as Edmondson points out, Augustine, for one, found this schema problematic in its subordinationalist implications:

> Thus, when Genesis says that we are created after the image and likeness of God, [Augustine] argues that this means in the image of the Godhead as a whole, Father Son and Holy Spirit, and not merely of one person in the Godhead.[12]

Augustine marks a major turning point in Western notions of christological mediation. Following him it was understood that humanity was not created in the image of the Son but in the image of the whole Trinity. From here it was thought that humans come to knowledge of God no longer through the Son *per se* but through the capacities endowed in them by virtue of their imaging of the Trinity (e.g., memory, understanding, will). Edmondson explains the significance of the shift: "The pattern, then, is simplified to Trinity <–> Humanity, and the Son is removed from his mediatorial position out of a concern for the unity of the Son with the Father in the divine nature."[13]

To further reinforce this line there was also Augustine's highly influential dictum, "*Opera trinitatis ad extra indivisa sunt*." Calvin himself drew Stancaro's attention to the way in which Augustine's authoritative line could be over-tightened to the point of its own misuse.

> As barbarous language had indeed spread throughout the world the common dictum that the work of the Trinity is undivided, being the more difficult to understand in isolation, was corrected or mitigated by adding the restriction, the word intrinsically. But we conscious, however, of our ignorance, are satisfied with an operation which is extrinsic, one by which God adjusts himself to the small measure of our intelligence. (*CR* 9:354)

---

11. See Edmondson, *Calvin's Christology*, 23, where he cites similar views in Athanasius' *On the Incarnation of the Word* 11–19.

12. Edmondson, *Calvin's Christology*, 23.

13. Ibid.

Calvin does not deny the validity of Augustine's point, he only says that when it is given too much attention "in isolation," when it is mitigated with qualifications abstracted from the divine economy—from "an operation which is extrinsic"—it can lead theology away from its proper concern with what is available in divine revelation.[14]

The tendency in the theology drawn on by Stancaro was to use Augustine's dictum to connect the being and act of God so closely that the *indivisa* came to refer not just to the inseparability of triune *opera* but to the indistinguishability of triune *persona*.

The point was supposed to be about the way the Father Son and Spirit always create and redeem together as the one God they are, but Stancaro and his ilk were taking Augustine's line to refer to the being of the God doing these acts. The shift was across the grey line between the act and being of God; not much further in this direction and one ends up saying that the economic acts of the Trinity are indivisible because of an immanently singular being of God somehow behind the three persons. Stancaro did not go quite that far—he was no modalist—but it is at least relevant to point out that the theology developed in Poland as a counter-response to his soon ended at the opposite extreme, tritheism.[15]

The crucial point for here is that there is absolutely no space for a *divine* mediator, such a thing is a theological misnomer. To be divine is to be one thing and to be non-divine, another so to mediate between these two things, whatever ontological contortions this might require, cannot involve a claim that the resultant mediator is in any respect properly God. Any denial of this theologic, as Stancaro relished pointing out, would appear to get one to Arianism: if God cannot mediate and the Son does, then the Son is not-quite God.

Although Arianism in its original integrity had been rejected at Nicea, the incipient theological impulse lived on, and the doctrine of the two natures of Christ had become an ideal Petri dish. Here the humanity

---

14. Tylenda does not address Calvin's gloss, "was corrected or mitigated by adding the restriction, the word intrinsically" (*interposita restrictione correctum vel mitigatum fuit: nempe quum addita fuit particula: intrinsecus*). Calvin's sense is unclear here but it is possibly 'by adding the restrictive word "intrinsically." Thus, *the* intrinsic *work of the Trinity is undivided*. This "corrective" would leave space between the immanent and economic "trinities" for Calvin's concept of accommodation; an idea to which we will return soon below.

15. Tylenda, "Second Reply," 144. We note here the parallels between sixteenth-century Polish theology and that of the mature John Philoponus. Both responded to what they perceived to be dualistic Christologies and ended up in tritheism.

and divinity of Christ held the same places once occupied by the One God and the so-called "firstborn" Son. Now whatever fudge made in the Arian doctrine of creation for the sake of divine transcendence could be re-made in christological terms for the sake of Christ's deity. In broad strokes it could be said that much late-Patristic and Medieval Christology wrestled with the idea that the mediation accomplished by Christ was done "through" his humanity; be it in his economic "flesh," as with Cyril, or in his "soul," as in Philoponus, or simply in his "humanity," as in Stancaro. Christ was indeed, as Chalcedon had required, a single person in two natures, but as Chalcedon had also stipulated, these natures cannot be confused. As we have seen, the ongoing distinction of Christ's natures was taken by many to mean that certain attributes ought to be ascribed only to his humanity—being born, growing in stature and knowledge, suffering and dying, etc.—and certain others only to his divinity—creating everything, healing the sick, and rising from the dead, etc. The trend illustrates the perseverance of a certain theological instinct; in both the Arian and this post-Nicean christological tradition, the mediation of God and world was achieved either by a being or by a "nature" that was necessarily non-divine.[16]

Augustine again stands as the influential example in this trend: "as man, he is our Mediator; but as the Word of God, he is not an intermediary between God and man because he is equal with God, and God with God, and together with him one God."[17] Jesus was uniquely qualified to mediate between humanity and deity because he was like other humans in his mortality and like God in his righteousness. The point here is that both mortality and righteousness were attributes of his *humanity*.

But this is where such a simplified account cannot avoid a second layer of historical complexity. Not only was Augustine arguably responsible for influencing the tradition that attributed the mediation of Christ only to his human nature, he also stands as the likely progenitor of a significantly different counter-tradition.

> Man is not mediator without deity, and God is not mediator without humanity. This is the mediator: divinity without humanity is not the mediator, nor humanity without divinity, but

---

16. See Edmondson, *Calvin's Christology*, 24.

17. *Confessions* 10.43, cited in ibid., 24. Edmondson rightfully continues, "Of course, Augustine adamantly adds, Christ's human nature is able to mediate only because of its unity with the divine nature—only thus is it just—and not in any sense apart from it."

between divinity alone and humanity alone the mediator is the divine humanity and the human divinity of Christ.[18]

Augustine here articulates a view of Christ as an ontological medium between God and humanity in his person as both. Now Christ is not between God and creation by virtue of shared attributes with both (righteousness and mortality), rather by virtue of simply *being* both. As the God-man Christ shares divinity with God and humanity with humans and this sharing *is* his mediation.[19] In his *Second Reply* Calvin himself quotes Augustine against Stancaro,

> To be mediator he must have something in common with God and something in common with men, lest being like men in both points, he would be far from God, or if in both of them like God, he would be far from men, and so he would not be mediator. (*CR* 9:357)[20]

Although this view stands in significant contrast to the other in which Christ mediates only in his humanity, both share a significant feature that will deserve some more attention in later chapters: in each case Christ is considered the Mediator insofar as he shares something with the parties he mediates, and it is this multilateral 'sharing' that puts Christ in his place; he is the Mediator because he is somehow *between* the divine and the human. In the first case, Christ has attributes in common with both humanity and deity, and in the second case, Christ mediates by virtue of his duality of natures. In both cases, the mediation of Christ is more about something he *is* rather than something he *does*.

Then, in the twelfth century, the pendulum between act and being began its return swing. Most likely due to the broad influence of Peter Lombard a new distinction emerged between the divine power to save and the atonement achieved via Christ's human obedience.[21] Edmondson connects this with our course:

---

18. *Sermon* 47.21 (*CCSL* 41:595); quoted in Tylenda, "Second Reply," 156.

19. Note that, although much of this has followed Edmondson, we here part from his account and identify Augustine as the likely source of both medieval perspectives on Christ's mediatorship instead of just the former. For the shift in Augustine's own view of Christ as Mediator, see Muller, *Christ and the Decree*, 194ff.

20. Citing Augustine at *CSEL* 33:277–278.

21. See Edmondson, *Calvin's Christology*, 24ff., for an only slightly slower pace across so much theology, and see n24 below.

> This distinction between divine and human activity, which is carried over as a distinction between the operations of the divine and human natures in Christ, begins to define mediation more as his activity—what Christ does through his obedience—rather than his ontological state—who he is either in his mortality and justice or in his two natures.[22]

Edmondson is tracking what was in fact a very slow shift from a focus on the being of the Mediator to one on the mediatorial effects of his acts. Nevertheless the trend is observable: Thomas Aquinas, well known for giving space to the humanity of Christ and its causal role in redemption, further strengthened the shift begun by Lombard. And his influential contemporary Bonaventure also cooperated with the trend.[23] The shift was gradual but eventually, and in complete contrast to the tendency in theology prior to Lombard, it was more widely presumed that mediation was something that Christ *did*; like a priest standing between God and people, offering sacrifices and expiating for sins.

With this quick sketch of the roots of late medieval notions of christological mediation we are ready to recall Stancaro's place within it. For Stancaro, whatever was to be said about the mediatorship of Christ it ought in no wise threaten his essential deity, his substantial communion with the Father and the Spirit. Consequently, whatever mediatorial activity Christ undertakes it is—like eating, sleeping, or suffering—something only properly attributable to his humanity. That said however, Stancaro would have been quite ready to admit some initiative to the eternal Son for the mediatorial results of Christ's human activity, but this initiative would be the same broad kind shared among the whole Trinity for every operative act *ad extra*. The second pressure characteristic to Stancaro's theology of mediation is one that it would seem he had inherited from the broader medieval theological heritage. In this respect Stancaro would have insisted mediation is a species of reconciliation, something Christ does to respond to the damages incurred on account of the Fall. For him, mediation was a way of talking about Christ's acts as the priest between

---

22. Ibid., 25.

23. For this account, see Landgraf, *Dogmengeschichte Der Frühscholastick*, 2/2:299–327. N.B., whether Thomas refers to Christ as Medium or to his activity as Mediator, he follows Augustine and generally connects both to Christ's *human* nature (cf. the discussion at Edmondson, *Calvin's Christology*, 25–6). See *Summa Theologiae* (*ST*) IIIa.q26.2. And regarding the shift from being to act in the Mediator, see *ST* III. q22.1.ad3; III.q59.4.ad.1. For Bonaventure, Edmondson refers us to Hayes, *Hidden Center*, 55–90 and 192–205.

John Calvin and the Problem of a Logos Asarkos   105

God and humanity. Operative here was a Christology that relied on the distinction of natures in Christ to preserve the ontological integrity of the Trinity and a doctrine of the Trinity so tightly imagined that no act *ad extra*, not even the incarnation of the Son, could cross the line between God's being and his acts without unwinding monotheism from the inside out.

Now for Calvin's response to all this.

∼

Calvin's first move was to reject the either-or binary alternatives offered by Stancaro (effectively: *agree with me or choose between Arianism and tritheism*). Instead of accepting Stancaro's starting-place and then choosing between the consequent options, Calvin began by rejecting the idea that the incarnation was necessary for mediation at all. He reorganized his doctrine of God so that the mediatorial activity of the Son is something God does primally as *Creator* and not simply something he does subsequently as *Redeemer*. For Calvin, mediation is not an effect of the incarnation, but *vice versa*. Already in his *First Reply* Calvin made his position against Stancaro plain:

> His arguments deny that Christ can be said to be mediator according to the divine nature, thus he would be inferior to the Father. But we maintain, first, that the name of mediator suits Christ, not only by the fact that he put on flesh, or that he took on the office of reconciling the human race to God, but from the beginning of creation he already truly was mediator, for he always was the head of the Church, had primacy over the angels, and was the firstborn of every creature, (Eph, 1.22; Col. 1.15; 2.10). Therefore, we conclude that not only after Adam's fall did he begin to exercise his office of mediator, but since he is the eternal Word of God, both angels as well as men were united to God by his grace so that they would remain uncorrupted. (*CR* 9:338)[24]

In direct contrast to Stancaro, Calvin not only denies that Christ mediates just in his human nature but more to the point, he insists Christ was mediator before there was a human nature of Christ at all. By the time Calvin had to reply a second time to the Polish Brothers he was even clearer on the crucial point: "Certainly, the eternal Logos was already

---

24. On this, see also Willis, *Calvin's Catholic Christology*, 70ff.

mediator from the beginning, before Adam's fall and the alienation and separation of the human race from God" (*CR* 9:350).[25] For Calvin, Christ is the Mediator prior to and in advance of the problem of sin. Although there are some unspoken implications here that will require closer attention soon enough, it is at least clear for now that Calvin intends to link the notion of mediation not just with the economy of reconciliation but somehow with the divine will to create. David Willis identifies this twofold aspect of Calvin's theology about the Mediator:

> As reconciler, the Mediator was ordained because of the Fall to restore the broken relationship between God and man. As sustainer, the Mediator always was the way creation was preserved and ordered.[26]

In his *Commentary on John,* Calvin drew this "reconciler"/"sustainer" distinction himself, albeit with different terms and in the opposite order:

> For there are two distinct powers of the Son of God. The first appears in the architecture of the world and in the order of nature. By the second he renews and restores fallen nature. (*Comm. Jn.* 1.5)[27]

Simply put, even a sinless humanity would require a Mediator to know God. In his *Institutes* Calvin makes it plain, "Even if man had remained free from all stains, his condition would have been too lowly for him to reach God without a Mediator" (2.12.1).[28] This recalls the way much Alexandrian "vertical" Christology tended to align what Calvin is here at pains to distinguish. For Calvin there is a deliberate distinction between the mediation the Son undertakes by virtue of there being a creation other than God and the mediation incumbent upon the Son once the creation requires redemption from sin.

There are two systematic maneuvers in play here. First, Calvin has affirmed and distinguished the twofold nature of the Son's relation to creation; he is the one through whom everything has been made and also the Lamb who takes away the sins of the world. Second and consequently, Calvin has dislodged the concept of mediation from theology

---

25. See also ibid.: "Christ was the head of angels and men in the still innocent state of things."

26. Willis, *Calvin's Catholic Christology,* 70.

27. ET in Calvin, *New Testament Commentaries*; cf. Wyatt, 36.

28. Translations of the *Institutes* will be from Calvin, *Institutes,* unless otherwise indicated.

strictly about the latter of these. Christ mediates not just as Redeemer but also in his role as Creator. Of course, this is playing loose with how Calvin uses the term "Christ," since the mediatorial role performed by "Christ" before the Fall is more accurately attributed to the one Calvin calls the "Eternal Son." But with the problem this raises about a *logos asarkos* aside for the moment—and only for the moment—the point here is about Calvin's basic response to not just Stancaro, but to the whole tradition of Patristic and Medieval concepts of mediation behind him. For Calvin, the Mediator is not just a rescue effort, he is somehow integral to the way God relates to creation. "In other words," explains Edmondson, "we will find that there is nothing 'before' Christ's headship over creation and the Church. He is the Mediator in all of God's relating to what is not God."[29]

Yet, by locating the mediatorial identity of the Son somehow before his incarnate economy, the concern to maintain Christ's consubstantiality with the Father would appear to be raised considerably. Calvin however, would disagree:

> [F]rom the title mediator he unskillfully deduces that Christ is less than the Father. These elements admirably fit one with the other, that the only begotten Son of God was the same God and of the same essence with the Father, and nevertheless, he was the mid-point between God and creatures, so that the life which was otherwise hidden in God would flow from him. (*CR* 9:338)

It is clear that Calvin has more in mind than what by his time was the typical view of Christ's role as Mediator. He speaks here in theological terms that are categorically prior to whatever Christ accomplished in his high priestly expiation for the sins of fallen humanity. Calvin rejects Stancaro's claim that a mediatorial role for the Son in the order of creation would require the Son to be ontologically inferior to the Father. He says, "these elements admirably fit one with the other"; namely, the eternal consubstantiality of the Son with the Father *and* his identity as what Calvin calls "the mid-point between God and creatures" [*et tamen fuisse quasi medium inter Deum et creaturas*]. This, Calvin argues, was necessary lest life somehow stay bottled up inside the being of God. The eternal Son's mediation here is, according to Calvin, the very possibility of life beyond the Trinity (again, an idea to which we will return in later chapters). The Son mediates "so that the life which was otherwise hidden in God would flow from him." In his *Second Reply* Calvin reaffirmed this

---

29. Edmondson, *Calvin's Christology*, 143.

claim: "and when John says that life was in him, he indicates the mode of communication from which otherwise hidden source, the grace of God flowed to men" (*CR* 9:350). Calvin suggests that Christ's claim to have life in himself (John 5:26) is valid insofar as Christ "communicates" this life from his "hidden source" in God. In his commentary on this passage, Calvin clarifies:

> Thus, 'God is said to *have life in himself*, not only because he alone lives by his own inherent power, but because, containing in himself the fullness of life, he communicates life to all things ... But, because the majesty of God, being far removed from us, would resemble an unknown and hidden source, for this reason it has been openly manifested in Christ. We have, thus, an open fountain placed before us, from which we may draw. (*Comm. Jn.* 5.26)[30]

As Christ speaks in this passage he is of course addressing a group of fallen humans, a group in need of mediation in the more typical sense of needing God to overcome the effects of their sin, but Calvin's commentary suggests he has something larger in view. Calvin speaks of the life available in Christ as that which, "because of the majesty of God," would be "far removed from us," and he suggests that only as this has been "openly manifested in Christ" can we now hope to draw from the fountain of life. Indeed, as Calvin sees it, the entire gospel of John is something of a grand-scale picture of Christ as the Mediator. In his *Second Reply to Stancaro* he says,

> [W]hat Christ elsewhere asserts: "I am in the Father, and the Father is in me" (John 14.11) cannot be predicated of the human nature alone. There to the life is the picture of a mediator! John's whole gospel, in fact, is brought to mind by similar statements of Christ as when he claims for himself what does not belong to either nature but concerns the complete person. (*CR* 9:352)

Here is the second way in which Calvin opposes the theology of Stancaro. Now Calvin rejects the presupposition that the mediatorial acts of Christ must be attributed to either his human or his divine nature. On the contrary, for Calvin, it is only the whole person of Christ, in both his natures, who could possibly perform the mediatorial task.[31] Calvin even

---

30. ET Calvin, *New Testament Commentaries*; cf. Edmondson, *Calvin's Christology*, 126.

31. Edmondson makes this point, but then skews it in the other direction: "If the

insists that the fact Christ's mediatorial acts cannot be simply attributed to the human nature alone is "to the life"—is itself!—a "picture of a mediator." It is the impossibility of reducing the Mediator to just one of his two natures, the inseparability of his humanity and divinity in his one person, that makes our picture of Christ undeniably one of the Mediator between God and his world.³²

Now we have all of the proverbial cards on the table. Stancaro for his part could not allow that Christ in any way mediated in his divinity since he believed this would require Christ's inferiority to the Father. Calvin, on the other hand, decisively flanked both claims by insisting that Christ's mediatorship is in the order of creation and not just redemption; and that even when it does come to Christ's redemptive mediation, this is only attributable to the whole person of Christ, humanity and divinity together. Yet if these are the opposing positions, from where did they begin? How did Calvin and Stancaro get to such radically different theological conclusions? Two basic observations:

For Stancaro, Trinitarian logic dictated how to understand the gospel story, for Calvin the priority was reversed. Stancaro began with the consubstantiality of the Father and Son and then tried to work out his Christology. In short, he did his theology as if eternity were superior to time, as if God in his immanent self was categorically distinct from how he appears to humans economically. An understandable decision, but one nevertheless stoutly rejected by Calvin:

> I retort that the mystery of the dispensation which the Scriptures everywhere recommend is poorly and miserably neglected by him. It is a wonder that he does not attend to the clear testimonies he quotes! If, properly speaking and according to the usual mode of Scripture, Christ is mediator between God the Father and us, that cunning speculation of his only entangles and obscures what is otherwise clear. (*CR* 9:352)

Word mediates between the Father and creation, it cannot be his nature that mediates, for he shares that nature with the Father. Rather, it is the Word, as a person distinct from the Father, who mediates) [*sic*], though he is only able to perform this mediation on the basis of his divine nature" (Edmondson, *Calvin's Christology*, 31).

32. "It is impossible for us to trust in Jesus Christ aright without understanding his human nature; as also it is necessary to have comprehended his majesty before we can put our trust in him for salvation. Moreover, it is not sufficient to understand that Jesus Christ is God and that he is man unless we add also that there is in him but one person" (*Sermon on I Tim. 3:16*; *CO* 53:324ff., quoted in Wyatt, *Jesus Christ and Creation*, 4.

Calvin is committed in his stance against Stancaro to the priority of the divine economy, what he calls "the mystery of the dispensation which the Scriptures everywhere recommend." And he has made a deliberate choice to remain bound to this economy over the appeal of any kind of "cunning speculation" since he believes such flights only land one in obscure tangles:[33]

> As long as Christ is placed in this medial position this is not a question of his essence, nor do we subtly dispute about what it is; we should rather direct our attention to the divine counsel which the ancients have called economy and dispensation. (CR 9:353)[34]

Somewhere near the root of the issue between the two, then, is a difference over the relation between doctrine and Scripture. For his part, Calvin was prepared to embrace some provisional ambiguity in the nature of doctrine for the sake of a firm grasp on the authority of Scripture. So when it came to the doctrine most valued by Stancaro—that of the Trinity, and in particular of the Son's consubstantiality with the Father—Calvin, neither denying Stancaro's basic claims nor the doctrines he began from, plays light with the extent to which this kind of theology can dictate a hermeneutical posture. For Calvin, too much theology about the Trinity was always suspicious.[35] He preferred to keep things grounded in the Biblical texts: "Leaving aside that profound and incomprehensible mystery, we only account what we have learned from Scriptures and the sacred lips of Christ" (CR 9:355). When Scripture and the "profound and incomprehensible mystery" of the Trinity seem to collide, Calvin argued, the right theologian will go with Scripture.[36] And although, as we shall

---

33. Thus, in his "First Reply": "In this matter we must consider the economy of divine wisdom and not give free reign to our speculations" (CR 9:341).

34. Thus Wyatt, *Jesus Christ and Creation*, 2: "It almost goes without saying that for Calvin authentic Trinitarian thought is related to the "economic" Trinity, that is, to the differentiated work of the persons of the Godhead *ad extra*."

35. Thus Willis, *Calvin's Catholic Christology*, 123: "Unleashed Trinitarian speculation was always distasteful to Calvin, but his experience in controversy over the years demonstrated to him that in addition to being empty and signifying the haughtiness of man, anti-Trinitarian speculation brought heretical tendencies jeopardizing the soteriological impact of the Biblical witness."

36. Thus Edmondson, *Calvin's Christology*, 39: "Trinitarianism is not negotiable on the basis of biblicism, but doctrine is properly sounded and heard only within the greater context of God's witness to Godself in Scripture . . . doctrines find their final place in his Christological thinking only when they have been placed in the greater

see with his use of the so-called *extra Calvinisticum,* Calvin does not always stay as close to the shore as he here advises, we can at least begin to feel his pull in this direction. Indeed, there are some difficult tensions in play here, and Calvin's apparent commitment to stay bound to the divine economy and its availability in Scripture gets us into their midst.

If, on the one hand we embrace a commitment to the way God reveals himself in the divine economy and if, on the other, we find cause to affirm the basic reality of this God as someone prior to and distinct from the creation in which he is revealing himself, we stand with Calvin in between two apparently contradictory theological desires. There will be much about this dilemma in later chapters but first we need come to grips with how Calvin dealt with it. And to do this we could hardly find a better handle than another grasp at the question of a *logos asarkos*.

∽

One approving modern commentator inadvertently highlights the dilemma: "[F]rom Calvin's perspective, in neither case is this subordination a threat to the unity and equality of the Son with the Father in eternity, for, again, we must separate God's essence from the economy that God has ordered for our salvation."[37] It is this "separating" of God's essence from how he gives himself in the divine economy that raises the issue. Calvin would not budge on his commitment to the economy as the starting-place for theological knowledge and the result was a tendency to "separate" God's eternal identity from how he reveals himself in the world.

When Calvin routed Stancaro by insisting theology about the Mediator ought begin back in talk about creation and not just when the need for redemption arises, he stopped talking about the mediation of *Christ* and spoke instead of the "Eternal Son" (*CR* 9:350).[38] There are two things to note here. First, talk of the angels in this context is a kind of theological short-hand for referring to the nature of original creation in its relation to God. Just as unfallen angels enjoy a kind of access to God not contingent

---

context of Scripture's witness to God's economy for our salvation."

37. Ibid., 37. Edmondson is also committed to the idea that Calvin deliberately "separates" the two natures: "The separation of his two natures is what ensures the lowliness of his flesh . . . Calvin emphasizes the separation of the two natures in Christ primarily so that Christ can share our condition" (ibid., 120).

38. "Christ was the head of angels and men in the still innocent state of things" (Tylenda, "Second Reply," 147).

on expiation, likewise did mankind before sin not need a reconciling Mediator. Talk about the angels is a theological paradigm for ontology about creation as distinct from soteriology about fallen creation. Second, Calvin's talk about the Mediator in the order of creation is very clearly not about the incarnate Christ but whoever this Christ was "before" his incarnation. This is the move that deserves some closer attention.

The first thing to note is what Calvin is not doing. Although it could likely be made clear enough from his letters about the Stancaro issue, Calvin's theology on this point comes into sharpest expression in his dispute with Andreas Osiander. Osiander's Christology can perhaps be best summarized as "Scotist" or "Franciscan" with regard to the priority of the incarnation. Peter Wyatt explains, "For Scotus, the Incarnation would have taken place irrespective of the fall since its cause is to be sought not in human rebellion but in the nature of God, who's essence is love."[39] This idea Calvin explicitly rejects:

> Osiander shows the same ignorance in saying that if Christ had not been man, men would have been without him as their king. As if the Kingdom of God could not stand had the eternal Son of God—though not endued with human flesh—gathered together angels and men into the fellowship of his heavenly glory and life, and himself held the primacy over men also by his divine power, quicken and nourish them like his own body by the secret power of his Spirit until, gathered up into heaven, they might enjoy the same life as the angels. (*Inst* 2.12.7)

Clearly Calvin is intent on the priority of the one he calls "the eternal Son of God—though not endued with human flesh." This eternal Son, and not Jesus Christ *per se,* is the Mediator in the order of creation. And this recalls a crucial claim in Calvin's replies to Stancaro: "Certainly, the eternal *Logos* was already mediator from the beginning, before Adam's fall and the alienation and separation of the human race from God" (*CR* 9:350). It is the appearance of this "eternal *Logos*" that suggests some dogmatic trouble may be on the horizon. In short, who is this?

---

39. Wyatt, *Jesus Christ and Creation*, 61, citing *Opus Oxoniense* I, d.17, q.3, n.31. He continues, for Scotus, "such a love could only be manifested by the union of divine and human natures in the eternal Word incarnate, so that Christ was predestined to assume our humanity not primarily as the Redeemer, but rather as '*supremus inter viatores.*' [citing *Rep. Paris.* I d.41, q.1, n.1] In point of fact, because of sin, Christ appeared as Redeemer, but his eternal predestination was to be the head and fullness of creation."

Peter Wyatt has a likely handle on what was driving Calvin's theology at this point: "As *Deus,* then, is the presupposition and foundation of *Deus manifestatus in carne, Logos* is the presupposition and foundation of *Logos ensarkos.*"[40] Just as the reality of God logically precedes that of a God manifest in the flesh, so too suggests Wyatt, does that of a divine Word precede the reality of an incarnate one. Calvin seems merely to have accepted what appears to be a necessary corollary to belief in a God distinct from creation. Yet a difficulty remains. Not only does Calvin have a central place for a *logos asarkos,* as it were, "prior" to creation, but there is something similar-looking at the end of it too. In his *Second Reply to Stancaro,* Calvin describes an end to Christ's mediatorial role:

> And so, without any injury, Christ will be placed as intermediary between us and the Father; in this nothing is taken from his immeasurable glory, even though he be perceived (in a more obscure way) under the veil of his humanity until the time when Christ in his human nature, and the course of his mediatorship being completed, submits to the Father, and his divine essence and majesty immediately shine forth in splendor. (*CR* 9:354)

In his *Commentary* on 1 Corinthians 15:27 Calvin explains his idea in better detail:

> Christ will then hand back the Kingdom which he has received, so that we may cleave completely to God. This does not mean that he will abdicate from the Kingdom in this way, but will transfer it in some way or other from his humanity to his glorious divinity, because then there will open up for us a way of approach, from which we are not kept back by our weakness. In this way, Christ will be subject to the Father because, when the veil has been removed, we will see God plainly, reigning in his majesty, and the humanity of Christ will no longer be in between us to hold us back from a nearer vision of God.[41]

The difficulty with all this is that it makes the humanity of Christ seem like something only loosely connected to the being and identity of the Son.[42] To repeat the problem as I put it with Cyril: it is as if what-

---

40. Ibid., 49.

41. Quoted in ibid., 42.

42. "Calvin conceives of an end to the Christ's mediatorial ministry. Although Christ's appointment to be Mediator has an eternal origin, he regards its duration as temporal" (ibid.). How something can have an eternal origin and a temporal duration opens questions about the relation of time and eternity, an issue to which we shall

ever was happening with Jesus was just an ontological episode in a larger biography of the Logos. Despite some of the unnerving destinations of such a train of thought—two of which we will come to briefly—there is an appealing parsimony about their starting-point. Indeed, the idea that there is a difference between how God is "in himself" and how he is "toward us" seems bound to follow from this kind of Christology. And this gets us to an idea arguably at the heart of one of Calvin's most notorious theological concepts. Calvin explains: "the mode of accommodation is for [God] to represent himself to us not as he is himself, but as he seems to us" (*Inst* 1.17.13).

The notion that God somehow "accommodates" himself to the abilities and capacities of the humans to whom he is revealing himself is as close to a hallmark of Calvin's theology as any other. The idea even comes out in his *Second Reply to Stancaro*:

> If it be a question about his essence, we know that nothing is more or less in God. But because God's eternal Son, taking account of our weakness, appeared in the role of mediator to be the intermediary between God and us, he is said with fitting reverence and following the rule of piety to be inferior to the Father. (*CR* 9:353)

Several important themes are converging here. Calvin has in view both the relation between what we today call the "immanent" and the "economic" trinities and at the same time the way in which the difference between these two hinges on the way God deliberately "takes account of our weakness" by "appearing" in certain "roles." F. L. Battles brings the point into focus: "Calvin makes this principle [i.e., "of divine accommodation to human capacity"] a consistent basis for his handling not only of Scripture but of every avenue of relationship between God and men."[43]

For Calvin there is what we might call a qualitative difference between how God is in himself and how he has chosen to "accommodate" himself in revelation. We might even want to say that for Calvin the whole enterprise of Christology is itself a species of precisely this observation.[44] Any discussion about the person and work of Christ is essentially discus-

---

return in the next chapter.

43. Battles, "God Was Accommodating Himself," 22.

44. "The effulgence of the being of God is so excessive that it dazzles our eyes until it shines upon us in the face of Jesus Christ" (*CR* 55:12). See also Niesel, *Theology of John Calvin*, 114: "Calvin suggests that Christ must become true man since God can only draw near to us in that disguise without annihilating us."

sion about what God has given of himself in revelation. At first glance this may seem like a relatively mundane theological tautology—all we have is what we have been given—but recall that some have seen in Calvin a tendency not just to distinguish but effectively to "separate" the God revealed in the divine economy and the one supposedly behind or above this "accommodation." The result appears to be a contradiction in Calvin's thought between the immanent and the economic "trinities."[45] Paul Helm, for one, has flatly rejected such a concern: "Calvin failed to perceive a contradiction here because there isn't one; and there isn't one because Calvin does not affirm an identity between the immanent and economic trinities." Helm, unlike many sympathetic to Calvin's ideas today, is unflinching in his Augustinianism, and so goes on to embrace the logical conclusion: "A 'wedge' is thus driven between the immanent and the economic Trinity. But this 'wedge' is necessary to preserve consistency in Calvin's account of the relation between God as he is in himself and God as he is to us."[46]

Even if Helm has boosted Calvin's contemporary currency with some polemic edge from his own agenda, his way of reading Calvin gets us quickly to grips with the issues at stake.[47] The fulcrum between Calvin's theology about creation and revelation emerges in Helm's question,

> [T]o what extent is the dogmatic construction of trinitarianism in the Patristic period, with its emphasis upon the subordination of the Son to the Father, based upon reading back into the Godhead itself those roles that were only freely undertaken by the Trinity for human redemption? And if it is based upon such a reading back, to what extent is this theological procedure justified?[48]

At least two crucial issues are raised in this question, the first—about the effects of a "reading back" from the economic to the immanent "trinities"—I will consider now. The second, about the way in which the

---

45. For an almost opposite reading of Calvin on this point, see Butin, *Revelation, Redemption and Response*, 57ff. And for the other extreme, see the following regarding Helm, *John Calvin's Ideas*, with discussion at 46ff.

46. Helm, *John Calvin's Ideas*, 47, 48. With the term "wedge," Helm is accepting and refuting a critique of Butin, *Revelation, Redemption and Response*, 59.

47. Helm's work is of course impeachably scholarly and characteristically insightful, but one tends to emerge from it with a picture of Calvin as more like a modern analytic philosopher of religion than a Reforming theologian-pastor.

48. Helm, *John Calvin's Ideas*, 48.

economic roles of the Trinity were "only freely undertaken" and the way such an observation gets to the thorny question about the role of voluntarism in Calvin's theologic, I will return to in passing at the end of the chapter.

So first, what of the desire to "read back" what we know of God from the divine economy to how and who he is in eternity? Calvin himself puts the matter as plainly as anyone could: "All thought about God which does not proceed from the fact of Christ is a fathomless abyss which utterly engulfs our faculties."[49] A poignant claim, and one especially in view of what may be the two most contentious elements of the theological tradition that even the visionary Calvin could not possibly have imagined himself to have started. Both of these warrant attention; first is how Calvin's construal of the relation between the eternal life of God and his revelation in Christ comes to bear on his theology about divine predestination, and second is how this same dogmatic intersection also effects the possibility of theological knowledge beyond the incarnation.

The basic contours of Calvin's doctrine of predestination are well known:

> We call predestination God's eternal decree, by which he determined with himself what he willed to become of each man. For all are not created in equal condition; rather, eternal life is foreordained for some, eternal damnation for others. Therefore, as any man has been created to one or the other of these ends, we speak of him as predestined to life or to death. (*Inst* 3.21.5)[50]

When this theology is laid alongside Calvin's sharp distinction ("separation"; "wedge") between the immanent and the economic life of God, a difficulty arises. Peter Wyatt makes an initial connection between this and voluntarism: "The implication of these formulae, abstracted as they are from the actual revelation and work of God in the Incarnation, is that the fundamental determination of our destiny seems to arise from a divine decision made independently of Jesus Christ."[51] Calvin's repeated

---

49. CR 55:226, quoted in Niesel, *Theology of John Calvin*, 116.

50. "The decree is dreadful, I confess. Yet no one can deny that God foreknew what end man was to have before he created him and consequently foreknew because he so ordained by his decree" (*Inst*. 3.23.7).

51. Wyatt, *Jesus Christ and Creation*, 44. Contrast Calvin's approach to the doctrine of predestination with that of Barth. For the Reformer, God elects individuals, while for the modern Swissman, he elects the Son eternally begotten as Jesus Christ. We will return to this difference with the treatment of a "neo-Barthian" in our next chapter.

appeals to an "Eternal Son," even in his constructive appropriation of theology about mediation into the doctrine of creation, would seem here to be home to roost. Helm's is a typical rejoinder, "[T]he work of Father, Son, and Holy Spirit in redemption is that of three fully divine persons who (in a way that is both hidden and inscrutable to us) decree to redeem."[52] But such a defense both dodges and dulls the point. The question is not whether or not Calvin is a modalist—he clearly asserts and employs theology about the eternality of the three divine persons—it is about the unknown, "hidden" and "inscrutable," identity of a "Son" who is somehow not quite the Jesus Christ of the divine economy. There are issues here that will be more central in later chapters but suffice it now to say that any God other than (or indeed "separated" from) the God who is so plainly merciful in the career of Jesus Christ can be nothing more than the same "fathomless abyss" about whom Calvin himself has already warned. It need not be said that this is not Calvin's God. But it could be suggested that tensions inherent to his Christology lean toward the edge of precisely this chasm. And it should be said that without the counterweights Calvin supplied in less popular elements of his theology, anyone coming in his train is at risk of slipping over this edge into something dreadfully atheological.

Calvin's somewhat perpendicular relation between the eternal Trinity and the life of the incarnate Son has a second implication. This is the way it seems to open up the possibility for knowledge of God from beyond his revelation in Christ. Simply put, if the real protagonist of creation is a *logos asarkos*—someone perhaps adventitiously related to Christ but not exclusively identical with him—then the way appears open for other similarly adventitious and non-exclusive avenues for knowledge of God. On an issue that has famously divided twentieth century theology, David Willis finds the point:[53]

---

52. Helm, *John Calvin's Ideas*, 47. Helm is, of course, aware of the tensions in play here, and has made his dogmatic choices plain: "[T]here is no identity between the economic and the immanent Trinities, there is a consistent relation between them; the activities of the former express the nature or character of the latter" (ibid., 48, and cf. 50).

53. Helm takes Willis's side: "Nor, finally, shall we be concerned about the significance of the *extra* for the nature of our knowledge of God, with whether, for example, there is a valid knowledge of God apart from reference to the Incarnation. Calvin clearly thought that there is" (ibid., 60). And contra: "It is not the case that the *Extra* constitutes the centre of Calvinistic Christology. Calvin does not teach that God is to be found in Jesus Christ but is also to be encountered fully apart from Him. No;

> When Calvin says that men know God only through Christ, he means primarily but not exclusively the man Jesus Christ. Calvin does not say that we have no knowledge of God *extra hanc carnem*; he says we have no knowledge of God *extra Christum*. *Christus* may refer in a secondary sense to the Eternal Son of God *extra carnem* as well as in a primary sense to the *Deus manifestatus in carne*. Calvin's doctrine of the knowledge of God is exclusively Christological only in the sense that a saving knowledge of God is available through Christ alone who as the Eternal Son of God cannot be isolated from or known without his manifestation in the flesh, but who is not restricted to that flesh.[54]

Willis's explanation of the issue pivots on a crucial element of Calvin's Christology that I have so far left untouched.

⁓

The question of the possibility of revelation extra-Christ, or "natural theology," and the christological pressures particular to Calvin's doctrine of predestination are linked with his concept of the so-called *extra Calvinisticum*. Subsequent Reformed developments notwithstanding, it is clear that Calvin himself held and taught the theology later dubbed "that Calvinist 'beyond' (*illud extra Calvinisticum*)."[55] The *extra* is essentially the idea that "in the Incarnation God the Son retained divine properties such as immensity and omnipresence and that therefore Christ was not physically confined within the limits of a human person."[56] Even though this is a quick gloss of a subtle idea, the awkwardness inherent here—i.e., in talk of a "relation" between Christ and the Son as if they were two distinct realities—is part of the idea's characteristic ethos. Calvin calls it "marvelous":

> [E]ven if the Word in his immeasurable essence is united with the nature of man into one person, we do not imagine that he

---

according to Calvin, God has disclosed himself only in Jesus Christ and we must therefore hold fast solely to this One and not attempt to seek God outside the Mediator" (Niesel, *Theology of John Calvin*, 119).

54. Willis, *Calvin's Catholic Christology*, 130–31.

55. This and much of the following account follows ibid., 128ff.

56. Helm, *John Calvin's Ideas*, 58. Or, in the words of Willis, "that the Eternal Son of God, even after the Incarnation, was united to the human nature to form One Person but was not restricted to the flesh" (*Calvin's Catholic Christology*, 1).

was confined therein. Here is something marvelous: the Son of God descended from heaven in such a way that, without leaving heaven, he willed to be borne in the virgin's womb, to go about the earth, and to hang upon the cross; yet he continuously filled the world as he had done from the beginning! (*Inst* 2.13.4)

Again I flag for later the idea that this metaphysical contortion began when the Son "willed" to descend from heaven, be born, etc. For now we see the *extra* in full force: The "Son" is up to something; without leaving heaven he is and does the life, death, resurrection, and ascension of Jesus. Calvin clarifies:

> [H]e is said to have descended from heaven in respect of his divinity, not that his divinity quitted heaven to conceal itself in the prison of the body, but because, although he filled all things, it yet resided in the humanity of Christ corporeally, that is, naturally, and in an ineffable manner. (*Inst* 4.17.30)[57]

The awkwardness returns. Here is a single subject—"he"—and a thing possessed by this one, "his divinity," that subsequently—as "it"—*resides*, in an "ineffable manner," in the humanity of Christ. There is a long tradition on this point of accusing Calvin and his theological successors of a crypto-Nestorianism. Although perhaps unfair, with a passage like this in view the accusation cannot be said to be groundless.[58] The modern patriarch in this critical guild was Karl Barth,

> [Reformed theology following Calvin] failed to show convincingly how far the *extra* does not involve the assumption of a two-fold Christ, of a *logos ensarkos* alongside a *logos asarkos*, and therefore a dissolution of the unity of the natures and hypostatic union, and therefore a destruction of the unequivocal Emmanuel and the certainty of faith and salvation based thereon.[59]

---

57. This translation is from Beveridge. Calvin here goes on to make the distinction between Christ in *totus* and *totum*. For a discussion, see Willis, *Calvin's Catholic Christology*, 30ff. The other classic texts for Calvin's use of the *extra* are: *Comm.* on Acts 20; *Comm* on John 3:13; and the preface to *Comm.* on Jeremiah.

58. See the literature cited at ibid., 2nn1–2.

59. Barth, *CD*, 1/2:170. Van Buren gets the point when he wonders if such a thing means when we get the incarnate Christ we have something less than a "full gift of God to us" (*Christ in Our Place*, 12). Helm's defense so perfectly misses the point as to reinforce it: "Calvin could avoid these charges merely by asserting that becoming incarnate as the Christ is an apt and consistent expression of the character of the Word" (this and the previous citations at Helm, *John Calvin's Ideas*, 63).

Here is a point at the crux of this project. In one sense, theology is about trying to state the ineffable without raising multiple problems with a response to just one. In Christology this requires knowing when and where to stop speaking. Calvin has brought us to this place in his theology about the *extra*. Yet having come to this conceptual hub, the question now is about whether Calvin's doctrine of the *extra* has sufficient stopping strength. The momentum established in his theology about predestination and the way it put more behind that about the *logos asarkos* means we need something equally rigorous to keep the problems accompanying these doctrines from exceeding their point. Barth's critique is about the way Calvin's Christology seems to produce exactly this effect; the way answers given to certain peripheral problems appear to render moot the central reason for replying to them in the first place.

Although there is something admittedly modern about my concern with Calvin's thought here, many commentators have seen the *extra* in Calvin's thought along the lines sketched by I. A. Dorner:

> The Logos is constantly both outside of and in the flesh: the Almighty Deity cannot be chained with its nature to one point of the world, not even to that with which He is personally united. Again, the humanity of Christ would no longer have been humanity, had it had for its own the predicates of the divine infinitude. For in that case its finite predicates would be done away with; in other words, its creatural nature lost. Its fundamental determination, finitude, which distinguishes it from God, being taken away, it itself would be annihilated.[60]

Dorner's last flurry of presumption—that finitude is creation's fundamental determination and consequently what distinguishes it from God—is far from granted, yet taken as such for the moment, it frames a question that has been so far under the surface of this whole study: In the words of David Willis,

> Can the infinite be related to the finite in a way not destructive to the finite? Or, can the Word of God be united to the humanity of Jesus Christ so as not to nullify that finitude without which his humanity is only illusory?[61]

In retrospect from here we might imagine that much of the theology since Calvin has in fact been on a long slow plod toward a finally

---

60. Dorner, *History of the Development*, 136–37.
61. Willis, *Calvin's Catholic Christology*, 18.

negative reply to this question. God as infinite is ultimately stifling and ontologically exclusive that he is necessarily incompatible with anything or anyone beside himself. Consequently most modern opinion about God has had mainly to do with the implications of the impossibility of his existence.

Calvin however did not go as far as his successors. He was determined to maintain a deep and strong distinction between God and the world; to avoid at all costs the kind of mingling or mixing of the human and the divine implied in other Christologies current in his day. In this respect, the *extra* was Calvin's way of sustaining a positive answer to Willis's question about the compatibility of God and everything else. His theology about the relation of the human and divine in Christ was a kind of ideological forum for imagining the relation of the infinite and the finite. In Calvin's view, the two ways of being are congenial because they are incomprehensibly distinct.

The tensions we have been tracking in Calvin's theology remain however. Indeed the crucial role played by the *extra* in Calvin's thought would appear to even further reinforce the problem of what Alexander Schwiezer calls the "absolute being of the Logos asarkos."[62] Wilhelm Niesel, in a gush of praise, highlights the difficulty along this direction of Calvin's thought:

> With such statements Calvin radically rejects the idea of any mingling of humanity and divinity in Christ. The Godhead is not merged in the manhood of Christ. For our salvation it remains what it is eternally. Hence as divinity it is also wholly without the manhood of the Son of God. It retains always its fundamental transcendence over human nature.[63]

It is this ominous "fundamental transcendence" and the idea that such a way of being allows the Godhead somehow to remain what it "eternally is" "without the manhood of the Son" that marks the problem. In short, what God *is* this? And conversely, if this is God, who (or what) is Jesus? The fact that these questions would appear to solicit unrelated replies suggests we are either nearing or past the edge of a deliberately *Christian* theology. On these readings of Calvin the "fathomless abyss" has reappeared, only this time it is not between faith and nothingness but between the two natures of Christ.

---

62. Schweizer, *Die Glubenslehre*, 296, 303, cited in ibid., 2n2.
63. Niesel, *Theology of John Calvin*, 118–19.

And why such a sharp distinction between the two natures of Christ? Commentators are divided, or content with ambiguity, about which of Christ's natures Calvin felt needed protection from the other. Most likely Calvin himself allowed the edge to cut both ways as polemic circumstances required. In any case, it is clear that he understood the loss of proper distinction between Christ's natures would mean the end of either divine immutability (Helm) or of Christ's authentic humanity (Edmondson).[64] Either way, the need to sustain a distinction for the sake of protecting one or the other nature of Christ is based on the presumption, to use Helm's image, that there is an ontological "asymmetry" between the divine and the human.[65] Such an infinite/finite asymmetry means that if the divine and the human were simply to somehow come up alongside one another, either the former would start changing within the flux of human contingence and thereby cease being itself, or the latter would inevitably suffer some kind of instant annihilation. This recalls, by contrast, the way Luther was willing to allow human and divine attributes to pass multilaterally between Christ's two natures. The difference between the two Reformers in this respect will come clearer into view through a brief look at Calvin's use of the *communicatio idiomatum*.

The clearest Calvin gets on his understanding of the *communicatio* is in his *Commentary* on Acts 20:28:

> There is nothing more absurd than to suppose that God is corporeal or mortal . . . But when [the Scriptures] set God before us made manifest in the flesh, they do not separate his human nature from his divinity. Yet because, on the other hand, the two natures are so united in Christ as to constitute one person, what properly belongs to the one is sometimes improperly transferred to the other. For instance, in this verse Paul attributes blood to

---

64. Edmondson, *Calvin's Christology*, 211ff.

65. "In Calvin's Christological thinking an important role is played by the thought that there is a strong asymmetry between the person of the Son and the human nature that he 'assumed.' This asymmetry is underlined by Calvin's emphasis on the *extra*. The person of the Son has ontological priority. In an ontological if not in a temporal sense (for Calvin thinks that God exists atemporally), he exists before the existence of the human nature that he assumed. The asymmetry is strikingly seen in the fact that while the person of the Word can act independently of the human nature he assumed—this is the heart of the *extra*—his human nature has never acted and cannot act independently of the person of the Word" (Helm, *John Calvin's Ideas*, 71; cf. ibid., 63).

God, because the man Jesus Christ, who shed his blood for us, was also God. This figure of speech was called the communication of properties by the Fathers, because the property of one nature is applied to the other. (*Comm. Acts* 20:28)[66]

Two points here characterize what Calvin was up to. One is his use of a "properly/improperly" distinction, and the other is his reference to the *communicatio* as a "figure of speech." The first comes out more prominently in the *Institutes*:

> Surely God does not have blood, does not suffer, cannot be touched with hands. But since Christ, who was true God and also true man, was crucified, and shed his blood for us, the things that he carried out in his human nature were transferred improperly, although not without reason, to his divinity. (*Inst* 2.14.2)

Calvin is here sounding a warning against the logical fallacies we studied with Luther. Both suggest certain things may be said of Christ *humanly* and others of him *divinely* but the two forms of predication must not be mingled.[67] In this respect Calvin used the *communicatio* in what could be called a qualified ontological sense. Like Cyril, he allowed the attributes of one nature to be applied "improperly" to the other since they are descriptive of a single subject, "one person . . . as human and divine." Joseph Tylenda draws an important distinction here however; he says that in none of the rare occasions when Calvin uses the communicatio "is the property of one nature applied to the other *nature as such;* it is always applied to a *subject possessing a nature.*"[68]

Tylenda's view stands in some contrast to that of Helm who understands Calvin to have been significantly less ambitious with his use of the *communicatio*. On Helm's view Calvin understood the *communicatio* as a kind of inverted and strictly epistemic version of his concept of

---

66 ET Calvin, *New Testament Commentaries*; cf. Tylenda, "Calvin's Understanding," 58ff.

67. For more discussion on this point see Tylenda, "Calvin's Understanding of the Communication of Properties," 62n18.

68. Ibid., 59; emphasis original. Tylenda then admits: "It is true that Calvin writes 'a property of humanity is shared with the other nature,' [*Inst.* 2.14.2] and that Scriptures 'assign to the divinity that which is proper to the humanity, and to the humanity that which concerns the divinity' [*CR* 1:66]," but then Tylenda somewhat unhelpfully reminds us that "these statements should be interpreted in accordance with Calvin's mind."

accommodation; like a rhetorical device by which the theologian admits the restrictions of human language about God and so knowingly says things about Christ which, although "true" in a figurative or pedagogical sense, nevertheless have little or no ultimate ontological weight:

> [Calvin] thinks that it is only figuratively and not literally true that God purchased the church with his own blood, and so this is an "improper" expression. Nevertheless it is a permissible way of talking—permissible on the grounds of vividness and economy.[69]

For Helm then, Calvin's use of the "properly/improperly" distinction and his reference to the *communicatio* as a "figure of speech" are just two ways of Calvin saying the same thing.[70] And with Helm and Tylenda thus divided, we would do well to heed the opening advice of Wilhelm Niesel, that is, we ought not resolve tensions in Calvin's thought which he himself clearly chose to sustain. On the one hand it is clear that Calvin does have a "figurative" notion of the *communicatio*:

> Thus ... the Scriptures speak of Christ: they sometimes attribute to him what must be referred solely to his humanity, sometimes what belongs uniquely to his divinity: and sometimes what embraces both natures but fits neither alone. And they so earnestly express this union of the two natures that is in Christ as sometimes to interchange them. This figure of speech is called

---

69. Helm, *John Calvin's Ideas*, 79; see also ibid., 77–9, 84, 88. Helm's reading, despite its corrective to the somewhat anachronistic undertones in Tylenda's, does, however, risk exposing Calvin unnecessarily to some of the Reformer's longest standing critiques. Helm is notable for the boldness with which he employs terms like "functional duplication," "substance dualism," or "contingently united" to describe Calvin's view of the relation between the Logos and the human nature of Christ. It is at least certain that Calvin himself is more agile than this around the fringes of Nestorius, and Helm's perspective on Calvin's use of the *communicatio* would seem to only further associate the Reformer with the Syrian. See ibid., 60, 62, 66, 68, 83, and 85ff. And cf. Edmondson, *Calvin's Christology*, 209ff. and Niesel, *Theology of John Calvin*, 115.

70. When van Buren suggests that "Calvin takes pains to suggest that [the communication of properties] is only a manner of speaking," he is making the more common claim that Calvin differed from the Lutherans by denying that the *communicatio* described a "real" ontological trafficking of attributes between the natures of Christ (*Christ in Our Place*, 22). Thus Wyatt, *Jesus Christ and Creation*, 34. And Tylenda: "To conclude, we may summarize Calvin's thought in this manner: the communication of idioms is not a real ontological communication of properties (whereby the characteristics of one nature ontologically belong to the other nature), but it is the assigning of attributes to a person or subject" ("Calvin's Understanding," 64). For Calvin himself on this, see especially the preface to his *Commentary* on Jeremiah (*CR* 20:74).

by the ancient writers "the communicating of properties." (*Inst.* 2.14.1)[71]

On the other hand, Calvin does not intend this "figure of speech" to be without ontological purchase. Moving too quickly here could mean treating the whole enterprise as just grammatical fidgetry. And so we come to the deeper question about whether Calvin understood his Christology to be describing a real ontological dynamic or if instead he simply used theological language as a kind of negative rhetorical tool to preserve the bounds around something essentially unknowable. By now we should realize that on Calvin's terms such a question does not warrant its either-or structure. For Calvin good Christology does both. There is real, albeit humble and provisional, content to theological speculation, and yet it is only viable as such when it both reinforces and stops short of the normative limits delineated by Scripture.

Returning, finally, to Calvin's disputes with Stancaro, he offers a quick but highly suggestive indulgence in precisely this kind of speculation:

> It is also true to say that all the actions which Christ performed to reconcile God and man refer to the whole person, and are not to be separately restricted to only one nature. Lest this opinion be subject to quibbles, a distinction will be helpful: certain actions, considered in themselves, refer to one nature, but because of a consequent effect they are common to both. (*CR* 9:340)[72]

Calvin here insists that contrary to Stancaro's opinion, whatever mediatorial things Christ does they ought all be referred to the whole person and not to just his human nature. While certain actions "considered in themselves"—and here we may want to gloss Calvin with his own words as adding, "that is, *properly*"—while these may refer to one nature, they nevertheless terminate in their reference in the single person, where actions are "common to both" natures. And then Calvin offers his "helpful

---

71. Cf. a similar teaching in 1536: "[S]ometimes they attribute to him that which can refer only to the humanity, sometimes that which belongs particularly to the divinity; sometimes that which is appropriate to the two natures and not to one alone. Finally, and by the communication of properties, they assign to the divinity that which is proper to the humanity, and to the humanity that which concerns the divinity" (quoted in Tylenda, "Calvin's Understanding," 55; cf. Willis, *Calvin's Catholic Christology*, 65).

72. The passage continues with Calvin offering some typical examples, then, "In this manner, nothing hinders the properties from remaining integral to each nature, nor does their communication argue against their distinction."

distinction": These actions have their source in this single person because of what Calvin calls "a consequent effect" [*quae tamen propter conscquentem effectum ambarum sunt communes*]. Although Calvin's exact intention with such a phrase is irremediably vague, the themes we have been following in this chapter suggest that Calvin lands on "effect" to reinforce the union of the Mediator's natures because it recalls the singularity of their cause. Whatever Christ does, all of his acts originate from a single divine will.

So it would seem that late medieval voluntarism lies at both the base and the fringes of what we have heard from Calvin in this chapter. The decision of God to predestine creation according to his own will, and the way this decision appears to have been made "before" the events and effects of the incarnation culminate in Calvin's use of his *extra*. The result is a systematic need, the want of which frames a simple question: Who or what constitutes the dynamic of mediation between God and world in Calvin's view? The answer can only be that at certain crucial junctures only the sheer will of God connects his identity "in himself" and the way he "accommodates" himself to the world *ensarkos* in Christ: the Son "willed" to become finite, while as a matter of fact remaining infinite. And the so-called "crypto-Nestorian" tones to this recalls the way that Nestorius himself tried to put grace at the intersection of God and humanity in Christ instead of a deifying union. The apparent intent in Antioch—to preserve a distinction by reference to a divine initiative—is repeated in Calvin, only now with the added weight of Calvin's theologies of accommodation and predestination.

And Calvin's use of the *communicatio* only slightly mitigates the presiding question about the ontological identity of the Mediator. Its design was for referring the human and divine attributes of Christ to the single person, yet the effect has become a further heightening of the need for precision about who exactly this person is. Indeed with Calvin we may be witnessing the expiration of the *communicatio*; the concept being capable of neither the precision nor the rigor required by the rest of his theology.

These final observations, though only general, rest on Calvin's high regard for absolute freedom. For him, one of the defining attributes of divine life—perhaps *the* defining attribute of divine life—is God's sovereignty. And the effect is undeniable. The fact that the pre-creative eternal decree has the, so to speak, final say in matters historical suggests that the divine economy, in its restriction to the particularities of contingent time, is somehow not part of God's own eternal identity, at least not in the way supposed in many modern Trinitarian theologies. Indeed, it may be that these kinds of concerns are themselves part of the modern milieu, and therefore ones that can only be raised properly by those within it.

6

ROBERT JENSON AND THE SPIRIT OF IT ALL

Christ as Space-time
(A Dialectical Concept of Mediation.)

> Ontology is accomplished not in the triumph of man over his condition, but in the very tension in which that condition is assumed.
> —Emmanuel Levinas

In keeping with the spirit of Jenson's work this chapter will take its shape around three interdependent subjects each of which has its own orienting centre yet nevertheless can only be properly understood in its relation to the other two. These three are: the relation of the being and act of God, the nature of time and eternity, and the possibility of causative narration. The presiding question will be whether or not these subjects really function as three modes of a single underlying movement in Jenson's thought; whether questions about the relation of the being and act of God, of the nature of time and eternity, and of the possibility of causative narration are in fact three ways of getting at a certain kind of pneumatology.[1]

1. I am aware that similar concerns have been raised differently by more able

Robert Jenson and the Spirit of It All   129

⁓

With the question of the relation of the being and act of God we already face the question of where to begin. Instead of choosing one entry point at random I will take two for their apparent contrariety and follow them into Jenson's thought until they either merge or collide.

The first line is one that we have already heard, and it is Jenson's first proposition about creation, "That God creates means there is other reality than God and that it is really other than he."[2] Or, as he has put it elsewhere, "one can only be or not be the Creator."[3] The second line is so essential to Jenson's thought that one could almost turn at random to a page in his *Systematic Theology* and find a version of it: When God introduces himself to his creatures he does not reveal something *about* himself, he simply gives *himself*.

As we have seen, the first proposition has been around in Christian theology at least since Irenaeus. As such, it is familiar enough to command an almost pre-supposed logical priority in the Christian doctrine of creation. But if Jenson is right I have the order of these two claims logically backwards. According to him, "*the* metaphysically fundamental fact of Israel and the church's faith' is that God is 'self-identified by, and so with, contingent created temporal events."[4] The logical ordering of these two claims is absolutely decisive for the shape of Jenson's theology. Even the structure of his *Systematics* bears the choice; chapters about the life, death and resurrection of Jesus are in his volume on the doctrine of God and not, as would be typical, in another about salvation or the divine economy. Jenson explains the rationale for his departure from tradition and thereby brings to the fore a question that has been at the periphery of this study several times already:

> Were God identified by Israel's Exodus or Jesus' Resurrection, without being identified *with* them, the identification would be

---

readers. See, e.g., Pannenberg, "Problems of a Trinitarian Doctrine of God." Also related are the contributions from Colin Gunton to the sustained debates he enjoyed with his mentor. See esp. Gunton, "Creation and Mediation," and idem, "Review: Robert W. Jenson," 364–65.

2. Jenson, *Systematic Theology*, 2:5; hereafter cited as *ST*.
3. Ibid., 1:99.
4. *ST* 1:47–48; emphasis added.

> a revelation ontologically other than God himself. The revealing events would be our clues *to* God, but would not *be* God.[5]

Jenson is not shy about his dogmatic choices and his placement of doctrine about revelation before his theology of creation is a case in point. The choice puts him on the radical edge of a larger trend in modern constructive theology in which the meaty second half of Rahner's maxim—"the immanent Trinity is the economic Trinity"—is taken with full ontological seriousness.[6] Although Jenson understands Rahner to have intended his maxim analogically, he himself is clearly determined to appropriate it in an *ontological* way.[7] Indeed, the effort to press the "is" between the "economic" and the "immanent" Trinity into full and unqualified service is arguably the engine driving all of Jenson's theological speculation.

This brings us to the threshold of our first subject. For Jenson, the immanent being of God is not something behind or removed from the act of this God in the divine economy, the eternal God is—and *is* without qualification—the God we meet in revelation. In this direction some of Jenson's most creative work has come from his sustained engagement with the idea's modern architect, Karl Barth. Commenting on Barth's achievement, Jenson agrees that,

> the triune reality of God is actual as an eternal meeting between the Father and the Son, a meeting in which, as in all personal meetings, something is decided. What is decided is that the eternal relation of the Father and the Son is in fact the relation between the Father and the man Jesus, and so also a covenant between God and Jesus' sisters and brothers.[8]

Here is an element in Jenson's thought that has heated up considerably in his more recent writing. And it is one that offers some needed purchase on our otherwise slippery subject. For Jenson, it is "the man Jesus" who is in an "eternal relation" with the Father. He brooks no *logos asarkos*. Jenson makes his position plain:

---

5. *ST* 1:59.
6. Rahner, *Trinity*, 22, 34.
7. On this, see Jenson, "Jesus in the Trinity," esp. 197 and n22.
8. Jenson, "You Wonder Where the Spirit Went," 301.

> [T]he man Jesus, exactly as his personhood is defined by the life-story told in the Gospels, is the one called the Son, the second identity of God. *Jesus* is the Son, with no qualifications.[9]

Jenson is simply unwilling to budge on this point. And for good reason. He believes that any compromise on the immediacy of God in Christ will unwind the gospel from the inside out. For Jenson, the events that constitute the story of Jesus' life, death, and resurrection also and directly constitute the being of the God revealed by them. As a theologian capable of infinitesimal subtlety, it is significant that Jenson refuses to nuance the point. On the contrary, he is clearly at pains to make the assertion as bald as possible: "where the deity of the Son is there must be Jesus' humanity unabridged as soul and body."[10]

Jenson is so committed to this point that he will re-fire the ancient christological controversies with all the conviction of an Alexandrian Archbishop if he thinks his readers deserve a reminder of the consequences of "Leonine" Chalcedonianism. And it is certainly the see of *Alexandria* that would host this American Lutheran:

> By the time Antioch had become Nicene and turned to Christology, the term *Logos* had ceased to be felt as denoting the deity of *Jesus*; "the Logos" had become an extra metaphysical entity that would have been the "person" he was with or without the man Jesus; and Jesus' relation to God was grasped as his relation to *this* "second" God.[11]

It is the stubborn recurrence of this "second' God' in the christological tradition that keeps Jenson fired up. Such a thing is simply anathema to everything he is striving for. God the Son is not somehow behind or other than what we are given in Christ, he simply *is* this Christ. No ontological fidgetry required. In Jenson's appraisal, what the "Antiochene" school stood for (and as he sees it, still stands for) is nothing less than a total evacuation of the gospel:

> The Antiochene escape is in fact just the Arian escape, move a notch . . . [And since they] set the terms of the debate, . . . the problems were created that have occupied "Christology" ever since . . . Now "the *Logos*" and "God the Son" came to be taken as identifying descriptions of a divine entity who as himself is

---

9. Jenson, "Jesus in the Trinity," 317.
10. *ST* 1:203
11. Jenson, "Jesus in the Trinity," 194.

> simply an other than the man Jesus. Thus theology was set a new problem: of construing a unity between two distinct and metaphysically polar entities.[12]

For Jenson, the whole project of Antiochene/Chalcedonian metaphysics is misguided from its outset. Alas, the many attempts I have so far charted to construe "a unity between two distinct and metaphysically polar entities" is simply a false agenda. As he has said elsewhere, "one does not need to fasten together what is not separated in the first place."[13] Here is a theme that will deserve more direct attention soon below: for Jenson, the idea that Christ is somehow "between" God and man is *itself* the problem. Unless the life of this creature *is* the being of the Creator, the church worships something that is not quite either—a superman or a demigod. And this would begin to explain why Jenson is so uneasy with the idea of Christ as ontological mediator. Indeed, it is clear from the tone in his *Systematics* that he regards his program as an *alternative to* the idea of christological mediation. We will get to what he offers in its stead before the end of this but for now I simply note that the idea of the incarnate Son somehow relating and distinguishing God and world rarely appears in Jenson's mature work, except, that is, as an item of heresy. As he sees it the idea is simply unthinkable,

> when theology has started with the notions of an entity on the creator's side of the Bible's great divide and of an entity on the creature side, . . . the identity of the two has proven impossible to think, and not in the sense in which the mystery of incarnation ought to be impossible to think, just in the ordinary sense that all attempts to state the fact of the matter lead to incoherent positions.[14]

For Jenson, Christology is not about crunching God and world together into the person of Christ, it is about confessing their essential union in him and getting on with the rest of the story. This is not to say that Jenson has no time for the duality of Christ's natures, there are even points in his thought where he relies precisely on this kind of duality to sustain the distinction between God and the world.[15] The point is rather

---

12. *ST* 1:126.
13. Jenson, "For Us," 82.
14. Ibid., 76.
15. See, e.g., Jenson, "Creator and Creature," 221. See n56 below on the feasibility of his "alternative" to christological mediation.

that for Jenson, the unity of deity and humanity in Christ is something of a theological non-issue—Jesus of Nazareth simply is the eternal Son and that should settle it. In one of his earliest works on the question, Jenson is characteristically explicit: "Across the Creator/creature distinction, no mediator is needed. 'Creator'/'creature' names an absolute difference but no *distance* at all, for to be the Creator is merely as such to be actively related to the creature."[16]

Whereas most in this discussion imagine time and eternity alongside one another in a somehow single Christ, Jenson's parsimony arises from the opposite route: Christ is first of all a single subject, and time and eternity must be somehow sorted out thereafter. But as we shall see in the next section, this move raises at least as many issues as it so deftly avoids. At this point I will only note that neither did Chalcedon settle the issue nor has Jenson's "Neo-Chalcedonian" reversion done so yet. As Jenson has himself observed, split opinions on this matter seem "to be there whenever the Christological task is taken seriously."[17]

And Jenson is indeed one to take the task seriously. Yet for all of his proposal's cogency it is one on which there is much at stake. If whatever it means to be Jesus includes creatureliness and whatever it means to be the Creator includes Jesus, there are some significant difficulties on the horizon. First in view is the proposition we began with: how is God both "really other than" his creation *and* defined by it? Jenson at least, never shy of an idea's stature, embraces the implications outright, "the gospel does not tell of work done *by* a God antecedently and otherwise determined, but itself determines who and what God is."[18]

For Jenson, the "act" of Jesus' life is in no way incidental to the being of God; indeed the precise opposite is the case. Simply put: God *is* what

---

16. His endnote on this raises the possibility of an entirely different option, but then drops it just as quickly: "Or, alternatively, the incarnation is the mediation, not the Logos as such" (Jenson, *Triune Identity*, 107). This is to leave aside Jenson's perplexing theology about angels: "They are in fact the everyday version of that ambiguous realm of mediation between deity and time which we have heretofore encountered in less representational forms" (*ST* 2:117).

17. Jenson, "For Us," 79.

18. *ST* 1:165. By relating the being and act of God so closely, Jenson must appeal to a kind of weak anthropic principle to explain his doctrine of revelation: "We know God in that the Word of God that is God, that is *homoousios* with the Father, is actual only as conversation with us. If we ask what the divine Word would have been without us, we—again—do not know what we are asking" (*ST* 2:226).

Jesus *does*. And it is the theological equation of the being of God with his acts in creation that gets us back to the concern. Jenson explains,

> If we attend to the maxim that in God doing and being are not different—though their identity is conceptually impenetrable—then the fact that God's Son is incarnate for us says that creaturely circumstances are involved in what it means for God to be God.[19]

But here at least is a claim that Jenson is not willing to let stand so starkly. Indeed his suggestion that "in God doing and being are not different" would appear to be 180 degrees from the more moderate line taken earlier in his *Systematics*: "There is a hypostatic being of God *that must be distinguished* from his act of being, as the antecedence of those who *do* the act."[20] Either Jenson has changed course on this fundamental question or there is some important nuance between these quotes that space here does not permit. In either case, the issue has been raised. If the being and act of God really are "not different" then we must take Rahner's maxim with as much ontological severity as possible—the immanent Trinity really *is* the economic Trinity—but if the being of God "must be distinguished" from his act, then much of Jenson's rhetoric teeters on the hyperbolic. (What we will find is that although Jenson does indeed indulge in the occasional blast of hyperbole, he nevertheless is committed throughout his work to the absolute immediacy of God in Christ.) I will leave this issue raised for the moment since with this we have arrived at a question that is already sizeable enough to exceed the scope of our attention to Jenson.

But before I move on, a moment to confirm our direction. Recall the two lines of thought with which we began, only this time with the order as Jenson would have it, and in the form of a question: If "creaturely circumstances are involved in what it means for God to be God" then how is the creation "other reality than God and . . . *really* other than he"? The question of God's relation to his creatures—to his "acts"—and Jenson's determination to hold onto both God's sovereignty and his self-identification with these acts is in fact a set-up for my next question; how Jenson relates time and eternity.

---

19. Jenson, "For Us," 77.
20. *ST* 1:215; emphasis added.

If there were a recurring theme across Jenson's wide-ranging writing, a strong candidate would be his sustained opposition to the presumption that divinity and time are mutually exclusive. As we have just seen, Jenson insists that God is identified by and with created events; from this it only follows that "the biblical God's eternity is not immunity to time."[21] If God is only who he is as he reveals himself to temporal creatures then whoever he be, he is ontologically compatible with time. For Jenson, whatever distinguishes God and world it cannot be "a distinction between the simplicity of timelessness and the differentiations of temporality." He says that if we must imagine God on one side of this distinction and the creation on the other then "eventful differentiation is real on both sides."[22]

Again we are dealing with one of the chartered propositions of modern trinitarian theology, and Jenson has done much to support the cause, but, again, Jenson exceeds the status quo. Instead of simply negating what many have seen as a weakness in the tradition, Jenson presses the issue into its affirmative implications. He makes the point by transposing an insight from Gregory of Nyssa into the twenty-first century like only he can, "[the] being of God is not a something, however rarefied or immaterial, but a *going-on*, a sequentially palpable event, like a kiss or a train wreck."[23]

Far from being the static bastion against time that is Jenson's theological *bete noir*, this God is "sequentially palpable." Or as he has put it elsewhere, "God is what he does among us."[24] For some it may take a moment to adjust to the significance of such a claim, but Jenson has had plenty of time to work it out, "the one God is an *event*; history occurs not only in him but as his being."[25]

Before I move on to consider how Jenson explains himself, I should note here that his affinity for temporality extends also to a re-imagining of creation, "the world God creates is not a thing, a 'cosmos,' but is rather a history."[26] Jenson explains,

21. *ST* 1:210.
22. *ST* 1:113.
23. *ST* 1:214.
24. Jenson, *God after God*, 7.
25. "[I]t is a particular event, the active relation of the triune persons . . . God is what happens between Jesus and his Father in their Spirit" (*ST* 1:221).
26. *ST* 2:14.

> God does not create spatial objects that thereupon move through time; he creates temporal-spatial objects, that is, in a more precise language, he creates histories.[27]

At one level this is simply a theological shift from Newtonian mechanism and absolute notions of time to something more compatible with relativity and a "spatiotemporal" universe. At another level however we are at a juncture in Jenson's thought in which two radically different streams converge, and it is one that gets us to the connection between questions about time and Jenson's knack for narrative: On the one hand, Jenson has the long Lutheran tradition of word theology to draw from, and, on the other, he is current with late-modern structuralist thought (although his dependence on the latter is never quite made explicit).[28] And the merger is powerful. Both enable him to reject the kind of theology that presumes "creation is itself effected not by a divine call but by a prior divine act of an other sort."[29] For Jenson, the call of God, his narrateable address to creatures, *is itself* constitutive of creation's being. It is only because this call is ongoing that creation continues to exist at all, "the world would not *now* exist did not God *now* command its existence."[30]

So far (I hope), so clear; but this is where Jenson contributes an important twist. It is not just the being of the creation that is contingent on the ongoing address of the Creator, God himself only exists as the conversation he is among the persons of the Trinity. God, Jenson suggests, is the mutually constitutive conversation among the Father, Son, and Holy Spirit.[31] To be awkward but to the point: God is a trialogue.

> The Trinity as such is a conversation, the only one that can never collapse into dialogue or monologue, because the three who make its poles *are* the conversation.[32]

At work here is another dart from the collective quiver of modern trinitarian discourse. Jenson—drawing on Aquinas where others typically look to the Cappadocians—insists that a triune person is only such as a "subsistent relation," that is, "a relation that itself subsists and is not

---

27. *ST* 2:46.
28. See *ST* 1:120.
29. *ST* 2:68.
30. *ST* 2:9.
31. *ST* 2:35.
32. *ST* 2:26; cf. 1:223.

merely a connection between subsistents."³³ Once this relational ontology is spun in narrative terms, Jenson can define a person as "one with whom other persons . . . can *converse*, whom they can *address*." And as we might expect, the circularity here is intentional. As Jenson explains, it "is constitutive . . . Father, Son and Spirit are persons insofar as they address one another in the conversation they are as God."³⁴

Again, Jenson has us on the cusp of our next section without being quite ready for it—what he is here calling "constitutive conversation" will soon look more like "causative narration"—for now, we need only realize that both creation and Creator exist in the personal address and exchange that *is* the Trinity. Both God and world are held in their being by the conversation among the Father, Son, and Spirit. That said, Jenson makes the crucial qualification,

> In the context of creation, the specification of God's being as conversation is privileged. We must therefore say: to be, as a creature, is to be mentioned in the triune moral conversation, as something other than those who conduct it.³⁵

To be a creature on these terms is to be "mentioned" in the ontologically constitutive conversation of the Father, Son, and Spirit.

If I may offer a loose sketch: it is as if there was internal triune discourse for an infinite history before creation but as soon as Someone mentioned the idea of a creature, everything popped into existence; and then, once creation existed, it is as if creaturehood is the being-in-act of eaves-dropping on the divine trialogue. For Jenson, creation is what happens when the Father speaks to the Spirit about Jesus, and the extension of creation—its time—is the fact that these two *keep talking* with and about this one. As we have seen, the Father, Son, and Spirit, are the three "poles" of their conversation, now we can add that as such they are also the three "poles" of contingent temporality. Jenson explains: "The specificity of the triune God is not that he is three, but that he occupies each pole of time as a *persona dramatis*."³⁶

---

33. *ST* 1:108–9.

34. *ST* 1:117; and cf. 2:14.

35. *ST* 2:35; and cf. 2:26, and 1:110. But if, as Jenson has said elsewhere (2:25), "the only fully reliable otherness is that of persons," what of the goodness—reality even—of non-personal creatures?

36. *ST* 1:89.

To hold these poles together—to keep the conversation moving as it were—Jenson commandeers and advances Barth's embrace of a "Whence" and "Whither" in God:

> The Father is the "whence" of God's life; the Spirit the "whither" of God's life; and we may even say that the Son is that life's specious present.[37]

Now, incidentally, I note the word here is "specious" and not "spacious." Jenson may be enjoying an historically convenient play on words. The present for Jenson (with a nod to Augustine), is "specious" in the sense that it is never truly realized. On the other hand, the present is also *spacious* since, for Jenson, space is itself one aspect of time; he calls it "the horizon of the present tense, . . . of what is all there for us at once."[38] And it is the fact that the Son—indeed the "spatially" incarnate Son—is God's "specious" present that means the Father and Spirit are reconciled in their whence and whither:

> If, then, whence and whither do not fall apart in God's life, so that his duration is without loss, it is because origin and goal, whence and whither, are indomitably reconciled in the action and suffering of the Son.[39]

With this point secure, Jenson, as ever, pushes through the inherited language to its logical conclusion. In volume two of his *Systematics* he says the structure of triune life is enabled by the difference between this whence and whither and then confesses, "which one cannot finally refrain from calling 'past' and 'future'; and which is identical with the distinction between the Father and the Spirit."[40] So time, be it the infinite history of God or the finite temporality of the world, is the dynamic between the Father and the Spirit as it is brought together (mediated?[41]) in the present of the incarnate Son: "What happens to the world with Jesus has three identities that are the origin of time, the goal of time, and what within time is what time is all about; the three bracket time and occupy time and just so reach through time."[42] Clearly Jenson is up to something truly

---

37. *ST* 1:219.
38. *ST* 2:46.
39. *ST* 1:219.
40. *ST* 2:35.
41. See n62 below.
42. *ST* 1:222.

revisionary.[43] Not only is God, and by proxy everything else, a "conversation," but in their triunity the Father, Son, and Spirit are the past, present, and future of this conversation. By addressing the Son as Jesus, the Father causes created time—is its "past"—and the Spirit brings it to its End—is its "future." The divine conversation is constitutive because it is inclusive.

Even if that is not entirely clear, this much at least is: For Jenson, time is no longer what separates God and world, it is what they have in common. For the further clarity we need, a direct question for Jenson might help: What *is* time?

In Jenson's program, time is neither Plato's turning wheel around a static eternal center nor Aristotle's external metric of sequentiality. Moreover, and perhaps most significantly, nor is time Augustine's brilliant synthesis of the two. Jenson explains: When Augustine "cut [Plato's] circle and stretched it out as a line, to model the biblical understanding of reality as history . . . he continued to think of the point of eternity as equidistant from all temporal points." Then Jenson makes his characteristically incisive observation, "Many puzzles within Western discourse about time result from the oxymoronic root metaphor, of a point perpendicular to a straight line yet equidistant from all points on it."[44] According to Jenson, the inherited problem within Western metaphysics is our fidelity to Hellenic notions of eternity as static timelessness.

Recall the "kiss and train wreck" idea at the start of this section: For Jenson, Gregory of Nyssa managed to take the gospel seriously enough on this point to somehow rewire his Greek mind around it. Jenson explains Gregory's accomplishment,

> Aristotle's and Plato's divinity is the stillness for which moving things long; the being of Gregory's God is that he keeps things moving. To be God is always to be open to and always to open a future, transgressing all past-imposed conditions . . . [this is] the eternity appropriate to the gospel's God.[45]

Sometimes one can be lost in the rush of reading Jenson. There is a kind of novelty adrenaline that both enlivens the reader and tempts her to move along too quickly. But with this, now second, mention of "future"

---

43. "[A]nswering these questions requires a major effort of revisionary metaphysics, which I have discovered that many find pressing reasons not to follow. Who knows? One of these reasons may be good" (Jenson, "For Us," 79).

44. *ST* 2:32.

45. *ST* 1:216.

with reference to God we should pause for a moment. The key move here is surely to suggest that "To be God is always to be open to and always to open a future." And recall we have already been told *who* this future is. For Jenson, the *Spirit* is the one "as whom God is future to himself."[46] He explains, "The Spirit is God as his and our future rushing upon him and us; he is the eschatological reality of God, the Power as which God is the active Goal of all things."[47] But what can this mean? Again we are at a crucial intersection in Jenson's thought and much if not all of his systematic traffic passes through it. So which way to go? For the sake of some coherence to our efforts, let us return to the question about a *logos asarkos*.

By suggesting the divine life coheres as the one God because this God as the Spirit of the Father and Son is the power of his own future, Jenson means to put some teleological weight on items in Christian dogmatics long stuck in protological conundrum. And the problem of the *logos asarkos* is a case in point. The question we left hanging above: how can God the Son be antecedent to *and* contingent on his identity as Jesus? Jenson's solution begins by reshuffling the terms of the problem.

First, he takes the now typical Barthian line,

> [I]t is the Incarnate Son who is himself his own presupposition in God's eternity: the Incarnation happens in eternity as the foundation of its happening in time.[48]

Then he gives it his teleological twist,

> Christ's birth from God precedes his birth from the seed of David in that in God's eternal life Christ's birth from God is the divine *future* of his birth from the seed of David.[49]

And this is possible because, "as the Spirit [God] is his own future."[50]

---

46. *ST* 1:158.

47. *ST* 1:159.

48. *ST* 1:140. Generally Jenson must coin concepts like, "the narrative pattern of being going to be born to Mary," to remain consistent with himself and somehow to refer to whatever ontologically precedes the history of Jesus (see, e.g., *ST* 1:141; 2:159). He does however—somewhat awkwardly—still seem to have a place for the *logos* in Israel's history; see *ST* 1:79.

49. *ST* 1:143. See also: "So from whence did Christ come to us? From heaven; indeed, that is from the eschatological future as this is available to God" (Jenson, "For Us," 82; cf. 83).

50. *ST* 1:143.

Whereas Barth kept a *logos asarkos* from unraveling his doctrine of revelation by loading the incarnation into eternity, by which he meant the pre-creative *past* life of God, Jenson flips the scenario. In an effort to avoid the same unraveling, he puts the bulk of God's life in what from the creature's perspective looks like the future.

Now another pause is in order; it hardly needs to be said that suggesting the future somehow precedes the past for the sake of an item of speculative Christology does not immediately inspire confidence. Jenson however is well aware of the counter intuitive tone of his theologic at this point and he has devised a plan to regain his listener's ear. His strategy involves two moves. The first we have already seen, it is to make the subjective center of time not the human self, but God. This we have heard when Jenson says "God is an event" or "God is what happens to Jesus and the world." His second move is just as radical. It is to plot created time *inside* the divine subjective center. Jenson packs both claims together:

> [T]ime is indeed, a la Augustine, the "distention" of a personal reality, and . . . just *so* it provides creatures with an external metric of created events. That is: the "stretching out" that makes time is an extension not of finite consciousness but of an infinite enveloping consciousness.[51]

Here is what may be the most contentious item of Jenson's already demanding paradigm. He wants us to imagine time and its effects on creatures' collective experiences are *internal* to the "enveloping consciousness" of God. Our perception of change and the metric against which we reckon sequential events are moments within the psychological distention of the divine self-consciousness. Jenson moves fast but let us try to keep up with the idea for we are nearing its center. For him, it is exactly the divine internality of time that is the possibility of creaturehood at all,

> for God to create is for him to *make accommodation* in his triune life for other persons . . . In himself he *opens room*, and that act is the event of creation . . . We call this accommodation in the triune life "time." . . . creation is above all God's taking time for us.[52]

Now to my question, and it is twofold: If God's eternity means he occupies the three poles of time, could the Trinity's personal

---

51. *ST* 2:34. We will note here and return below to the significance of Jenson's footnote, "This is undoubtedly a Hegelian sort of solution—and why not?"

52. *ST* 2:25; and cf. 1:226.

movement—their perichoretic liveliness—bring eternity back around on itself, make it circular in some respect?[53] And if time is somehow internal to this eternity, has Jenson inverted Plato so that time is the "specious" center-point to the enveloping circle of God's eternity around it?

I have been quick in my treatment, and come to some correspondingly tentative results. Moreover my concerns are, in this case at least, ones that it would seem Jenson has anticipated:

> This answer will seem circular only if we, perhaps subliminally, persist in plotting the triune life on a time *line*, or as a timeless *point* from which all points on the time line are equidistant. But the triune God's eternity can be plotted neither way.[54]

So how then ought we "plot" God's eternity? Jenson is not so easily pinned down. But he does have at least one more important move to make, and it is one that finally gets us to the namesake of this chapter. Next we will look at the Spirit's role in Jenson's effort to explain the possibility of narrative causation.

~

The question of the possibility of narrative causation is the question of the possibility of Jenson's theology. If a story can be not just *about* something but actually responsible for the reality of the events so told, then Jenson's is perhaps one of the most insightful and constructive theological systems of the twentieth century.

Once again there are many possible ways into this aspect of Jenson's thought, but to achieve the important first impression I will start with his doctrine of God. Jenson asks rhetorically, "Is his [God's] life ordered by an Outcome that is *his* outcome, and so in a freedom that is more than abstract aseity?"[55] We should note here that Jenson distinguishes "abstract aseity" from the idea of being "ordered by an Outcome" and he suggests the priority among these two is decided by whether or not God is authentically free. If God is *a se* in a simply abstract sense then all that is meant is he somehow causes himself. But Jenson raises the possibility

---

53. Space here does not permit a proper look at this. For now, we only note Jenson's own willingness for flexibility, "Here we follow, or perhaps trade on, a line of Orthodox theology that sees the triune life more in the pattern Father-Spirit-Son than the pattern Father-Son-Spirit" (*ST* 1:143n95).

54. *ST* 1:140–41.

55. *ST* 1:159.

that the tradition of abstraction at this point has meant a fatal oversight: The problem with aseity is that it establishes an absolute difference between God and creation without a corresponding notion of their relation. Jenson's point here is about the way this restricts the freedom of God to participate in his creation, it puts the being of God at odds with his freedom—not a desirable tension in Jenson's view. On the other hand, if as Jenson says, "God's life is ordered by an outcome that is *his* outcome," then God's own freedom—his "ordering Outcome"—is deeply compatible with contingent creation.

Another way of putting this would be to say that the relation between God and the world is not ontologically *determined*, it is freely *narrated*. And indeed, the only way something can be freely narrated and also causative is for the "Outcome" of the narrated events to somehow order them. It is this idea of being "ordered" or, effectively, *created*, by the end or "outcome" that is the essential characteristic of narrative for Jenson. He explains,

> The order of a good story is ordering by the outcome of the narrated events . . . the power of a self-determinative future to liberate each specious present from mere predictabilities, from being the mere consequence of what has gone before, and open it to itself, to itself as what that present is precisely not yet. The great metaphysical question on the border between the gospel and our culture's antecedent theology is whether this ordering may be regarded as its own kind of causality.[56]

In short, can a story cause itself? Our Greek intellectual ancestors said *No* and Jenson says *Yes*. For his "Yes" to hold at least two things must obtain. The first is simply the possibility for an "End" to cause the events that lead to it and the second is the possibility of this possibility: Can an "End" even be narrated at all? We will look at each of these in turn.

The first question: Is it possible for an End to cause the events that lead to it? Jenson has clearly worked hard to bring us to a place at which this is at least conceivable. We have already covered some of his groundwork when he told us that "the specificity of the triune God is not that he is three, but that he occupies each pole of time as a *persona dramatis*."[57] The present course is essentially a second pass at this terrain. This time we aim not to identify the divine characters so much as consider the genre of

---

56. Ibid.
57. *ST* 1:89.

their conversation. Broadly speaking, narrative causality is contingent on the generative function of the story's outcome. In Jenson's words, this is whether a story's "ordering may be regarded as its own kind of causality." Is this possible?

Of course Christian theology has from its inception acknowledged that the sovereignty of God extends to his ability to bring creation to its intended goal. The question we must face in Jenson's theology is however not so straightforward. Having inverted the metaphysic that lets God drive time from outside it by locating time inside God, Jenson must find a new engine to get creation to its final destination. Moreover, for Jenson, it is not just *creation* that has a *telos*, but God too. As the event he is, God must also come to some kind of narratable "End" or "Outcome."

Now all that effort to imagine the triune persons as the "three poles" of time might start to pay off. As we have seen, Jenson understands the Spirit to be the "power of God's future," and since this power is a conversationally constituted triune "identity," this future is one of the three among whom God finds himself. For Jenson, the Spirit is the End of the narrative and so "the dynamism of God's life is a narrative causation in and so of God."[58]

This is a difficult concept and a new way of trying to think about it so some more familiar terms might be helpful: Following Pannenberg, Jenson suggests our traditional conceptions of the Trinity have been too protologically driven. Although he freely employs the established use of "relations of origin" to imagine the immanent triune life, Jenson argues that when these terms are used exclusively for a doctrine of the Trinity our theology diverges from the essentially eschatological character of the biblical narrative. To correct the overuse, Jenson suggests we give due weight to what he calls the triune "relations of fulfillment":

> The divine beginning at which the relations of origin focus is acknowledged as the Father's Archimedean standpoint. Equally, the divine *goal* at which relations of *fulfillment* focus should be acknowledged as the Spirit's Archimedean standpoint; but this the tradition does not do, in West *or* East.[59]

When we recall that these "relations of fulfillment" are, of course, "subsistent relations," we arrive at a doctrine of God that would seem to

---

58. *ST* 1:160.
59. *ST* 1:157.

allow for telic determination—or, to return to Jenson's language, a God "with his own kind of causality."

But Jenson is not content to leave alone what some might think is well enough. To further secure his point he insists on the *priority* of the divine-future-Spirit over the divine-origin-Father: "[God] is *temporally* infinite because 'source' and 'goal' are present *and* asymmetrical in him, because he is primally future to himself and only thereupon past and present for himself."[60] Again Jenson is standing firmly among some of modern theology's most able trinitarian thinkers. The attempt to warrant an ontological priority to the future is a feature of similar theology from, among others, Jüngel, Pannenberg, and Moltmann.[61] But Jenson's effort to identify the "End" with the Spirit in such an explicit fashion puts some unique strains on this concept. To get a better handle on these strains, we need to look at the second issue raised by the idea of narrative causation.

Again a question will set the course: is it possible for an End to be absolute and still be narratable? Or in the terms Jenson has used in some recent writing: can there be a "sublation which is itself not sublated"?[62]

Here we should note one of the laudable characteristics of Jenson's work—its constructive reception in so many different theological circles. With this mention of "sublation" we should acknowledge that in certain of these circles G. W. F. Hegel keeps company with the likes of Arius, Pelagius, and other similarly suspect characters. Yet while even the most junior theologian could likely offer some explanation for why certain villains of church history should be named among the dogmatically disadvantaged, many would be reduced to incoherent mumbles about "synthesis" and "immanence" when it comes to Hegel. Even Jenson himself appears to have deliberately waited until after publishing his *Systematics* to make his affinity for Hegel explicit. There is doubtless an important story behind the theological taboo sometimes associated with Hegel but it need not be retold here to make the necessary observation: the question is not whether Jenson is "Hegelian" but rather, what exactly could "Hegelian" mean as it applies to him. Although this is an issue that requires more attention than I have here to offer, we can at least afford to get started in the right direction.

---

60. *ST* 1:217.

61. Contrast the call for a "reaffirmation of the centrality of the present" in Gunton, *One, the Three and the Many*, 93. We will consider Gunton's thought in chapter 8.

62. Jenson, "Great Transformation," 40.

The first step gets us to the alternative to christological mediation we have been expecting from Jenson since the first section of this chapter.[63] Whereas in some of his earlier work Jenson was comfortable with Irenaeus' mediatorial metaphor of the Son and the Spirit as the "two hands" of God,[64] he has clearly traded this concept for a specific kind of Hegelian dialectic. He clarifies which kind this is by rejecting the essentially "binitarian" structure of "I-Thou" relations:

> How is an I-Thou relation ever to be other than an overt or covert struggle for power? How is its "bond" ever to be love? . . . Surely we must acknowledge that if there is to be a freely given love there must be a third party in the meeting of "I" and "Thou." If you and I are to be free for one another, someone must be our liberator . . . if another, whose intention for you and me is precisely our mutual love, objectifies us by that very intention, we are free to love each other.[65]

In order for God to be free, according to Jenson, he must be liberated into the kind of loving relations that cannot deteriorate into a

---

63. It would have been possible at this point to ask if Jenson has in fact offered an *alternative* to christological mediation or just so radically altered the terms of the dilemma that we cannot immediately recognize the typical solution. When we recall how he has ontologized time it may be that, instead of somehow being both fully divine and human substance, Christ on Jenson's terms participates simultaneously in both the divine and human histories. Perhaps where we once had a consubstantial Christ, Jenson has simply given us a "con-historical" one—i.e., Christ is not a "mediatorial being" because he is a mediatorial "event." See *ST* 1:138: "That Christ has the divine nature means that he is one of the three whose mutuality is the divine life, who live the history that God is. That Christ has human nature means that he is one of the many whose mutuality is human life, who live the history that humanity is."

The fact that this is one of the rare few appearances of "two nature" talk in Jenson's work means we can make the point that, although it is absolutely clear in Jenson's theology that Jesus participates in the divine history, it is less clear that he does so as fully in human history. Much more could be said here about, for example, his understanding of Christ's "biological" body; as in his sustained hesitation over the importance of the empty tomb (*ST* 1:194ff.), or in his claim that Christ's "body" was "born of Mary and risen into the church and its sacraments" (*ST* 1:129); or his claim that "the church is ontologically the risen Christ's human body" (*ST* 2:213); or indeed about his more general concept of the body as one's "availability," so that, "*prior to the resurrection, my embodiment is of course not separable from a biological organism—or is only exceptionally*" (*ST* 2:88; emphasis added). Cf. Jenson, "The Body of God's Presence." These are questions we will address when we come next to similar theology in John Zizioulas.

64. See, e.g., Jenson, *Triune Identity*, 69.

65. *ST* 1:156.

struggle for power. As God there is no one beside himself capable of doing such a thing for him, so Jenson appeals to the Spirit as the best way to understand how the Father and the Son are freed for one another. The implications become clearer with some more familiar language: Jenson insists this God is himself love because he "is the archetype of thesis, antithesis and synthesis."[66] When this dynamic is put in eschatological terms, Jenson has a Spirit who freely transforms God and world into their future together:

> We need not here decide the controverted question whether or not Hegel's own system allows this reconciliation to be truly free transformation—to be eschatological—or compels it to be what we more usually mean by "synthesis," mere result, mere product. We will unambiguously posit the former.[67]

This is indeed the first question of any theological reading of Hegel. Is the synthetic end only a product of the events that lead to it or is it somehow responsible for realizing its own outcome? In other words, does *Geist* "transcend" the world, or is it ultimately immanent within it? To be sure, the brilliance of Hegel's theology is its resilience to precisely this kind of either-or simplicity (which probably begins to explain Jenson's affinity for it), yet the sense of these questions nevertheless remains. The point here, let me be clear, is not about the "accuracy" of Jenson's reading of Hegel—this is something I am neither equipped nor inclined to ask—the question, rather, is about how Jenson has commandeered Hegelian ideas. Conveniently, Jenson is clear with how he imagines himself to have done so: "We will unambiguously posit the former." For him, the "End" is indeed brought about by a free transformation and this freedom *is* the Spirit: "This 'economic' Trinity is *eschatologically* God 'himself,' an 'immanent' Trinity."[68]

God and world are not ontological opposites somehow mediated in Christ, for Jenson we are simply dealing with the "mystery of personal love":

> The true mystery here is simply the mystery of personal love. Gifts of love can genuinely belong to the recipient, without transforming the recipient into the giver, just as they are plural and in their plurality are not individually identical with the self

66. Jenson, "Great Transformation," 41.
67. Jenson, "Cosmic Spirit," 169.
68. Jenson, "Pneumatological Soteriology," 155.

of the giver. Yet in their mutual completeness they are nevertheless nothing but the giver.[69]

As Jenson would have it, Creator and creation do not exist in a kind tension between otherness and relation, rather the Spirit unites the two by freely opening their one future together. There is a long tradition behind Jenson on this point, albeit one that made it with significantly different terms. Jenson sees himself standing with Luther and Jonathan Edwards in their essentially affirmative answer to Peter Lombard's question: "[I]s the love which unites believers the same love as that between Father and Son, or that given by this [Spirit]?" Like Luther, Jenson is not content with conventional ideas about grace. Whereas Augustine had argued that we are united to God by a created *gift*, Jenson sides here with those who imagine that we are united to the Father in the Son by *their Spirit*. With this idea, Jenson is getting to the climax of his theology—and one to which we have already been with Cyril—to "what the church has called *theosis*." Simply put: "God and only God is the creature's future."[70] As with any concept of deification, this will not meet with intuitive approval for some readers.[71] But typical concerns notwithstanding, does not Jenson have some especially acute difficulties here?

Aside from the fact that his way of preparing the debate about deification tends to make grace look rather dull beside its theotic alternative, our train of thought here recovers some of the momentum from concerns previously raised: although it is apparent to some modern readers that Augustine may not have been altogether trinitarian enough in his concept of created grace, it is at least clear that he realized that something created could genuinely imbibe a degree of derived goodness. And caution about the slighting of creation's own goodness is an echo of my original concern about the eliding of God's being and act. Does God give his acts their own contingent reality—do creatures have space to be something other than him—or is creation somehow an event within the

---

69. *ST* 1:149.

70. *ST* 2:26.

71. "One must indeed fear that many of those theologians who dislike the notion of deification misconstrue it because they do not at bottom conceive of God as alive in himself but rather as a timeless essence, so that being taken into God would mean exchanging one essence for another, would mean the abolition of humanity by divinity" (Jenson, "Great Transformation," 41). Cf. *ST* 1:71; 1:226; 2:69. And see Jenson, "Theosis."

"enveloping" divine consciousness and so only good or real insofar as it serves God's own self-discovery?

On the one hand, for all of its "immanence," Jenson's theology is a remarkably constructive way of maintaining what may be the only way to finally distinguish Creator and creature. In his words, "God is in himself the one as who and among whom he finds himself . . . Creatures are not triune; therefore God and our fellow humans must present us with ourselves."[72] Whatever happens in Jenson's retelling of the gospel it is clear that God is triune and everything else is not.

On the other hand, however, it is perhaps especially significant, given what Jenson has invested in the futurity of God and creation, that he recurs to protology—to relations of *origin*—to maintain this distinction between God and everything else in the End. Triune and created persons are finally distinguishable because,

> a divine identity, as we have said, is nothing but a "subsistent relation" to the other identities; each of the three is primeval to the other two. Therefore, one who comes *into* this life does not thereby become a divine identity, does not become one of those whose life it is.[73]

But the question is, can there be anything left of primeval beginnings once everything has been brought to its eschatological End?[74] Does the "conversation" continue or is the End really only music?[75]

On our first pass at the problem of a *logos asarkos* we heard Jenson retort that with regard to the supposed two natures of Christ "one does not need to fasten together what is not separated in the first place." And perhaps here Jenson might simply reply that with regard to what he has called "the Great Transformation" one ought not separate what is fastened together in the last place. If this is a fair gloss, the issue stands: With the being and act of God so immediately "fastened," and with created time a distention internal to the divine consciousness, how can the End we are talking about preserve that which it finishes?

---

72. *ST* 2:131.

73. *ST* 1:226.

74. Thus Pannenberg, 252: "[D]espite his bold thesis that the Spirit eschatologically grounds the unity (the 'self') of God [Jenson] continued to hold to the conception of the triune God as a single Subject, thinking of the Trinity in terms of its self-unfolding."

75. If the Trinity is a communion of *personae dramatis,* are there certain parts of the divine life that do not end up in the Spirit's final Director's Cut of God?

Whatever the case, Jenson would perhaps be the first to remind us at this point that concerns as abstract as these verge on (or into) the theologically absurd. Yet of the many lessons Jenson has to offer, surely one among them is the absolute centrality of a doctrine of God for all of Christian life and thought. The issue at the crux of this chapter is whether or not Jenson's doctrine of the Trinity finally affords appropriate space to the Spirit, and thereby to everything that is not this Spirit. And it is concern about the particularity of this person of the Trinity that raises the same for another. Does not Jenson's affinity for Hegel and its corollary in his absolute rejection of a *logos asarkos* risk idealizing Christ to such an extent that, as in Hegel, there remains no theological place for the *particular* Jesus?

Clearly, Jenson's system is one in which pneumatology is both subtle and supreme. Yet, despite the fact that his work often seems to be of an aesthetic caliber beyond reproach, there remains a nagging sense that it—to use his fine phrase—"fudges the particularity of the Spirit."[76] When it comes to the future, and without being precisely able to capture how or why, his theology sometimes leaves one wondering about the influence of Hegel so that when it comes to the Spirit one might even wonder where everything else went.[77]

With Jenson the questions charted in the patristic and medieval eras about Christ and mediation have come blazing into the twenty-first century, and these in turn have raised more about the nature of the God responsible for this mediation. Jenson serves us well as a theologian capable of bringing theology about God, the world and Christ into tight systematic relation. His clarity on questions about the triune being of God and in particular about God's freedom means we have more pointed ones to ask of our next figure, John Zizioulas.

---

76. Jenson, "Cosmic Spirit," 165

77. This chapter is based largely on my "Robert Jenson and the Spirit of it All."

7

JOHN ZIZIOULAS AND BEING FREE
Christ as Personal Paradigm
(An Existential Concept of Mediation)

> For things, whose existence originated in change, must also be subject to change, whether it be that they perish or that they become other than they are by act of will. But if things are uncreated they must in all consistency be also wholly immutable.
>
> —John of Damasacus

The clear intent of John Zizioulas's work is to establish ontological space for personal freedom at a time when various monisms have much of modern culture still gasping for air. But if I am right, there is a familiar theological irony afoot. In this chapter I will investigate areas in which the central intent and the overall effect of Zizioulas's program are at odds in certain important respects.

Before I proceed with what will be a mainly critical evaluation of Zizioulas's theology however, a word first about his fundamental achievement is in order. Whereas ontological speculation, generally speaking, tends to imagine persons as first of all substantial and somehow thereafter capable of various kinds of relations, Zizioulas's insight rests on an inversion of that order. For Zizioulas, a person does not exist first as a substance and somehow later enter into relationships, but rather is realized first by and in those relations and as such is somehow later "substantiated" by them. The ambiguity of the point of difference is part of its characteristic ethos and we will have occasion to consider some of its more constructive elements in later chapters. For now, I will focus on the apparent contradictions loaded just beneath the surface of this quick gloss—on how the implications of Zizioulas's primary ontological thesis find expression in his particular theology.

What we will discover is that although Zizioulas's work has been a profoundly effective alarm, his warning comes laden with the danger itself. Three of his central themes converge to suggest monism is a risk *internal* to Zizioulas's theology and as such immune to his own struggle for freedom from it. I will try to explain each theme in turn: first his doctrine of God in which his emphasis on the primordiality of the Father risks undermining the cohesion of triune communion. Second, his soteriology, in which he tends to problematize creaturely being at the expense of its own contingent integrity. And finally, we will look at his Christology, where Zizioulas's emphasis on the singularity of Christ's person over against the duality of his natures seems to open the doors to a final absorption of humanity into the divine.

∼

I will start with an image that will be familiar to Zizioulas's readers; it is a scene from Fyodor Dostoevsky's *Demons* in which the character Kirilov explains his rationale for suicide:

> Every one who wants to attain complete freedom must be daring enough to kill himself . . . This is the final limit of freedom, that is all, there is nothing beyond it . . . Who dares to kill himself becomes God.[1]

Kirilov's morose conclusion comes at the end of a train of thought best understood according to Jean-Paul Sartre's familiar terms: Kirilov's "existence" precedes his "essence"—he simply *is* before he *chooses* how to be—and so his "existential" life always qualifies his essential freedom.[2]

---

1. Dostoevsky, and in particular the scene here of Kirilov's dilemma, appears at many of the crucial junctures in Zizioulas's theology. See esp. Zizioulas, "Human Capacity and Human Incapacity," 432; idem, *Being as Communion*, 108n105 (and cf. 42–43); Zizioulas, "Preserving God's Creation (3)," p. 2.

2. "What do we mean by saying that existence precedes essence? What we mean

Kirilov's thirst for absolute freedom means a desire to reverse this order, to be his essence freely and in advance of the restrictions imposed by the conditions of his existence. The appeal of suicide for Kirilov arises from the fact that it seems to be the only act available to him that would accomplish this reversal. By "daring" to kill himself Kirilov would finally exert his freedom over the conditions of his existence by ending it. On Kirilov's logic this reordering of his essential freedom before the givenness of his existence would place him in the domain of absolute freedom, and so make him "God."

Now to bring this scene into the scope of this chapter. The shift requires focusing on Kirilov's subtle equation of freedom and divinity. On Kirilov's terms, to "attain complete freedom" is to "become God." Being "God" for Kirilov is to exist on one's own terms, to have essence first as it were, and so be "existentially" free to choose how to *be* that essence thereafter. Thus, crudely put, to *be* fully is to be fully *free*. This equation of being and freedom is the crux. And it forms the theological connection between Dostoevsky and Zizioulas: if being and being free are conceptually synonymous then the only way to *be* truly is to *cause* one's own existence.

The question we face in Zizioulas's theology is whether or not Kirilov's dilemma holds at the ontological scale, whether the precedence of existence over essence is a metaphysical matter of fact for everything. This is the existential crisis at the heart of Zizioulas's thought. If the essence of everything is bound or restricted by the conditions of its own existence then everything only exists as it must according to these conditions. And this brings us to the "necessity" that is so regulative in Zizioulas's work: "If God's existence is determined by the necessity of his *ousia* . . . then all existence is bound by necessity."[3] Against this Zizioulas offers a twofold response. His first move is against necessity head-on; his second is more subtle—coming around behind his nemesis to outflank him as it were. Let us look at each movement in turn.

First, Zizioulas confronts necessity by rallying us behind the absolute freedom of the Father as cause. That the being of God must be caused and cannot simply be accepted as a "dead ousianic tautology"[4] is the conviction at the conceptual hub of Zizioulas's theologic. This

---

is that man first of all exists, encounters himself, surges up in the world—and defines himself afterwards" (Sartre, *Existentialism and Humanism*, 28).

3. Zizioulas, "Doctrine of God the Trinity Today," 25.

4. Ibid.

causation—the absolutely free act whereby the Father generates the Son and spirates the Spirit—is "meant to indicate that divine existence does not 'spring,' so to say 'naturally' as from an impersonal substance, but is brought into existence, it is 'caused,' by *someone*."[5] Zizioulas explains the significance of this:

> If God's being is not caused by a Person, it is not a free being. And if this Person is not the Father alone, it is impossible to maintain the divine unity or oneness without taking resort into the ultimacy of substance in ontology, i.e. without subjecting freedom to necessity and Person to substance.[6]

Leaving aside the questions about the accuracy of his repeated claim for Patristic—and particularly Cappadocian—support for these ideas,[7] we should notice here that there is a direct relationship between causation and freedom: "If God's being is not caused . . . it is not . . . free." And this is where the orienting theme of Zizioulas's theology begins to threaten its common effect. Most of Zizioulas's contemporary beneficiaries have capitalized on the importance of relation for conceptualizing divine and human persons, yet when Zizioulas himself comes to tell how it is that the Father is the single primordial Person his explanation has distinctly autonomous overtones.[8] Even when we grant that Zizioulas surely does not mean by "freedom" simply the ability to choose among a number of given possibilities, but rather intends it in the larger sense of being free from the existential restrictions of givenness, the concept nevertheless retains the operative term *from*. The result is that the Father is ultimately defined in terms of his freedom from necessity, and only subsequently in terms of his communion with the Son and the Spirit.[9]

---

5. Zizioulas, "Teaching of the 2nd Ecumenical Council," 37.

6. Ibid., 45

7. Some recent critique has focused on Zizioulas's attempt "to give his concept of relational person a normative Greek patristic content" (Turcescu, "'Person,'" 536).

8. This point has been well made already by A. Torrance: "An *a posteriori* ontology of intra-divine communion risks being subsumed by a cosmological category of causality" (*Persons in Communion*, 291).

9. It would be possible to conduct the same argument according to Zizioulas's doctrine of the *imago dei*. Here, too, man's likeness to God is understood first in terms of freedom and subsequently in terms of his relationality. See, e.g., "Whatever involves succumbing to the given, this man has in common with the animals. Whatever is *free* from it, constitutes a sign of the presence of the human" (Zizioulas, "Preserving God's Creation [3]," p. 2). And cf. Berdyaev, who suggests that for Dostoevsky, "freedom . . . is the mark of the highest dignity of man, of his likeness to God" (*Russian Idea*, 195).

The second movement of Zizioulas's response confronts the problem of necessity from another angle. This aspect of necessity is most apparent in the words of his own open query: "It is the question of knowing whether otherness can make sense in ontology, whether ontology can do anything more than rest on the idea of totality."[10] The crucial connection comes into view when we see that this ominous "idea of totality" is the quieter alter-ego of his just mentioned and more familiar nemesis, necessity. If being is restricted by certain existential qualifications—if it is "necessary"—then it is also bound by these qualifications in some respect. These boundaries would hem-in being, making it circumscribable within an "idea of totality." Necessity and totality are thus two sides to the same coin; one is more familiar because it is "existentially" relevant (necessity), the other—"totality"—is its ontological correlative.

Against the would-be monotony of this "idea of totality," Zizioulas deploys a subtle variation on his emphasis on the Father as cause. Here he develops the idea of the Father as the *principle* of the divine unity.[11]

For Zizioulas there are only two options: One must either predicate God's unity of divine substance, or attribute it to the Father.[12] Either God is one because the three persons are somehow substantiated by divine being, or God is one because there is only one *arché*—the Father. The question "What makes God be one?" cannot be evaded.[13] And, for Zizioulas,

---

Thus Kirilov also epitomizes the problem here: "I am still God against my will, and I am unhappy, because it is my *duty* to proclaim self-will . . . For three years I have been searching for the attribute of my divinity, and I have found it: the attribute of my divinity is— Self-will! That is all, by which I can show in the main point my insubordination and my new fearsome freedom. For it is very fearsome. I kill myself to show my insubordination and my new fearsome freedom" (Dostoevsky, *Demons*, 619).

10. Zizioulas, *Being as Communion*, 86, emphasis original. N.B. at this point Zizioulas refers us to E. Levinas, *Totalite et Infini* (1971).

11. *Arché* ("principle") is often used by Zizioulas synonymously with *aitia* ("cause"). It is generally unclear whether he intends these terms to carry an efficient (i.e., productive) or a formal (i.e., explanatory) sense. The morass is deepened when Zizioulas equates "principle" and "cause" with the "constitutive element of beings," since "constitute" can refer to both how a thing has come to exist and what the thing exists as (ibid., 39). It is likely safe to suggest that Zizioulas usually intends something like the overlap of these terms; this would at least mean there is always a sense in which both efficiency and componency (*quiddity*) are at stake. Cf. Zizioulas, "Teaching of the 2nd Ecumenical Council."

12. This is to leave aside the strictly apophatic option (a view Zizioulas associates with Lossky).

13. Zizioulas, "Doctrine of God the Trinity Today," 22.

anything like the "typical" Western view[14] or the now vogue "perichoretic" views he is often wrongly aligned with are only variations on the same theme.[15] Both beg "the question of whether being is due to an impersonal factor like *ousia* or to a *person*, like the Father."[16] But to dismiss substance and communion as impersonal raises a rather awkward question: *Which is more personal, a particular person or persons-in-communion?* Zizioulas, at least, would appear to have an answer:

> [C]ommunion is a *dimension* of personhood, not personhood itself. Without communion there is no Person, but Person does not mean communion. If we wish to attribute God's personal existence to a Person we cannot attribute it to communion, for communion is not a Person.[17]

It is crucial for Zizioulas that divine unity be attributed to something more than a featureless "structure of communion existing by itself."[18] To avoid recourse to the kind of flat ontology he sees as the only alternative, Zizioulas insists that communion must be "a *dimension* of personhood." For him, the particular—i.e., the Father—must be ontologically primary otherwise being is unavoidably unfree.[19] When this conviction is applied to his doctrine of God, anything that smacks of Heidegger's "single horizon" is nauseatingly close to the "idea of totality" that he is at pains to avoid.[20]

14. On the validity of the paradigmatic East/persons-first-then-substance vs. West/substance-first-then-persons, see Barnes, "Augustine in Contemporary Trinitarian Theology." Cf. Zizioulas, "Teaching of the 2nd Ecumenical Council," 49: "It is in the light of this absence of an ontology of the Person in the West that we must place the entire history of East-West relations in theology."

15. Zizioulas argues that "Augustinian-substantialist" doctrines of the Trinity are ultimately indistinguishable from "Buberian relationality" views (Zizioulas's modern example for this is Alan Torrance); see Zizioulas, "Father as Cause," unpublished typescript, 14. See Cross, "On Generic and Derivation Views," where he argues similarly that a properly sympathetic reading of the Western "generic" view is basically the same as an emphasis on perichoretic mutuality. He suggests that in both cases "the divine substance is simply the metaphysical overlap of the persons."

16. Zizioulas, "Doctrine of God the Trinity Today," 25.

17. Zizioulas, "Father as Cause," 14.

18. Zizioulas, *Being as Communion*, 89.

19. "Ancient Greek philosophy knew of causation, but it always posited it *within* the framework of being . . . And so the particular is never the ontologically primary cause of being. This leads to necessity in ontology. Being is not a gift but a datum to be reckoned with by the particular beings" (Zizioulas, "On Being a Person," 38; cf. 36).

20. "If the three Persons of the Trinity are ontologically conceived as simultaneous

At play here is another version of the existential Hellenism I signaled with Cyril and Philoponus. For the earlier Greeks the question was, what is it that finally secures being against change? The problem then was the insecurities inherent within time, the extreme end of which was a dissolution into nothingness, a falling-off the bottom of the vertical continuum of Irenaeus' opponents. For their modern spokesman the question is the converse one about what can keep being free from the ontological restrictions of that flux and nothingness. Whereas the Alexandrians achieved their stability through substantialist notions of divine impassibility, Zizioulas finds his existential catharsis in the absolute freedom of a particular member of the Trinity, the Father.

In sum, the Father is to be identified by and in his being-in-communion with the Son and the Spirit but he is also particularly responsible for the unity that keeps this communion together. It is this deliberate emphasis on the Father's particularity that raises the concern. Zizioulas emphasizes his point for clarity: "This principle of personal causation of being means that particularity is to be understood as causative and not derivative in ontology."[21] The question is whether or not the emphasis placed on the particularity of the Father at this point does not dissolve the unity of the triune communion from the other way round. At the very least, the suggestion that the principle of unity is identifiable with a particular person does seem to lead us to the somewhat awkward idea that there is a single champion over the problem of singularity.[22]

---

and mutually co-emerging we are applying to God a Heideggerian 'panoramic' ontology rightly criticized by Levinas. The absence of personal causation in ontology would make ultimate reality identical with relationality as a metaphysical concept. We are thus driven to a 'platonizing' or 'idealizing' ontology of the divine being, something that would replace *ousia* with the metaphysics of 'Tripersonality' or 'Trinity' etc. All these are nothing but backdoors for the return of substantiation to theology" (Zizioulas, "Father as Cause," 13–14. Cf. Zizioulas, *Being as Communion*, 45n40. Cf. the comments at n52 below. And for a completely opposite reading of the Cappadocians on this point, see Jenson, *Triune Identity*, 90.

21. Zizioulas, "On Being a Person," 38.

22. Zizioulas might respond to this quip by suggesting the typically Western alternative vis-à-vis the *filioque* would lead to an even more incongruous conclusion: "Is the Father the only *aition* of divine being, of the Trinity? If he is not, then the dilemma arises: if we accept another person (the Son) as *aition* next to him we have to choose between two options: either we make the *ousia* of God the first generating principle or else we end up with two causing principles, i.e. with two Gods" (Zizioulas, "Doctrine of God the Trinity Today," 26–27; and cf. Zizioulas, "Human Capacity and Human Incapacity," 46). But a polemic based on the *filoque* at this point relies on its own internal presuppositions about the necessarily derivative nature of unity.

When Zizioulas's double movement is observed together what emerges is a choice between necessity and freedom made for the Father as *cause* and a choice between totality and particularity made for the Father as *source*. Freedom prevails over necessity because the Father causes being, and particularity prevails over totality because the Father is the source of divine unity. The decisive maneuver was to make both of these choices in a single answer; to make freedom and particularity correlative aspects of the one person of the Father.

The issue that has arisen however is whether or not this crucial correlation is theologically sustainable. It would appear that certain tensions internal to Zizioulas's theologic have taken us in directions that lead to ideas which are themselves very much contrary to Zizioulas's stated objectives. On the one hand, Zizioulas defines personhood in terms that seem to give priority to freedom over communion. On the other, he has located the unity of God in such a way as to give priority to particularity over relation. Combined, these pressures suggest Zizioulas is at risk of identifying the Father by his *freedom from* the Son and the Spirit. Our task now is to ask whether or not Zizioulas's programme can support these tensions on its own terms.

∽

As an entry into the dilemma, let us begin to grapple with Zizioulas's soteriology. For this we need to see the human predicament on his terms:

> This rupture between being and communion [i.e., the fall] results automatically in the *truth of being* acquiring priority over the *truth of communion*. This is *natural* for created existence. It is inevitably the case when you have a created being as the ultimate point of reference, because "created" means "given": man may wish to make communion ultimate but the fact of existence is a "datum" with which he is presented, and thus he can never escape from the fact that being precedes relationship. The "substance" or *ousia* of things becomes the ultimate content of truth, if truth is to relate to being. The only alternative to this would be to make communion *constitutive* of being, but in this case a denial of the fall—or a redemption from it—would be implied.[23]

First of all, it is clear that to be created is to receive one's existence as a "given datum" and that this "givenness" is somehow existentially restrictive.

---

23. Zizioulas, *Being as Communion*, 102; emphasis original.

Zizioulas explains that "creaturehood, taken in itself, has its being rooted in beginning and thus under the constant threat of nothingness."[24] Creaturehood is defined first in terms of being given—having an *ex nihilo* beginning—and then in terms of the restriction "beginningness" has on the creature's being.

This is Kirilov's existential dilemma at the anthropological scale: "[H]ow can a man be considered absolutely free when he cannot do other than accept his existence? . . . [since] . . . as a creature he cannot escape the necessity of his existence."[25] What we seem to arrive at therefore is a three-part train of thought: to be created is to receive one's being as a given; to receive one's being as a given is to be restricted by necessity; and being restricted by necessity is antithetical to existing as an authentic person. Thus it would seem that for Zizioulas, "created" and "person" are fundamentally incommensurable. The drive for absolute freedom and the "natural" course of created existence are not only headed in opposite directions, they are moving on entirely different planes of being.[26]

The second way Zizioulas explains our condition is similar. In this case humanity suffers from a wrong ontological ordering of nature and personhood. He suggests that the "*priority* of nature over the person"[27] is humanity's main problem. This is closely related to the terms we have just met, since this wrong ordering of nature and person is "due to the fact that human existence is a *created* existence, i.e. it is an existence with a beginning."[28] Once again however, the key concepts have slipped from a nuanced logical antagonism into an effective ontological opposition. Created being and given nature have become antithetical to personhood and relationality since the first two concepts are defined in terms of ontological limitation and the latter two are defined in terms of absolute freedom.

24. Zizioulas, "Human Capacity and Human Incapacity," 419.

25. Zizioulas, *Being as Communion*, 42, 43. And cf. another important reference to Dostoevsky: "The youth in adolescence, in the very period in which he becomes conscious of his freedom, asks: 'and who consulted me when I was brought into the world?' Unconsciously he articulates the great theme of the ontological necessity which exists in the biological hypostasis" (ibid., 51n45).

26. It is important that we recall that Zizioulas intends this in an absolutely *ontological* sense, i.e., and not as a moral or volitional freedom. See ibid., 121–22n126. We note the difference in this respect between Zizioulas's theology and that of Jenson; for the latter this distinction would be unthinkable.

27. Zizioulas, "Doctrine of the Holy Trinity," 53; emphasis mine.

28. Ibid., 53.

The crucial task is locating the cause of these oppositions. Are we talking about a dynamic that is intrinsic to creation or something that is a result of the fall? Zizioulas is not entirely consistent in how he might answer this. At points, he clearly associates the priority of substance over communion with the fall.[29] At other and, it must be said, more frequent points, the distinction between creation and fall seems to have been dropped entirely.[30] For Zizioulas, the bondage of communion to substance is "a servitude which applies only to created existence."[31] He explains approvingly,

> For the Greek Fathers the fall of man—and for that matter, sin—is not to be understood as bringing about something new (there is no *creative* power in evil), but as *revealing and actualizing the limitations and potential dangers inherent in creaturehood, if creation is left to itself*.[32]

What we are beginning to see here is a vision of the human condition as an inherently frustrated one.[33] It seems that to be a created person is to *be* tragically. Until "created"—i.e., oriented toward substance—is finally reconciled with "person"—i.e., oriented toward the other—any attempt to be a created-person is an attempt to be an oxy-moron. But how, then, can we be freed from this existential angst? One gets the sense from Zizioulas that creaturehood and personhood are definitively at odds until one is transformed into the other. Such a logic is by now familiar territory in this study. Zizioulas explains: "[T]here is hope also for the creature which by definition *is* faced by the priority of substance, of 'given realities,' to be free from these 'givens,' to acquire God's way of being in what

---

29. See Zizioulas, "Human Capacity and Human Incapacity," 428n3: "[T]he fallen state of existence . . . is characterized by the dialectic of good and evil . . . As well as the individualization and fragmentation of being which are inherent in it." And cf. especially ibid., 434.

30. Thus: "Creation and Fall coalesce into a single entity in Zizioulas's thinking. The Fall consists merely in the revelation and actualization of the limitations and potential dangers inherent in creaturely existence" Volf, *After Our Likeness*, 83–84.

31. Zizioulas, "Doctrine of the Holy Trinity," 50.

32. Zizioulas, *Being as Communion*, 102; emphasis original.

33. "Tragedy is the impasse created by a freedom driving towards its fulfillment and being unable to reach it . . . It is impossible to have a complete definition of Man without reference to the tragic element, and this is related directly to the subject of freedom" (Zizioulas, "Preserving God's Creation [3]," p. 2). Cf. Kirilov above.

the Greek Fathers called *theosis*."[34] The good news, according to Zizioulas, is that God's way of being is not an exclusive affair.

> If the ground of God's ontological freedom lies simply in His "nature," that is, in His being uncreated by nature, whereas we are by nature created, then there is no hope, no possibility, that man might become a person in the sense that God is one, that is, an authentic person. But no, the ground of God's ontological freedom lies not in His nature but in His personal existence, that is, in the "mode of existence" by which He subsists as divine nature. And it is precisely this that gives man, in spite of his different nature, his hope of becoming an authentic person.[35]

Theosis for Zizioulas is not merely a resolution of the dialectical tensions we have observed between givenness and necessity on the one hand and substance and personhood on the other, it is their absolute final synthesis in the free communion of God's own being. As with Jenson, there may be need to pause here on Zizioulas's own grounds. A question comes to the fore when we recall that for Zizioulas the Father is *the* primordial Person[36]: if *theosis* is the process by which we become authentic persons, and the Father is *the* authentic Person, there appears to be a suspiciously unilateral—indeed "vertical"—connection between Zizioulas's doctrine of God and his doctrine of creation. Once freedom is located in the particular person of the Father and necessity presides as the defining characteristic of creation, any construal of salvation in terms of freedom from necessity seems to suggest (if I may) one is bound on a long walk off a short dock into the great sea of being.

Zizioulas is aware of this lure however. So aware in fact, he has taken recourse to a surprising safeguard: "So, whenever the question of the ontological relationship between God and the world is raised, the idea of *hypostasis*, from now on ontological in an ultimate sense, must be

---

34. Zizioulas, "Doctrine of God the Trinity Today," 25.

35. Zizioulas, *Being as Communion*, 44. Cf. Zizioulas, "Human Capacity and Human Incapacity," 436.

36. "[O]nly God can claim to be a personal being in the genuine sense . . . When we say, therefore, that God *is*, we do not refer to a being as being but to the *Father*—a term which denotes being in the sense of hypostasis, i.e. of Person" (Zizioulas, "Human Capacity and Human Incapacity," 410). Cf. Zizioulas, *Being as Communion*, 43: "[T]he authentic person, as absolute ontological freedom, must be 'uncreated,' that is, unbounded by any 'necessity,' including by its own existence"; and Zizioulas, "Father as Cause," 11: "They [the Cappadocians] wanted to say that divine being in its personal existence is due to a *free agent*, to a Person in the fullest sense of the term."

completed with that of substance if we do not wish to fall back into ontological monism."[37] Whether or not there is sufficient ontological weight left in the concept of substance for such an important task after Zizioulas has had his way with it is not immediately clear. I suspect the direction of Zizioulas's theology is problematic in this regard, but let us take a closer look at the issue by way of its conceptual nexus, his Christology.

∼

For Zizioulas, the union of a divine and human nature in Christ is a soteriological paradigm: "Christology consequently is the proclamation to man that his nature can be 'assumed' and hypostatised in a manner free from the ontological necessity of his biological hypostasis, which, as we have seen, leads to the tragedy of individualism and death."[38] In Christ we are shown that it is possible for human nature to be assumed by a divine nature and thereby incorporated into a way of being that is free from the restrictions inherent to humanity's "biological" condition.[39] The meaning of "biological" in this context is perhaps best glossed to refer to those ontological restrictions inherent to (fallen?) creaturehood. These restrictions can be broadly set into two categories: there are those that we suffer by nature, by virtue of the fact that we have a beginning and so are not absolutely free (Kirilov), and there are those that we suffer due to our isolation from one another in bodies (i.e., individualization and death).[40] Although this explanation doubtless raises more questions about Zizioulas's doctrine of creation than it answers, let us press on to the central point: what is clear from this is that with the term "biological" Zizioulas

---

37. Zizioulas, *Being as Communion*, 89. This confession arises regarding Athanasius's "relational" concept of substance; on this, see Zizioulas, "Teaching of the 2nd Ecumenical Council," 32.

38. Zizioulas, *Being as Communion*, 56. And cf. Zizioulas, "Human Capacity and Human Incapacity," 442: "Personhood, I have argued, is the mode in which nature exists in its ecstatic movement of communion in which it is hypostatised in its catholicity. This, I have also said, is what has been realized in Christ as the man *par excellence* through the hypostatic union. This, I must now add, is what should happen to every man."

39. "Christology is found precisely upon the assertion that only the Trinity can offer to created being the genuine base for personhood and hence salvation . . . True life, without death, is impossible for us as long as our being is ontologically determined by creaturehood" (Zizioulas, *Being as Communion*, 107, 108).

40. It is difficult to represent Zizioulas sympathetically at this point. A reader more familiar with Maximus the Confessor may be able to appreciate the crucial nuances at play here. See especially ibid., 50ff.

intends to summarize the problem overcome by the incarnation. The assumption of humanity's biological condition by one of the Trinity is *the* saving event. Our next step is to investigate Zizioulas's understanding of this event.

In the years following Chalcedon, the Antiochene-Alexandrian irresolution it solidified was re-doubled as a contest for Cyril's endorsement. Zizioulas's reading of Cyril is accordingly telling: "The patristic idea of *hypostatic union*, such as developed principally by Cyril of Alexandria, makes the *person (hypostasis)*, and not the natures, the ultimate ground of Christ's being."[41] Leaving to one side the accuracy of Zizioulas's exegesis of Cyril, the point for our present purpose can be seen in how he commandeers him. Two things deserve our attention. First is the suggestion that the person of Christ and his two natures are theological alternatives. The symbiosis of "one person" and "two natures" is, after all, precisely the point of Chalcedon, and suggesting otherwise is a classic Alexandrian attempt to trump the Council with Cyril.

A second and even more fundamental point is the basic assumption that there need be a "ground" to Christ's being at all. If we accept the search for such a thing, then his person is clearly the best choice. But it is precisely the theological validity of pursuing single underlying grounds that is in question here. What does one presuppose by enquiring after the *ground* of the being of Christ? I suspect this kind of ontological method is based on held-over presuppositions from the discipline's Greek founders. But I will return to this point later; a particular example of this ground-oriented tendency in Zizioulas is already to hand: "The real issue, therefore, between Antiochene and Alexandrian Christology in the Early Church must be seen against the background of the question: can human personhood be true personhood if taken *in itself*?"[42] Again, if one accepts the terms of the question then certainly the answer is "No" and the Alexandrians were right "precisely because they would not conceive of man . . . apart from communion with God."[43] But painting the Antiochenes as radical atomizers is to misconceive the real foe of Chalcedon. Humanity "*in itself* . . . apart from communion with God"—be it Adam's or Christ's—is simply an ontological impossibility, and to suppose it can function as a conceivable alternative to orthodoxy is to undermine one's own doctrine

---

41. Ibid., 109n107.

42. Zizioulas, "Human Capacity and Human Incapacity," 435n2; emphasis original.

43. Ibid.

of creation from the inside.⁴⁴ If the Antiochene-dyophysite error was to suppose that humanity and deity could be conceived in ontological isolation from one another then the Alexandrian-miaphysite counter-claim is surely right. But if the dyophysite rationale began from the possibility of genuine otherness between humanity and deity, and miaphysite thought sought to end inexorably at single ontological "grounds," though it may not be immediately clear who was right, it is at least clear why they were each sure the other was wrong.

With this we are quickly approaching a new version of the dilemma we have already met: Is Christology about the conceptual pursuit of a single ground for Christ's being and the consequent rejection of humanity "*in itself*"? Or is otherness a real ontological possibility—even at the very heart of Christian theology—in the person of Christ himself? Something like the reply Zizioulas might offer is already before us.

It could be said that the resurrection of Christ is to Christology what eschatology is to one's doctrine of creation—it is where subtle nuances come into their own—and Zizioulas's theology is a case in point.⁴⁵ If what I have suggested so far is true, and Zizioulas's Alexandrian commitments have eclipsed Christ's real humanity, we would expect as much to manifest itself in how he describes Jesus' victory over death. And such is the case: at the resurrection, Zizioulas suggests, "the real hypostasis of Christ was proved to be not the biological one, but the eschatological or Trinitarian hypostasis."⁴⁶ The resurrection is demonstrative for Zizioulas, exposing the fact that the divine hypostasis of the Son triumphed over the passions and restrictions inherent to (fallen?/"biological") humanity. And it is here, finally, that we can just touch on the themes that are most important to Zizioulas himself. For him, the resurrection inaugurates the "de-individualization" of Christ:

> If one accepts the resurrected Christ, then it is no longer possible to have an individualistic Christology. Any reference to the person of Christ will inevitably imply what we have called here a de-individualization, i.e. it will present Christ as a *person* (not as an individual), as a being whose identity is established in and

---

44. That Zizioulas accepts and indeed emphasizes the conceivability of humanity "in itself" is borne out in his exposition of the doctrine of *creatio ex nihilo*. On this, see esp. Zizioulas, "Preserving God's Creation (2)," 43.

45. "All things in Christology are judged in light of the resurrection" (Zizioulas, *Being as Communion*, 55n49).

46. Ibid.

through communion... The raised Christ is unimaginable as an individual... establishing His historical identity in and through the communion-event which is the Church.[47]

The point here is emphatically ecclesiological—Zizioulas is getting to the climax of his efforts, a doctrine of the Church—but we should not miss one of the apparently peripheral implications of this "full and organic" synthesis between Christology and pneumatology:[48] What has happened to the ascended Christ? There is, at this point, no ambiguity. For Zizioulas the ascended Christ is absolutely and ontologically co-terminus with his Church.[49] And this means something very unusual has happened to this carpenter's apprentice. The (fallen?/"biological"/"individual") humanity of Christ has been so thoroughly superseded that he can now *be* the communion of saints in the world.[50]

∼

So far we have heard Zizioulas suggest freedom from necessity is only thinkable when the Father is both the cause and principle of personal existence, and that this personal existence is made available to human creatures in the being of Christ. The nagging problem with this theologic is its tendency to elide a confessional belief in a single God with a metaphysical predilection for single grounds. All of the three dogmatic areas under consideration have been found to defer in their various ways to themes of singularity. In Zizioulas's doctrine of God we found the primordiality of the Father to be at odds with the divine communion. In his soteriology we were left wanting at the crucial distinction between creation and reconciliation; and this led to a doctrine of the person of Christ in which we found an implicit absorption of the human into the divine. If I may press the point: In each case, the pressure is toward oneness. In God, the one is the Father, in creation/salvation the one is via *theosis*, and in Christ the one is the "triune hypostasis."

---

47. Ibid., 113n116.
48. Ibid., 126.
49. Ibid., chapter 3. See, e.g., 137: "There is no Church without the community, as there is no Christ without the Body, or the 'one' without the 'many.'"
50. This is possible due to the process by which "Human nature in Christ . . . becomes a nature which can have a hypostatic catholicity in its reference to being" (Zizioulas, "Human Capacity and Human Incapacity," 435).

The dilemma is only heightened when we note the *direction* of this ontology. The three tendencies toward unity do not stand in isolation from one another; each is systematically linked to the one above it in a unilateral—or again, "vertical"—fashion. To be brash for the sake of clarity, it would appear as if creation's substantial problem is to be overcome by its absorption into the divine through the being of Christ and then finally nullified in its union with the primordial Father. The question that remains is the one we met at the crux of this chapter: "It is the question of knowing whether otherness can make sense in ontology, whether ontology can do anything more than rest on the idea of totality."[51]

It has been pointed out before that monism is the only logical alternative to Trinitarian theism and as such functions as the rubric for everything other than the gospel.[52] Zizioulas is well familiar with the longstanding allure monism has had in Christian thought and has indeed sounded his alarm loudly against certain modern versions of this ubiquitous other option.[53] The question however is whether monism needs to be rooted out from inside a Christian ontology or if it should rather be excluded as a possibility from the outset. The effect of my argument so far would suggest Zizioulas is taking the former approach. He is wrestling with a dilemma that is intrinsic *within* his theology. But what if the problem of ontological totality was rejected as an incarnational matter of fact? Or, to put this in positive terms, what if ontological otherness was simply accepted as axiomatic for Christian theology?

These issues come into sharpest contrast in the doctrine of the person of Christ. In this one person we can focus at the same time on the "totality" of Creator and creation, and consequently on the possibility of

---

51. Zizioulas, *Being as Communion*, 86; emphasis mine.

52. The point about monism or Trinitarian theism has been variously made by such diverse thinkers as S. T. Coleridge, Kierkegaard, and most recently and perhaps most poignantly for our present purposes, by Žižek: "Thus monotheism is the only logical theology of the Two . . . This is why Christianity, precisely because of the Trinity, is the only true monotheism: the lesson of the Trinity is that God fully coincides with the gap between God and man, that God *is* this gap—this is Christ, not the God of beyond separated from man by a gap . . . This fact also allows us to pin-point what is false about Levinisian-Derridean Otherness: it is the very opposite of this gap in the One, of the inherent redoubling of the One—the assertion of Otherness leads to the boring, monotonous sameness of Otherness itself" (*Puppet and the Dwarf*, 25). Cf. Zizioulas, *Being as Communion*, 106.

53. "This 'closed ontology' or monism of the Greek mind constitutes in our opinion the crucial point of conflict between Greek thought and biblical thought in the period of the Greek Fathers" (ibid., 70). Cf. references in n53.

their relation and otherness. Zizioulas's understanding of the person of Christ is crucial in this regard. He explains that in Christ we

> avoid the dilemma "divine *or* human person" as well as the curious composition "divine *and* human person," precisely because we cannot speak of the person as if it were an object—as we do about natures—but can understand it only as *schesis*: as that "schesis" (relation) which is *constitutive of a particular being* and in which or by virtue of which natures are such a particular being (or beings) and thus are at all.[54]

The difficulties arise when we come to apply this insight. For Zizioulas the "'schesis' that is constitutive of Christ's particular being is the filial relationship between the Father and the Son in the Holy Spirit in the Trinity." Zizioulas is committed to his position: "[T]he one and the same 'schesis' is constitutive of Christ's being, both with regard to his humanity and with regard to his divinity."[55] For Zizioulas there is *one* set of constitutive relations to the being of Christ: the divine. And when we recall that for Zizioulas relations are what make the person, it becomes difficult to find much of Chalcedon in such a confession. Indeed it would seem subtle Alexandrian tendencies have here become explicit dogma. The only identity-forming relation that makes up the being of Christ is his eternal divine relation with the Father in the Spirit; "and in this sense Christ's person can be called 'divine person.'"[56]

We can find the source of Zizioulas rationale for this and thereby connect it with our start:

> In order to give to the particular an ontological ultimacy or priority it is necessary to *presuppose* that being is *caused* and cannot be posited as an axiomatic or self-explicable principle. This causation must be absolute and primary in ontology, not secondary.[57]

Only divine relations—and in particular the one with the Father—are capable of connecting Christ with an absolute cause, and so it would be counter-effective for Christ to have his being in constitutive human relations. Creatures, as we have seen, have a finite beginning, and are thus bound to necessity, "individualization" and eventually dissolution into

54. Zizioulas, "Human Capacity and Human Incapacity," 436.
55. Ibid.
56. Ibid.
57. Zizioulas, "On Being a Person," 37–38.

death. Properly speaking, creaturely relations as such are misnomers. But the problem is, little if any space remains for whatever ontological value Jesus' relations with the rest of creation might have. What we are observing here are the christological implications of the essentially existentialist choices made in advance of Zizioulas's theology about Jesus. The result is a model in which the "ontological ultimacy or priority" of "the particular" presides absolutely. Any relation not grounded in the freedom of the Father—any relation not *immediately* sourced in the divine cause and unifying principle—is categorically unfree and so a-particular. The effect is a Christology that is all but displaced by its own soteriological agenda. It is as if Christ is the metaphysical conduit we observed at the end of chapter three. His "divine person" is the medium in which humanity becomes God "in and through the one filial relationship which constituted Christ's being."[58]

Two observations will prepare us for our next chapter. First, a doctrine of God in which relations of origin hold priority of place over the divine economy tends to put being and relation—existence and essence—at odds with one another at the very core of Christian ontology. And this in turn tends, secondly, to put the absolute freedom of the Creator at odds with the creaturely contingence of everything else. Zizioulas's specific route to his prioritization of particularity has meant a leaving behind of the particularities of Jesus' human life and thereby the particularities of humanity in general and indeed of the rest of creation. Such a route stands in contrast to a very different one toward a very similar end sought by our next figure, Colin Gunton.

---

58. Ibid. On this point, see Farrow's contribution to the forthcoming collection of papers for the King's College Research Institute in Systematic Theology (September 2003). This chapter is based in part on my "Looking for Personal Space."

8

COLIN GUNTON AND THE INTEGRITY OF CREATION

Christ as a Particular Human
(An Economic Concept of Mediation)[1]

> No wonder so many sermons are devoted exclusively to "spiritual" subjects.
> If one is living by the tithes of history's most destructive economy,
> then the disembodiment of the soul becomes
> the chief of worldly conveniences.
>
> —WENDELL BERRY

THAT GOD IS NOT everything and that everything is not God is an item of Christian dogma as plain as they come. Yet on the terrain of this claim can be found much if not all of Colin Gunton's wide-ranging achievements. There may be few simpler items of Christian dogma but with Gunton we shall see that there are also few less difficult to sustain in the push and shove of dogmatic commerce. That God remains distinctly himself while at the same time sustaining everything else as distinctly itself was for him

---

1. For her friendship and support, especially after her husband's death, and for access to his library, I thank Mrs. Jenny Gunton—a constitutive relation when this student almost got lost in too much space.

the most basic and therefore least appealing item of a gospel against the grain of a sin-bent creation. And the gospel was indeed good news for this theologian; that God is something other than what he has made is crucial since, according to him, this otherness is itself the possibility of God's relation to it. Simply put, "Only that which is other than something else can be related to it."[2] And it is the tension between these two—otherness and relation—that pulls together all of what I will ask of Gunton in this chapter. These are the two dynamics at the crux of his theology: "if God and world are ontologically other, some account of their relation—some theology of *mediation*—is indispensable."[3]

Quickly on the heels of Gunton's call for a theology of mediation was another for more of that about the Trinity. For Gunton, to look for one is to find the other: theology about the Trinity is theology about a God who mediates himself to his creation, and theology about a creation that is other than and related to God is theology about the triunity of this God. And it is this idea that creation can have what he called its own "relative independence" that has earned Gunton a place in this study.

> [A] distinction between God's reality and that of the world serves the world's interest. The doctrine of the eternal Trinity serves as a foundation for the relative independence and so integrity of worldly reality . . . It is because God is a communion of love prior to and in independence of the creation that he can enable the creation to be itself . . . God's personal otherness from the world is needed if there is to be a true establishing of the world in its own right, as truly worldly creation.[4]

In this chapter we have come to the place at which we do finally need to ask exactly the kind of questions that Gunton did: How can we confess a "distinction between God's reality and that of the world" and not thereby undermine the "integrity of worldly reality"? Although the attempt to have both—to affirm both God's sovereignty and the relative independence of his creation—does seem to, in Gunton's own words, "want to have one's cake and eat it too," he makes the stakes clear:

> Are the two claims incompatible? One reason for the modern world's rejection of the gospel is that is has come to the conclusion that this is indeed the case. To affirm the world, and

---

2. Gunton, *Promise of Trinitarian Theology*, 202.
3. Gunton, "Creation and Mediation," 80.
4. Gunton, *Father, Son and Holy Spirit*, 24.

especially to establish the freedom of the human agent within that world it has been thought that it is necessary to deny God.[5]

Gunton would of course differ from "the modern world" on this matter, yet not without taking seriously the breadth and depth of its rejection. That God and freedom have become alternatives today was a matter of fact for this theologian; a fact that has, as do they all, a theological explanation. And a need for an explanation for this fact brought him to the doctrine of the Trinity. For Gunton, a reply to today's anti-metaphysical critique emerges from the way the triune God is a "communion of love prior to an in independence of the creation." He comments, "the doctrine of the Trinity enables us to think both the otherness, and so relative autonomy of the world, from God, and the relatedness of the world to God."[6]

Anyone familiar with his work will know how important Irenaeus of Lyons was for Gunton in this respect, especially his use of the "two hands" metaphor for understanding the co-existence of God and world.[7] Unless the Father "holds" himself, so to speak, both to and apart from creation via his "two hands" he is bound to 'overwhelm and depersonalize" this creation. Much hangs on this. And, as we shall see, the placement of the *Father,* and not God *simpliciter,* at the top of this metaphor will require especial attention.

A further Irenaean influence will get us started: "[B]ecause it is through the economy that scripture's God makes himself known, an account of the economy is essential to any doctrine of God's being."[8] For Gunton, the divine economy is the only place to begin Christian theology:

---

5. Gunton, "Creation and Mediation," 82.

6. Gunton, *Promise of Trinitarian Theology*, 14.

7. "I do not think we can do better than to hold to Irenaeus' straightforward characterization of God's action in the world: the Father works . . . by means of his two hands, the Son and the Spirit. That is not as inappropriate to the 'spiritual' nature of God as may appear: When you use your hands . . . it is you who are doing it. That is not mere metaphor, but a metaphor that conveys a great and important Christian truth. Our God's action is not immediate but mediated action. Immediate action would overwhelm and depersonalize, if not worse" (Gunton, *Father, Son and Holy Spirit*, 80). Cf. Gunton, "God, Grace and Freedom," 127. According to such a conception, God acts mediately but directly.

8. Gunton, "Christian Dogmatic Theology," 2.7.33.2. Hereafter cited as CDT with part, chapter, paragraph and manuscript page number referring to the version in my possession.

> We must place ourselves theologically where the action is, because if we turn away from God's actual historical self-identification in Jesus, we simply manufacture an idol, or a series of idols. One central value of the doctrine of the Trinity, therefore, is that it ties our speech of God to Jesus, and thus helps to prevent the creation of idols or of any God projected conveniently to confirm our wishes or prejudices.[9]

We listen to Gunton today for many reasons and it is a comment on our times that perhaps chief among them is our need to be reminded of a redundancy: specifically Christian theology is such only when it starts with Jesus. Yet there is a complex problem with such simplicity, and it is at least as old as Chalcedon. If Jesus is somehow one with us and with God, starting from him could slip easily back round to speculation about the latter. And such indeed would be the circle were we swimming with only *one* hand. For Gunton, starting with the economy of Jesus means starting 'paradigmatically' from the Spirit:

> In sum: all divine action whether creation, salvation or final redemption is the action of God the Father; but it is all equally brought about by his two hands, the Son and the Spirit. And these hands do not act separately, like someone holding a baby in one hand and trying to bang in a nail with the other—though I fear that our talk of the Spirit might sometimes suggest that. The Spirit works through the Son, paradigmatically as Jesus' ministry was empowered by the Spirit.[10]

To begin with Jesus for Gunton is to begin from the Spirit, and only as such to truly begin with Jesus. "Christology which is abstracted from a discussion of the relation to it of pneumatology is not Christology rooted in the actual human career of the incarnate Lord."[11] Thus, in a version of his incomplete and unpublished *A Christian Dogmatic Theology*, Gunton proposed a specific plan, and we will follow it here too.

> We shall accordingly approach the doctrine of the Trinity according to the way of knowing, beginning with the economy of the Spirit and moving from there to the economy of the Son, the economy of the Father, and thence to the doctrine of the triunity of God.[12]

---

9. Gunton, *Father, Son and Holy Spirit*, 26–27.
10. Ibid., 80.
11. Gunton, *Promise of Trinitarian Theology*, xxx.
12. CDT 2.7.33.1.

Colin Gunton and the Integrity of Creation 173

And so we begin with the economy of the Spirit.

∼

There are two kinds of action Gunton most commonly attributed to the Spirit. Both center on Christ and both deserve our attention. The first is the way in which the Spirit is iconic, always pointing away from himself to Jesus: "The Spirit's characteristic action is self-effacing, because the Spirit is the one who enables people and things to be themselves through Jesus Christ."[13] At issue here is getting people and things to *be* themselves. Gunton has taken a traditionally epistemological form—we know the Son by way of the Spirit—and applied it to his specifically ontological concern. This is then set to serve his theology of mediation—in the traditional grammar, a way of having both the immanence and the transcendence of God:

> [W]hile in the economy, the Son realizes God's immanence in history—he becomes flesh, history—the Spirit, contrary to what is often assumed, *is God's transcendence*. The restriction of the Spirit to forms of immanence . . . is a symptom of what is wrong with the whole tradition . . . The Spirit may be active *within* the world, but he does not become identical with any part of the world . . . That is the function of the Son, who becomes flesh; and if without more ado we think of the Spirit also as a form of God's immanence, we may be in danger of being unable effectively to distinguish between Son and Spirit.[14]

There are two distinctions at work in this: The Spirit is neither the Son, nor is he identical with any part of the world like the Son. The first distinction—the ontological two-handedness of the Father so to speak—is the possibility of both immanence *and* transcendence. The second distinction—that the Father keeps, as it were, both hands on the world—is God's economic actuality. And the point here is the Spirit's "place." For Gunton, the Spirit's is transcendent because he is self-effacing. The Spirit directs creation not to himself, but to the immanent Son. Put differently: "If the Son is the *content* of God's redemptive movement into the world, the Spirit is its *form*, and that form is its freedom."[15] In this respect, the

---

13. CDT 2.7.34.14. This quote continues, "The Spirit is the one who enables the church to represent Jesus Christ in her teaching and to live in his way, so that there is a sense in which it is truer to say that she speaks *from* than *about* the Spirit."

14. CDT 2.7.34.15.

15. Gunton, "Spirit in the Trinity," 130.

Son may be the content of God's immanence in the world but this is only true as he is (and this is a concept to which we will need return) *enabled* to be such by the Spirit. Similarly, the Spirit may be the "form" of God's transcendence but he is only such as he is forever directing creation to the Father *through* its immanent content, the incarnate Son.

Yet such a picture—God holding creation to and apart from himself through the immanent content and transcendent form of his two hands— is an image too static and spatial to be left alone. And so we come to the second kind of action Gunton typically attributes to the Spirit: "Where the Spirit is, there do creatures *become* that which God created them to be."[16] Thus:

> The Spirit is God's eschatological transcendence, his futurity, as it is sometimes expressed. He is God present to the world as its liberating other, bringing it to the destiny determined by the Father, made actual, realized, in the Son.[17]

Now we can see that the Spirit is God creating according to a particular intention; he is God's *eschatological* transcendence. Following Basil, and likely Barth and Jenson, Gunton understood the Spirit to be what the former called the "perfecting cause" of creation, "the one who directs the creatures to where the creator wishes them to go, to their destiny as creatures."[18] It would be difficult to overstate the significance of this claim for Gunton's work. Everything about his doctrine of creation hinges on the way in which everything that God has made is intended to "go somewhere"; creation is not simply the finished work of an absent watchmaker but is somehow a project in progress.

> [O]ur being in time is not a defect of being, but part of its goodness . . . human life is eschatological *in its structuring:* it is created with a view to an end that is more than replicating its beginning, because it is given *to be perfected.* That is to say, it reaches its perfection only at its end and so needs time to become what it truly is.[19]

---

16. Ibid.; emphasis added.
17. Ibid.
18. Gunton, *Father, Son and Holy Spirit*, 81.
19. Ibid., 136.

Contrary to what we have seen from the Patristic era, this need for time is not a problem: "Creation's temporality is its glory."[20] Much of the argument in Gunton's acclaimed *The One, the Three and the Many* arises from this idea.[21] Where God and creation were held by Greek and Enlightenment theology at static odds with one another, there followed an unavoidable pinch on human freedom, an ontological opposition between the "One" and the "many." Gunton's reply to such a situation relied on a recovery of the dynamism available from within the doctrine of the Trinity, and in particular on the way this kind of dynamism opens the possibility of conceiving God's creative participation in time. As Gunton sees it, hesitation here—or any outright belief in a timeless God or instantaneous view of creation—would introduce "a divorce between God's creating action, which is timeless and his saving action which takes time."[22] Gunton's tone in the debate about God's relation to time was similar to that in one of his favorite quotes from Bruce McCormack: "[I]f God does something in Christ then it is obvious that he can do it."[23] For Gunton, the matter was simple: in Christ we see that God "takes time" to save his creatures and since this saving is what our creating has in fact entailed, in Christ we also see that God "takes time" to create us.

This "taking time" is a specifically pneumatological dynamic since God creates and saves by opening and reopening his eschatological intentions. The position of the Spirit is specifically *transcendent* here insofar as these eschatological intentions are not yet fully realized. And yet a transcendent and atemporal divine position for the Spirit is far too deistic an image since it is talk of just one hand. God is also immanent and temporal by the Spirit's self-effacing focus, Christ.

With both hands firmly in place, Gunton was able to affirm a divine immanence in history without identifying God *with* history. The result is an alternative to the modern idolatry of progress. By the Spirit, God is bringing the creation into a future that is more than simply an immanent unfolding of itself. We might say (with respect to the Apostle), *when the Spirit of the Lord is, there is future*. This brings the two characteristic

---

20. "There is nothing intrinsically fallen about time in itself . . . Creation's temporality is its glory . . . It is not time that is the problem, but the fact that those who live in it find themselves beset by sin, suffering and evil . . . The problem with time is what happens in it" (ibid., 140).

21. See also Gunton, "God and Freedom," 119–33.

22. Gunton, *Father, Son and Holy Spirit*, 137.

23. McCormack, "For Us and for Our Salvation," 33.

actions of the Spirit conceptually together. The eschatologically transcendent Spirit directs creation to its intended end, and, like everything else about creation, the "end" to which the self-effacing Spirit brings us is the same Christ to whom he has brought us all along. Thus we enter the second movement of Gunton's dogmatic composition, Christology.

～

For Gunton, if you want to explain the humanity of the Son, the best thing to do is talk about the Spirit. According to him, humanity is a particular form of relation to God:

> [W]e must conceive the Spirit as the one who indeed maintains the Son in truth as his being the only one who, after the Fall, is enabled to be in true relation to God the Father and so truly human.[24]

To be human—"truly human"—is to be enabled by the Spirit to obey the Father, and so to suggest the Son is really human is to make a pneumatological claim: "[T]he whole of Jesus' authentically human life is made what it uniquely is through the action of the Spirit."[25] Having made this clear enough, Gunton goes on to introduce another big idea: "at the incarnation the eternal Son took to himself the fallen flesh that all human beings share." Gunton continues,

> [This] is not, of course, to teach the sinfulness of Christ, but to give an adequate account of the representative nature of his humanity. If salvation is really to be communicated to us, then our flesh must be healed . . . Our sinfulness, then, is not conceived *mathematically* as the accumulation of wrong acts, but *relationally* as that which universally qualifies human existence in the flesh. If so, then, as the anti-Apollinarian theologians had argued, precisely *that* fallen flesh must be assumed by the saviour.[26]

For Gunton the dictum that "the unassumed is the unhealed" applies even to peccability. The "representative nature" of Jesus' humanity is due neither to the fact that Jesus is also divine—his especial humanness needs

---

24. Gunton, "And in One Lord, Jesus Christ," 46, citing Rahner, *Trinity*.

25. Gunton, *Father, Son and Holy Spirit*, 157.

26. Ibid., 192, citing Edward Irving. Cf. Gunton, "Two Dogmas Revisited," with citations of John Owen, 375n20.

to be due to something about his humanity[27]—nor can Christ's headship be contingent on an unfallen caliber of his flesh, since this too would not just distinguish Jesus from other humans but categorically separate him from us. Gunton's start in this theological direction came in a hybrid of insights borrowed from John Owen, Edward Irving and Thomas Smail: if Jesus is the Spirit enabling the Son to live a fully human relation to the Father then "[h]e was sinless because he was enabled not to sin by the Spirit who maintained him in truth before the Father."[28] Gunton explains with a dig at his favorite foil, Augustine:

> [Jesus's] human persona must be, like ours, liable to sin. That it was so without falling was due to the action of the Holy Spirit . . . The Spirit, therefore, is not conceived, as tends to be the case with Augustine, as the immanent possession of Jesus, but as God's free and lifegiving activity towards the world as he maintains and empowers the human activity of the incarnate Son.[29]

This critique of Augustine is indeed critical.[30] The Spirit can no more be an "immanent possession" of Jesus than he could be immanent within the creation at all. As God's eschatological transcendence the Spirit is the one who opens to Jesus the particular future his obedience to the Father makes possible. In this way God's hands are, so to speak, no longer tied. The Spirit is here "free and lifegiving," and this mobility finds its "paradigmatic" expression in the resurrection: "The Lord, [the Spirit] the giver of life, transforms the body of Jesus so that it may partake of the life of the age to come, the first-born of the new creation."[31] For Gunton, therefore, the Spirit enables Jesus to transcend both the constraints of his fallen flesh and the constraints of his death, and so partake of eschatological life. Even the resurrection of Christ, as any of his acts, is neither accom-

---

27. On this point, see Gunton, "And in One Lord," 40ff.

28. CDT 1.1.7.8, citing Smail. See Smail, "Holy Trinity," 63–96.

29. Gunton, "Spirit in the Trinity," 127.

30. "It is in the incarnation and particularly in relation to the humanity of Christ in general that we discern a unique particularizing of the activity of the Spirit as the lifegiving power of God in and towards his creation . . . [following Augustine's contention that Jesus could not have received the Spirit at his baptism *because he already had it,* in the West] there has always been a tendency to minimize the particularities, in contrast to assertions of a general presence, of the Spirit's action in relation to Jesus. The outcome has been a corresponding stress on the divinity at the expense of the humanity of Christ, along with developments emphasizing the virginal—and eventually immaculate—conception of Jesus as the real source of his sinless humanity" (ibid., 126).

31. Ibid., 127.

plished by the Son alone nor by a somehow immanent Spirit behind him. Instead, the resurrection is an event in the human life of the incarnate Son that Gunton insists we understand *humanly*, as a straightforward result of this human's particular relation to the Father as it is mediated by the Spirit.[32]

Gunton's Christology will not appeal to Jesus' special case ontology to account for the remarkable in his life. The fact that this human is also divine is just that, a matter of fact; it is not a kind of hermeneutical ace up the sleeve to explain certain episodes in his historical career.

> [N]one of Jesus' acts is, on its own, unparalleled . . . In a certain sense even miracles belong among the "ordinary" . . . What is unique is that through this particular combination of finite historical particulars God achieved the salvation of his world.[33]

For Gunton, Jesus is an (indeed *the*) ordinary human being. And if that way of putting it whiffs of Schleiermacher, the irony signals the revolutionary nature of Gunton's thought. Simply put, Jesus must be ordinary because it is ordinary people that need saving. If Apollinarius represents one of the tradition's failures to grasp mediation, Gunton is saying that the "unparalleled" is the unhealed. As for the converse truth—the matter of fact divinity of this ordinary human—this too is commandeered to serve Gunton's doctrine of creation:

> [N]ot the human race as a whole but Jesus Christ "is the image of the invisible God" . . . As Pannenberg has pointed out, when it is used of Jesus, it implies that he is not only the one of whom we are copies—the prototype—but also the one who actualizes the true human destiny by what he achieves.[34]

Now we see that Christ is not just ordinary like Adam but also extraordinary as the one who is already what Adam was intended to become. Put in Gunton's terms: the incarnate Son is immanent within history as the human "content" according to which the eschatologically transcendent Spirit "forms" us. He is humanity's type as the first (and so far only) one to have been enabled by the Spirit to realize our "true human destiny." Such is the fullness of the christological intersection of

---

32. Gunton, *Father, Son and Holy Spirit*, 153.

33. Ibid., 158–59.

34. Gunton, *Promise of Trinitarian Theology*, 186, citing Pannenberg, *Systematic Theology*, 2:215–17.

soteriology and the doctrine of creation in Gunton's thought. And, once again, the Spirit is the one who keeps things moving:

> [O]nce the Son is incarnate, it is the Spirit and not the Word—for he is become fully human while remaining the eternal Son—who provides the so to speak motive power behind Jesus' actions.[35]

This is a remarkable claim. There is "space" enough for Jesus to be truly human since it is neither "the Word"—a *logos asarkos* behind Jesus—that is responsible for the extraordinary in the life of Christ nor even a pneumatic power possessed by him; everything is done by the incarnate Son *as human*. That the theological traffic here is about both Christ and creation signals the fact that Gunton is indeed offering some new direction. And if Apollinarius was a wrong turn then the tradition's response to him was a bottleneck: Gunton also rejected the *communicatio idiomatum*. He explains why with John Owen:

> One implication of this [account of the human Christ] is an assertion of the hypostatic union which does not entail "a transfusion of the properties of one nature into the other, nor real physical communication of divine essential excellencies unto the humanity." The humanity remains authentically human and is not subverted by the immanently operating Word, because he *is*, to repeat, that Word become human. Wherein, then, consists Jesus' capacity to do the word of God? "The Holy Ghost . . . the *immediate, peculiar, efficient* cause of all external divine operations."[36]

Gunton clearly saw the pneumatology he received from Owen and others as an *alternative* to various *communicatio*-Christologies.[37] Abstractions about ontological transfusions only appeal when the Spirit is an afterthought.

The result is what we might tentatively call a post-metaphysical Christology. The incarnate Son is human in the same way as, more or less, everyone else. In this respect Gunton may indeed have much to offer whatever is beyond the current anti-metaphysical critique. But that

---

35. CDT 1.1.7.6.

36. Ibid.

37. "[T]he communion of attributes is more of a problem than a solution, for it inevitably tends towards the truncation of the human story" (CDT 2.7.32.12).

assessment is not entirely accurate. To explain why, I need to proceed further.

⁓

Although according to Gunton's own scheme we ought move now to his patrology, we are not yet—for reasons that will soon become clear—ready for that. Gunton's concern for the authentic humanity of Christ is an instance of his wider concern for the ontological integrity of creation as a whole; the movement from the economy of the Son to the Trinity has as its correlative a movement from Christ to creation. The latter move does not give us different questions, however. Instead, it gives us different ways of asking the same ones. And when we recall the centrality of the concept of mediation for Gunton we have the key for understanding the connection between the two: just as we heard worry about an "overwhelming" or "subversion" of the humanity of Christ without a mediating Spirit, so now we hear Gunton similarly work to establish sufficient "space" for creation. And, as we saw at the outset, it is this need for creation's ontological space that leads into Gunton's theology proper: "Because God lives in a dynamic order of Trinitarian space, he is able to create a world that has space to be the world."[38]

There are two sides to this claim. The first concerns God's "space" and the second is about the effects of this space on that of creation. In the former, God has personal space because he is triune:

> What flows from the conception of God as three persons in communion, related but distinct? First, there is something of the space we have been seeking. We have a conception of *personal space*: the space in which three persons are for and from each other in their otherness. They thus confer particularity upon and receive it from one another. That giving of particularity is very important: it is a matter of space to be. Father, Son and Spirit through the shape—the *taxis*—of their inseparable relatedness confer particularity and freedom on each other. That is their personal being.[39]

---

38. Gunton, "Creation and Mediation," 88. This immediately follows a quotation from Barth: "God is spatial as the One who loves in freedom, and therefore as Himself . . . God possesses His space. He is in Himself as in a space. He creates space" (*CD* 2/1:470).

39. Gunton, *Promise of Trinitarian Theology*, 110.

Here the centrality of the concept of particularity identifies Gunton's thought like a theological moniker.[40] Unless the Father, Son, and Spirit are particularly themselves—unless they are other than one another—there is no way to understand their relation to one another and so no way to affirm the unity of God. The particularity of the three is the 'personal being' of the one. And this begins to explain why Gunton could not accept the now vogue attempts to reify relation:

> For Basil the persons are not relations; rather, persons are constituted by their relations to one another . . . Without a distinction between persons—as the ones who are each particularly what they are by virtue of their relations (*scheseis*) to one another—and the relations between them, the danger is that their particularity will be lost, as has been the case notoriously in the West with its excessive stress on the principle that the acts of God *ad extra* are undivided.[41]

Without a distinction between the concepts of relation and person the theologian has no way to distinguish between the persons themselves. Gunton's caution about the supposed indivisibility of God's acts *ad extra* gets us to the point: "If all divine actions are actions of the one God, so that the actions of the Trinity towards the world are undivided in an absolute sense, the persons are irrelevant for thought, and a kind of monism results."[42] Although he accepted the principle's value as a barrier against Tritheism,[43] he saw in its overuse a more subtle and prevalent tendency toward the opposite extreme. Simply put, when theology reserves any "undivided-in-an-absolute-sense" notion of God it thereby loses the possibility for particularity in *any* sense "and a kind of monism results." Here is Gunton's nemesis: it is a single-continuum metaphysic in which God and not-God are relative extremes in the same ontological spectrum. And this gets us to his second sense of theological "space": There is space

---

40. Thus Christoph Schwöbel's eulogy: "If God is not simply 'a sea of essence, infinite and unseen' but first of all this particular God, the Father, the Son and the Spirit . . . the particular must have paramount significance in theology . . . If we still followed the ancient custom of venerating the great doctors of the church by a particular title, Colin Gunton would have to be the *doctor particularis*, the teacher of the significance of the particular," King's College Chapel, September 2003, unpublished manuscript, 2.

41. Gunton, *Father, Son and Holy Spirit*, 46.

42. Gunton, *Promise of Trinitarian Theology*, 57.

43. Ibid., 198.

between the divine persons and thereby there is some too for the relation and otherness of God and creation.

Gunton's thinking on this matter began to flourish when he came to grips with S.T. Coleridge:

> [T]he only real alternative to Christianity is pantheism, [this is] Coleridge's view . . . Atheism and deistic mechanism are, in effect, identical with pantheism, for all of them swallow up the many into the one, and so turn the many into mere functions of the one. There is, that is to say, no basis in any such unitary conception of God for freedom because there is in it no space between God and the world.[44]

Coleridge is notoriously arcane,[45] but Gunton found in his thought exactly the scheme he needed to think clearly about "space between."[46] He continues, "the doctrine of the Trinity allows for such space because it enables us to conceive the world as other than God while yet in relation to God."[47] And it is this "other than . . . yet in relation to" that signals the parallel between his doctrine of God and his doctrine of creation.

Let me try to clarify the point. Gunton's concern for space between the divine persons and between God and the world is for the possibility of both relation (->) and otherness (<-). From here the grammar deteriorates somewhat since without space enough for these two dynamics to occur together (<=>), "relation" is not possible. The language is awkward because "relation" is used to describe both the whole dynamic (<=>) and one of the two within it (->). But there is another word for the

---

44. Gunton, "Immanence and Otherness," 23.

45. For the best available theological introduction to this, and the likely source of Gunton's own interest in Coleridge as a theologian, see Hardy, "Coleridge on the Trinity." See also McFarland, *Coleridge and the Pantheist Tradition*, esp. 268ff.

46. Summarizing Coleridge on the way to his own thought, Gunton explains, "According to the Phoenician scheme, there is no space between God and the world, and so no human freedom. According to the kind of Hellenism we have viewed, the space is placed in the wrong place: between mind and matter, so that there is too little space between the human mind and God, too much between one person and another: space is here at the expense of relation. In the third, Hebrew, scheme, their is space, because of the freedom of the immutable God to create *ex nihilo* but, we need more than space. Indeed, from one point of view, space is the problem: individualism is the view of the human person which holds that there is so much space between people that they can in no sense participate in each other's being. There is clearly space and space, and our requirement now is to find a conception which is correlative with that of relation" (*Promise of Trinitarian Theology*, 109).

47. Gunton, "Immanence and Otherness," 23.

whole-dynamic-relation (<=>), and although Gunton does not himself use it for describing the triune communion, it is what we have heard him call *mediation* in his doctrine of creation.[48] I suggest that communion and mediation are functionally the same concept for Gunton. Communion is about the otherness-in-relation of the three divine persons and mediation is about the otherness-in-relation of God and creation. Both describe the way God confers particularity, freedom and space to be, either within the triune life of Father, Son, and Holy Spirit or through the mediatorial economy of Jesus and the Spirit in creation. In this sense, mediation is not just something that God does as the need arises when he creates something, it is a way of describing the event that he *is*.

~

Such a close call between the being and act of God would not sit well with Gunton however, and it signals a shift in his thought that brings us now to his patrology. If communion and mediation are theologically synonymous, it is only because both are attempts to secure their respective forms of particularity.

In Gunton's doctrine of God the concept of particularity functions explicitly: it is what keeps the Christian theologian from talk of an absolute monotheos. In his doctrine of creation, however, it is less explicit—appearing as "relative independence" or *Selbständigkeit*.[49] Nevertheless, its function is the same, here keeping us from the correlative collapse into pantheism.

Before particularity was paramount for Gunton, the idea of communion held pride of place in his thinking. What we need see now is the way these two key concepts appear to have slipped, at the mature end of his career, into a kind of loose opposition. Whereas his earlier and perhaps less metaphysically ambitious thought seemed to allow him to hold particularity and communion in a sort of sustainable mutuality, this was a mutuality with tensions which it would seem he later chose to resolve. This produced a crucial shift in his thought.

Before the "shift," Gunton would commonly say things like,

---

48. He does, however, come close: "To be a person is to be constituted in particularity and—to be given space to be—by others in community. *Otherness* and *relation* continue to be the two central and polar concepts here. Only where they are given due stress is personhood fully enabled" (Gunton, *Promise of Trinitarian Theology*, 114).

49. On this, see Gunton, "Creation and Mediation," 90.

> God *is* no more than what Father, Son and Spirit give to and receive from each other in the inseparable communion that is the outcome of their love. Communion is the *meaning* of the word: there is no "being" of God other than this dynamic of persons in relation.[50]

But then, seven years later,[51] we hear something very different: "the personal should be primordial, and it follows that any concept like 'being' or 'communion' which is secondary to the persons should not usurp their pride of place."[52] This, we should note, was not a minor change for Gunton. His most influential work, for example, hinges on the finality of communion in God:

> The theology of God conceived to exist in the interrelationship of persons in which neither the one nor the many has priority over the other provides an alternative to the two poles of modern political thought, individualism, which elevates the many over the one, and collectivism, which does the reverse.[53]

There came a time when the implied apophasis in this "neither the one nor the many" would not suffice for Gunton.[54] And although we will find pressures in his own thinking that brought him to this change of course, it did not arise without external influence. Gunton found himself between two of his most respected theological interlocutors, T. F. Torrance and John Zizioulas:

---

50. Gunton, *Promise of Trinitarian Theology*, 10.

51. As with any dynamic thinker, the "shift" in Gunton's thought is not a clean cut. Even in 1988 we had a foretaste of his later position: "[I]f something other than the Father is the ontological foundation of the being of God, the world and everything in it derives from what is fundamentally impersonal. What under (or over) lies is some*thing* other than the God made known in the economy . . . But if the Father is not the substratum of the Godhead, what is?" (ibid., 54)

52. Gunton, "Persons and Particularity," 3.

53. Gunton, *Promise of Trinitarian Theology*, 171. Thus, "[M]odernity cannot do justice to the being of the human person because it has an impoverished theology. Oscillating between collectivism and individualism—which represent ultimately one and the same failure—it calls desperately for an understanding of the person not as *a relation*, but at one who has his or her being *in relation to* others. This Trinitarian and *ethical* insight flows from a theology of the Trinity in which both the one and the many are given due and equal weight" (Gunton, *Father, Son and Holy Spirit*, 53). At both points, he is citing his thesis in *One, the Three and the Many*.

54. Apophatic theology was always suspect for Gunton, but, as we shall see, this was not the rationale for his change of mind on this point.

> Now, I do not wish to adjudicate here on the dispute between, on the one hand, John Zizioulas' view that the only way of maintaining a truly personal basis for reality is by making the Father the source of all things, especially the source or *aitia* of the triune communion; and, on the other, Torrance's view that in some way or other we must understand the triune communion as a whole to be the metaphysical source of unity.[55]

Here Gunton is declining the opportunity to adjudicate a dispute, the central concern in which had to do with *source*. For Zizioulas, as we have seen, the Father must be this or else a "dead ousianic tautology" smothers freedom from the top down.[56] For T. F.—and more recently and pointedly Alan—Torrance, if one of the Trinity is somehow prior to the other two than the identification of being and communion unravels from the inside out.[57] There was a time in Gunton's career when he quite literally sat as a mediator between these two positions and we could say that his own thought on this point follows a movement from Torrance's side of the table to Zizioulas's. It is clear that he once sat firmly *across* from Zizioulas:

> Whence does this communion derive? According to Zizioulas, it derives from the Father, who is to be conceived as the cause of the communion in the Trinity. While such a claim preserves the due priority of the Father in the Godhead, I do not believe that it allows for an adequate theology of the mutual constitution of Father, Son and Spirit.[58]

This is Gunton in polite disagreement. He continues by offering his own view:

> Should it not rather be said that communion is a function of—a way of characterizing—the relations of all three, just as freedom

---

55. Gunton, *Father, Son and Holy Spirit*, 55. A problem already on his mind when he wrote the second introduction to his re-published *The Promise of Trinitarian Theology*, "[T]he chief [problem] for our purposes concerns whether Zizioulas' description of the Father as the cause of the Trinity endangers his own identification of being and communion" (xxiii).

56. Zizioulas, "The Doctrine of God the Trinity Today," 25.

57. "An *a posteriori* ontology of intra-divine communion risks being subsumed by a cosmological category of causality" (A. Torrance, *Persons in Communion* 291).

58. Gunton, *Promise of Trinitarian Theology*, 196.

is to be conceived as a relation between things, rather than as some contentless absolute?[59]

This reference to "all three" is classic Gunton. Crucial here is his implicit critique of Zizioulas' view of freedom as a "contentless absolute." At this point, he not only refused to look for a single cause of divine unity but found in the plurality of the triune communion a constructive rubric for his theology of mediation. Gunton continues in this important passage by going on to locate the "cause" of the divine communion:

> Whatever the priority of the Father, it must not be conceived in such a way as to detract from the fact that *all three persons are together the cause of the communion in which they exist* in relations of mutual and reciprocal constitution . . . Beyond this, it would be better to preserve an element of reserve, and to say that God's unknowableness prevents us from further enquiry into the *cause* of his being who and what he is.[60]

Here Gunton does not accept the pursuit of a divine "cause" behind the three persons and is instead content with "an element of reserve." Then, several years after this reserve, in a manuscript to his unpublished *Dogmatics*, he asks a question that, on its face at least, would appear to overstep it: "[I]f the unity of God is not located in a single substance in which the persons inhere, but in three persons perichoretically united, what is the principle of their oneness?"[61]

That Gunton would even ask for such a thing—a "principle" of God's oneness—is evidence of his high regard for Zizioulas's theology. And as with anything theological, more is decided in the framing of the question than in its answering. Gunton is searching for something, and he is now looking East. And though the turn may have been charted by Zizioulas, it was Gunton's own pursuit of particularity that fueled it:

> Being may indeed be understood in terms of communion, but there is for Zizioulas no communion that is not grounded in the particular. If it is not, it will be based in some general theory of being, and that is the beginning of the end, for where the particular person is not central, the person is in danger of being submerged into the abstract and impersonal.[62]

59. Ibid.
60. Ibid.; emphasis added.
61. CDT 2.7.31.1
62. Gunton, "Persons and Particularity," 1.

Now we are told that communion is no longer a "way of characterizing the relations of all three" but is something that needs to be "grounded in the particular." Thus, he made a choice between Torrance and Zizioulas, and particularity was the deciding feature:

> T. F. Torrance's conception of the unity of God . . . seems so to stress the utter equality of the persons that their particularity is submerged in a dangerously telescoped conception of their unity. To place the concept of being in the center . . . is to endanger the particularity of the persons.[63]

And, having made his choice, Gunton does follow through with his new orientation:

> Whatever we do we must not suggest that "being" unifies. The Father unifies the Godhead by virtue of the fact that he is Father of the Son and breather of the Spirit, and is therefore eternally the "cause" of the being of the Son and the Spirit.[64]

With the idea that the Father is somehow the "cause" of the other two persons of the Trinity we have Gunton's shift in full relief. Originally, it was "The priority of the Father is not ontological but economic,"[65] but later, in one of his last works, "Ontologically speaking . . . the Father is prior."[66] We should recognize that the idea that the Father ought to be understood as ontologically causative would not have been accepted lightly by Gunton, if for no other reason than it seems, on first impression at least, to leave him liable to the very indictment he so often laid at the feet of Augustine: "The charge against Augustine and many of his Western successors is that . . . he allowed the insidious return of Hellenism in which being is not communion, but something underlying it."[67]

And so a question presents itself: What else is the Father as cause of the Son and the Spirit but "something"—indeed some*one*—"underlying" the triune communion? Augustine aside, such was indeed the problem in Zizioulas's theology.[68] Is it Gunton's problem too?

~

63. CDT 2.7.31.1.
64. CDT 2.7.31.3.
65. Gunton, *Promise of Trinitarian Theology*, 197.
66. CDT 1.Preface.5.1.
67. Gunton, *Promise of Trinitarian Theology*, 10.
68. Or so I suggest in "Looking for Personal."

There was a time in Gunton's thought when we heard much more of Coleridge than Zizioulas, more about triune "space to be" than the causative particularity of the Father. And if Gunton had simply traded space for particularity, we would need to ask whether the identification of the Father as cause did not put *too much* space between him and the Son and the Spirit. Such a move would only secure the Father's particularity at the expense of theirs. But such a question would miss the significance of other concurrent developments in Gunton's thought.

We recall his knack for pneumatology. Unlike Zizioulas, Gunton has a pneumatological route back, so to speak, from the primordiality of the Father.

> Augustine called the Spirit the bond of love between the Father and the Son, but this is in danger of leading us to think of God as a kind of self-enclosed circle. The medieval, Richard of St Victor, provided the basis of a correction by making it possible to suggest that the Spirit is the focus of a love beyond the duality of Father and Son, of a love outwards to the other. The Spirit's distinctive inner-Trinitarian being is oriented not on inwardness, but on otherness: as perfecter both of the eternal divine communion—in which there is real distinction, *otherness*—and of God's love for the *other* in creation and redemption.[69]

This is the inner-triune corollary to the Spirit's economic action as God's "eschatological transcendence." Not only does the Spirit enable creation to live freely into its intended future, so also does he "free" the Father and the Son for a love that would without him be a static duality. Gunton is saying that the Spirit opens the triune life within God *and* outwards to creation. And, we might say, so too does the Spirit open new

---

69. Gunton, *Father, Son and Holy Spirit*, 86. Thus, prior to the shift we are observing, "Similarly, because the Holy Spirit is the agent of the Father's perfecting and transforming work as it is realized by relating the creation to God through Jesus Christ, it follows that we can cautiously draw conclusions from the Spirit's perfecting work to a speculation that he may, similarly, perfect the being of God, in a way parallel to, but distinctly different from, Augustine's teaching that the Spirit is the bond of love between Father and Son" (Gunton, *The Promise of Trinitarian Theology*, xxvii). Similarly, citing his paper in the same collection at 105ff.: "[This] might be rather near to Augustine's doctrine of the Spirit as the bond of love, but I hope that it says more than that, particularly about the Spirit's being the focus of God's movement outwards. The Trinity locked up in itself, to use Rahner's characterization of much post-Augustinian trinitarianism, by conceiving the Spirit as the closure of an inwards-turning circle, militates against a link between the Spirit's being in eternity and his action in the world" (Gunton, "And in One Lord," 46).

possibilities for Gunton's theology. Where Zizioulas's ontology tends to move unilaterally upward into the Father,[70] Gunton's does not because for him it is the Spirit who "completes" the divine being:

> [T]he Spirit is the perfecting cause not only of the creation, but also of the being of God . . . the Spirit perfects the divine and holy Trinity. As the one who "completes," the Spirit does indeed establish God's aseity, his utter self-sufficiency.[71]

This is a crucial move. Were the Father simply the "cause" of the Son and the Spirit in a kind of Hellenic-absolute sense, we would be hard-pressed to distinguish belief in this God from the fount-of-being theisms of Irenaeus' opponents. But by suggesting that it is the Spirit (and not the Father) who is finally responsible for God's aseity—for "completing" the divine life—Gunton has developed a doctrine of God that looks less like the top portion of a vertical continuum and more like an open dynamic of personal love. What we have here is a revised—or perhaps, "completed"—version of his use of the concept of perichoresis. Whereas the idea of divine interpenetration was formerly for him a kind of general description for the constitutive function of triune communion, it is here given a specific shape.[72] Now we see that the Father "causes" and the Spirit "completes" the divine life.

And here we must note the likely influence of Robert Jenson on his protégé. Yet Gunton's view of the Spirit's "futurity" is unlike similar theology from Jenson in at least one important respect: Gunton's version of

---

70. Although Gunton does indeed find occasion to critique the Western *use* of the *filoque*, his affinity for Zizioulas's theology did not extend to abandoning this classic bone of contention altogether. The remaining differences between the two at this point are crucial to the possibilities we are tracking here; there are ones available for Gunton and unavailable—or unlikely—for Zizioulas.

71. CDT 2.7.31.3.

72. Gunton's different answers to the question of what perichoresis means for the divine life is another way of representing the "shift" in his thought. Whereas he once said things like, "[T]he concept [perichoresis] is a way of showing the ontological interdependence and reciprocity of the three persons of the Trinity: . . . so that for God to be did not involve an absolute simplicity but *a unity deriving from a dynamic of plurality* of persons" (*The One the Three and the Many*, 152, emphasis added), he later came to say that "perichoresis cannot *do* anything as an abstraction, because it is the *outcome* of the relations of the persons, not their cause" (CDT 2.7.31.2; emphasis is Gunton's); and, "It [*sic*] its place it [the concept of perichoresis] serves to demonstrate the character of personal being, not to constitute it" (CDT 2.7.31.3).

this kind of speculation about the Trinity is bound especially close to the divine economy:

> We should be careful of mere projection, but we can at least ask whether it is right to suggest that because the Spirit is the agent of the begetting of Jesus in the womb of Mary, he is also the agent of his eternal begottenness. The Son is the kind of eternal Son that he is by virtue of the way . . . in which he is related to the Father in the Spirit, in the eternal triune love.[73]

As the agent of the Son's begottenness—both economic and eternal—the Spirit is the divine person who mediates the triune love of Father and Son. Without such an agent in the Trinity, God would be an immediate dyad of Father and Son, and—with a nod to Coleridge—we can suggest that for Gunton such a thing would be ontologically nothing more than a homogeneous *monotheos*. And herein lies the crucial contrast between Jenson and Gunton. Where the Spirit for Jenson tends to function like an End in himself, for Gunton the Spirit's role is always about relation *and* otherness. In this respect Gunton's understanding of the triunity of God is more like what we observed in Calvin and is similar even to the early Pannenberg, although there is also an important difference here, too. The likeness is in the importance of the Son's real distinction from the Father, the difference is in the identity of the one responsible for this distinction.[74] For Gunton it is the *Spirit* and not the Son who is the "agent of the Son's eternal begotteness," completing the causal initiative of the Father and thereby making God an *a se* communion of love. This achieves what Calvin and Pannenberg sought—it finds in the triune being the christological possibility of creation's otherness—but, unlike Pannenberg, Gunton manages to avoid placing the initiative for such a crucial distinction on the one being distinguished. Where Calvin and Pannenberg may be leaning on voluntaristic or neo-Hegelian categories, Gunton names the Spirit as the one responsible for the Son's eternal begottenness and so draws plainly from the divine economy.[75]

---

73. Gunton, "And in One Lord," 46.

74. For Pannenberg's concept of the "self-distinction of the Son from the Father," see *Systematic Theology*, 1:319ff.

75. Gunton makes the point best himself: "Pannenberg's emphasis upon the Son's self-distinction . . . does not in itself guarantee the ontological distinctness of creation, and might indeed endanger it. If the Father is not to be too much all in all, an adequate doctrine of creation requires to stress not only the Son as the focus of the creation's coherence but also the Spirit as the mediator of particularity and difference" (From a

Having dabbled in the heights we can now return to Jesus, noting that the proximity of Christology and the theology of creation is precisely the point of all this. For Gunton, a doctrine of Christ with ample space for the humanity of Jesus has as its correlative a doctrine of creation with ample space for the contingency of everything else. And so we might say—with respect again to the Apostle—there is indeed "one mediator between God and humanity," *the one enabled to be fully human by the Spirit* "the man Christ Jesus." With anything less than such a deliberately two-handed Christology, the mediation between God and world collapses.

> The danger here is that without a strong pneumatology the outcome will be the excessive separation of God and the world, corresponding to Nestorianism, that in fact became deism.[76]

A line between Antioch and the Enlightenment is a classic Gunton broad stroke and its historical validity need not occupy us. Instead we should notice the theological symmetry between an unmediated *logos:sarx* "conjunction" in Nestorianism and an unmediated Creator:creation duality in deism. Both establish an otherness by juxtaposing the divine and the contingent but neither can truly relate them. Such a failure is mitigated according to Gunton not by, as we have seen, Cyril's use of the *communicatio*, but by what he calls a "strong pneumatology." Gunton continues by typifying the division we have charted between Alexandria and Antioch in terms of their modern equivalents in, respectively, Lutheran and Reformed Christologies:

> One can be overschematic, but perhaps it is not too much of a simplification to say that each tendency seeks to conceive the relation-in-otherness of God and the world, the first stressing the relation, the second the otherness—again, in parallel with their corresponding Christological emphases.[77]

If such a scheme is even loosely allowable—that Antioch is reborn in Reformed theology and Alexandria in Lutheran—we have a recapitulation in this of all that we have been through together. There appears

---

review by Gunton of the second volume of Pannenberg's *Sytematic Theology*, a review shared with and unhappily received by the work's author and so, to my knowledge, left unpublished. This is from p. 2 of a typescript given to me in 1999).

76. Ibid., 91.

77. Ibid.

a broad line from Irenaeus through Cyril and Philoponus to Zizioulas, on the one hand, or from the same start through Luther to Jenson, on the other. The other possibility is another line from Irenaeus to a certain version of Nestorius, through Calvin, and on to Gunton. These are lines that mark out the bounds of this study and so ones that bring us right to the heart of Gunton's "overschematic" but helpful distinction: there are those theologies that tend to stress relation, and there are those which tend to stress otherness. What we are seeking in this final chapter is a way of having the proverbial cake and eating it too. We seek "the relation-in-otherness of God and the world," and so a way of locating this mediation of Creator and creation in its own christological hub.

∽

For Gunton, what the theologian does in her Christology she will do in her doctrine of creation: '. . . differences between Christologies generate differences in the conception of the mediation of creation.'[78] And these are differences which came for him into sharpest relief in his ongoing dialogue with Jenson. Despite their recent efforts at a Lutheran-Reformed rapprochement, the two sustained important differences in their respective doctrines of Christ. And, as we might expect, these differences came to a point over the question of a *logos asarkos*. In their co-authored paper, *The Logos Ensarkos and Reason*, Jenson and Gunton had successfully negotiated the terms of the dilemma:

> We both can begin with the strange logic of a passage in Irenaeus: "[God's] only begotten Word who is always present with the human race, united to and mingled with his own creation . . . and who became flesh, is himself Jesus Christ." One of us will go so far as to deny that what eternally precedes "became flesh" is any actual unincarnate state of the Logos; the other would stress more the historical newness marked by the birth to Mary, and so speak somewhat more definitely of a pre-incarnate Logos.[79]

It need not be said that Jenson is the "one" and Gunton "the other" in this. For Jenson, the Son is Jesus, and for Gunton, it would be better put other way round: Jesus is the Son. The point of difference has to do with the tense of the *is* in the identity statement here, for Gunton there *is* no such thing as a *logos asarkos,* and for Jenson there is and *never was* such

---

78. Ibid., 85.
79. Gunton and Jenson, "The Logos Ensarkos and Reason," unpublished, 81.

a thing. Once again, the concern is with what we might call the "timing" of the incarnation. We are asking after the chronology of what happens in God, after the *when* and *how* of the mediation accomplished in the incarnation between God and his world.

There are at least two issues on the table here. On the one hand there are the implications the incarnation has for theology about creation, and on the other there are those it has for theology about revelation. And although Jenson and Gunton are together on the latter—"We are in any case agreed that great ascesis must be exercised in saying anything *about* a Logos not incarnate as Jesus"[80]—it is the former that concerns us. What does it mean for Gunton to recognize the "historical newness marked by the birth to Mary," to sustain a theological place for a "pre-incarnate Logos"?

I will simplify for the sake of contrast: for Jenson, as we have seen, talk about the incarnation is first of all about a doctrine of God and then about one of creation, for Gunton the order is, again, the other way round; the doctrine of creation is the presiding theo-logic and doctrine about revelation ought to be set within it. Of course, both theologians would want it both ways, and so we are dealing with a difference of emphasis here and not a choice between alternatives. But as with any direction of even a few degrees, differences at an outset establish widely different results. Jenson can reject a *logos asarkos* because for him the incarnation is primarily an event in God; there is no unincarnate Logos because the Father has always addressed his Son as Jesus. For Gunton, however, the incarnation is first of all an historical event—something that happens in the space and time of creation—and only *as such* an event in the God responsible for this creation. In Jenson's theology, as we have seen, the creation occurs "within" God's life and so to say that Jesus has always been somehow interior to the being of the Trinity is not for him too much of a stretch. But Gunton cut his theological teeth in response to the monisms of process theology and so was always wary of his mentor's panentheism. Gunton's concern was for the ontological integrity of creation as something other than the Creator and so he felt that any concession on the way the life of Jesus occurs in this other is the first step onto a slippery slope toward a collapsing of the two: "We need a little more of a concrete not

---

80. Ibid. This continues: "We agree: there is not and never has been (whatever 'has been' can mean in this context) a Logos not eternally shaped to the flesh he bears, or who can be reliably referenced or evoked apart from reference to that flesh in its historical concreteness" (ibid.).

yet incarnate Son than Jenson has allowed if we are not to evacuate the actual historical event of the incarnation of its full significance."[81]

As we have seen, for Gunton, if God is not first of all other than his creation there is no possibility that he could be somehow related to it. And so any slight against the lodgement in time of Irenaeus' "became flesh" is the thin end of a wedge that would eventually separate the temporal creation from the creator of time. Clearly Gunton wants both. He wants to say that God is also somehow *in* the time he has created through Christ and that he is also *other than* this time. If Jenson's theology is one that has the first but not the second dynamic—an "in" without an "other"—the opposite theology was embodied for Gunton by Augustine and his modern spokespersons. As he saw it, such a view achieves the otherness of God from time without his participation in it. This he rejected because it "introduces a divorce between God's creation action, which is timeless and his saving action which takes time."[82] Gunton saw himself between these two extremes. If Jenson puts time in God, Augustin(ians)[83] put God beyond time, and Gunton tried to "mediate" these two positions by confessing a God who is both in *and* beyond time: "If there is to be true redemption for a temporal but fallen world, it must consist in enabling things to come to their due perfection in and through the process of time."[84] Such a view has its limits however, and we are at their edge in Gunton's Christology:

> It is not a Logos with no relation to Jesus whom we confess but "One Lord Jesus Christ . . . Begotten not Made." Jesus of Nazareth, the one who was begotten in time *is* also and at the same time the one who is eternally begotten. But what is the meaning of that "at the same time"? Here is the place at which our categories simply fail to encompass the mystery, for we have to say two things which appear to be contradictory: that he is Son quite apart from and in advance of being Jesus of Nazareth—for Jesus of Nazareth has a begetting in time—and yet he is not Son apart from being Jesus.[85]

---

81. CDT 2.7.33.12.

82. Gunton, *Father, Son and Holy Spirit*, 137.

83. Gunton's longstanding interlocutor from this school was Paul Helm. See, e.g., Helm, *Eternal God*.

84. Gunton, *Father, Son and Holy Spirit*, 142.

85. Gunton, "And in One Lord," 44.

It is the perennial christological task to say these "two things which appear contradictory" but it is a rare theological skill to say them in a way that opens instead of closes the discussion for further reflection. There is a note of humility between the lines of this theology, a skill rarer still—it is a call for more of the same.

Conclusion

GOD FOR THE TIME-BEING
The Need for a Christological Concept of Mediation

> Until our minds become intent upon the Spirit, Christ, so to speak, lies idle because we coldly contemplate him as outside ourselves—indeed far from us.
>
> —John Calvin.

In the run across so much theology several recurring themes have been reminders of both the scope of questions about the relation between God and world and of the way these questions come to their center in theology about Christ. And although questions about the deity and humanity of Jesus are certainly not any simpler than ones put more broadly in terms of the relation of deity and humanity as such, Christology has proven to be not only a repetition of these questions but also a constructive matrix for their consideration. In a way, the confession that Christ is simultaneously and fully both human and divine is itself an invitation to seek exactly the kind of mediatorial dynamic that has been the aim of this whole study. That there is a creature who exists as the second person of the Trinity may even be just another way of saying that creation only exists in its relation to God as something other than him. Yet again, however, reaching for the doctrine of the Trinity to grapple with the Christology has not made the task much easier; indeed the opposite would at times seem to be the case. Although a doctrine of God in which being is somehow about unity in plurality opens some of the most hopeful ways to understand life in our world, with the need also to confess the singularity of this God come difficult questions about the so-called "principle" of divine unity, and with these even more questions about the source and goal of not just the divine but also human persons. We are clearly within a systematic matrix in which adjustments to certain lines of thought have every affect on most if not all of the others. The task now is to identify some of the effects certain of our themes have had within this web, and so to offer some brief judgments about their feasibility.

~

The most crucial claim in these pages is the one with which I began: Gnosticism is different from the gospel not because it distinguishes God and world too sharply but because it distinguishes them insufficiently. Irenaeus' opponents were theists who thought within the ontological framework bequeathed to them by their Hellenic heritage, and their theology displays its characteristic strengths and weaknesses. The central challenge faced by these Gnostics was to explain the possibility of a benevolent source of being without also imputing to this One the responsibility for evil. Such efforts followed what I called "fictive distance"—various theo-myths compounded to emphasize the very great amount of space between the One God and the world. But so much space proved to have an undesirable effect on the need for theology about a salvific return to this One. With so many mediatorial beings between the source and its worldly affluent, the return journey became clogged, so to speak, to the same degree as its complex theodicy. But complexity is not the heaviest charge Irenaeus laid against this "knowledge falsely so-called"; he also refused the broader way that Gnostic thought plotted God and creation on a single ontological continuum. Placing something—indeed everything—underneath God in this vertical way effectively reduced God from what Irenaeus' faith required of him. For Irenaeus, God is first of all something other than the world and only thereafter a Creator who is related to it through the mediating activity of his "two hands," the Son and the Spirit.

The primary lesson to be learned from Irenaeus is thus the one about Christianity's single ontological alternative. The dualisms for which

Gnostic thought is so well known were but a minor plotline within their larger attempt to do theology about creation and redemption within an essentially monistic metaphysic. Irenaeus realized that without a theology that could say the creation is both *ex nihilo* other than God and at the same time held "two-handedly" in relation to him, there would indeed be only One, and this was plainly at odds with his Biblical starting-point. So it would seem that a very simple metaphor about a Creator with "two hands" established the possibility of exactly the kind of theology required in view of the anti-metaphysical critique of our own era.

But such a possibility had only been established with Irenaeus, and although there were hints of its use in his theology about Christ, they were strained and undeveloped. Cyril and Nestorius offered the chance to see the issue set squarely within a specifically christological framework. Now the need was not for a reply to monistic Gnosticism but to various slights against the integrity of Christ's real humanity and full divinity. Traditionally, Cyril is the hero in this dispute, but his own theology has benefited overmuch from scholarship that often teeters on the hagiographic; this study, with its implicitly Protestant ecclesiologic, has also found space for the merits of Nestorius' efforts. Both pastors thought at a time when the theological preservation of divine immutability was the hallmark of orthodoxy; it was a time when to change meant to go from being one thing to being another altogether. On these terms, Christ's immutability was understood as his irreproachable possession of divine substance. This common commitment offered two alternate forms of confession, and the Alexandrian-Antiochene divide is charted along the differing choices between them. On the one hand, one could say the divine Son took on generic humanity—or "flesh" in Cyril's most common terminology—and in so doing had not himself changed, but had instead changed this flesh into something new. On the other hand, one could say that neither the divine nor the human substance—or "natures" in Nestorius' terms—had changed at all. In the first case there is a "change," and in Alexandria this change is the good news about going from mortal flesh to divine life. In the second case, the good news is very different; it is that humanity has been preserved against such a change and that in Christ it enjoys a kind of gracious "conjunction" with the divine being. With Cyril the dilemma tended toward terms about the "timing" of the incarnation whereas Nestorius seemed more bent on finding "space" for it. In this respect, the opposition between Nestorius and Cyril is a christological version of the choice between otherness and relation. And the fact that neither appears to have been able to imagine a way of having both is one indication that with them we had neared but not yet found our theology of mediation.

Philoponus is a peculiar figure in our study. His own achievements stand squarely within the tradition established by Cyril, but his historical location at the other end of the council of Chalcedon means his theology is a further sharpening of the possibilities available from their common Alexandria. Of particular importance was the way Philoponus recognized the need for some kind of mediatorial locus within the being of Christ. Yet having established space in the creation for an authentic divine-human composite at the incarnation, he was still hard-pressed to explain the actual relation of these two. By making the soul of Christ the intersection of divine and human attributes, he only drove deeper into Christ the presiding conundrum about what is actually happening there. In this respect the idea that the soul of Christ somehow mediates between the divine and the human is similar to Cyril's use of theology about the communication of attributes. Both concepts attempt to describe a metaphysical event in the being of Christ with distinctly mechanical terms. Cyril and Philoponus both referred to the way that the duality of humanity and divinity in Christ is a dynamic that could be discerned "only in theory," and their similar but different appeals to either a concept (the *communicatio*) or a thing (the soul of Christ) for describing or locating the mediatorial event in Christ is the corollary to this deferral. The cause and result of this trend coincide: for both Alexandrians the single agent of the incarnational economy is the Logos, and so there is a both a distinctly mechanical tone to the relation of divine and human at the incarnation and a conspicuous absence of the Spirit at points where our later interlocutors had much to say of him.

By the time we reached the Reformers our sense of the dilemma about how God and the world could coexist in a way that meant neither the collapsing of God into the world nor the submerging of the world into God had reached a point where our strictly ontological concerns needed some theological grounding, and Luther provided that. The especially dialectic nature of Luther's thought offered a reminder of the epistemic tensions within this issue and also one about the impossibility of its purely abstract consideration. Yet Luther's theology also recovered certain Alexandrian contours and his development of the communication of attributes is perhaps especially important in this respect. With Luther we came again to the climax of this school of thought in its theology about the way the traffic of human and divine attributes in Christ functions as a paradigm for the deification of the Christian. We heard talk about the way the humanity of Christ was transformed into the power of the Godhead when it was assumed by the Son, and about the way his flesh, when taken hold of by faith or at the Eucharist, extends this same effect to the believer through a salvific union with Christ. For Luther, there is a deliberate immediacy of God in Christ. And his specific drive to secure the sovereignty of this God in salvation was an opportunity to observe the way his theology, much like Cyril's, tends to offer very little space for human agency, be it that of Jesus or his followers. But Luther does not simply repeat Alexandrian tensions. His specific mandate was to grapple with the substantialist foundations to the way Augustinian notions of grace had been repackaged by Aquinas. His suggestions opened the way for a specifically "theological" theology—the possibility that Christian thought might provide its own rationale for understanding how God and the world are related.

Having embraced a degree of faithful ambiguity with Luther we returned to the more ambitious tone of this project with the thought of John Calvin. Up to this point, with the exception of Irenaeus, theology about creation *followed* theology about salvation, but not with Calvin. Of especial significance in his replies to Stancaro was Calvin's insistence that even prior to the fall, the Son was already the Mediator between God and man. Calvin rejected categorically the false alternatives offered by Stancaro—either Christ mediated only in his human nature or he is not fully God. For Calvin, such logic only betrayed the critical flaw in Stancaro's Arius-paranoia. In Stancaro's logic, any suggestion that Christ was somehow *between* God and creation meant that he was therefore less than God. And this led Stancaro to simply adapt the then established practice of displacing the theological intent of the communication of attributes (i.e., the preservation of a single subject Christology) with its unfortunate hermeneutical convenience of splitting up various actions of Christ between his two natures. Like his apparent ignorance or his suffering in the flesh, Stancaro concluded, the mediation of Christ ought to be ascribed only to Christ's human nature. And in this respect Stancaro's theology exhibits the crucial flaw with the communication of attributes: it tends to reify the natures of Christ and so eventuate either Nestorian or Eutychean theologies of creation and redemption. Calvin's response was both brilliant and laden with another recurring problem: "the eternal Word" is always the one through whom God relates to his world, both as

Creator and Redeemer. There is indeed a single subject in Calvin's Christology but, once again like Cyril, this single-subject "Word" is effectively a *logos asarkos,* and so not necessarily the one Christians know as Jesus Christ. For Calvin, God creates via his divine *fiat* and not necessarily his divine *filius.*

At this point we had covered much of the christological possibilities available for imagining the relation of God and world in late-Ancient and Medieval theology. Certain constructive ideas had emerged, a number of problematic directions had been observed, and difficult questions had several times recurred. The leap into our own era loosened the dilemma afresh by providing another level to this study and with it the last locus for consideration: the being of God.

Despite the fact that my appraisal of John Zizioulas had a mostly critical tone, the critique took for granted the fundamental break-through of his thought: being is not first substantial then relational, but *vice versa.* The new possibilities made available by such a restructuring are immense, and although Zizioulas takes his own insights in a distinctly Alexandrian direction, they need not go that way. By embracing what I have called "existential Hellenism" at the center of his theology, Zizioulas retains a need for personal security against necessity and non-being. The result is a theological metanarrative that plots salvation history along lines very similar to the "vertical" ones in the Gnostic thought opposed by Irenaeus. With the particularity of the Father ontologically prior to the triune relations, and by imagining salvation in terms of freedom from "biological" restriction, Zizioulas binds himself to repeat a Christology in which the incarnation is a soteriological paradigm for *theosis.* Together these doctrines establish not just a priority of soteriology over theology of creation but a functional opposing of the two. The cause of this opposition in Zizioulas's thought is likely the way his theology tends to wrestle with monism as an internal possibility and the way this leaves him to imagine freedom as a kind of existential catharsis from "totality." The effect, in short, tends to suggest a salvation *from* creation instead of one *of* it.

The parallels between Zizioulas and Robert Jenson are perhaps a nod to the oft-suggested ones between Luther and Alexandria, but the parallels are only broad and the particular strength of Jenson's thought is in its finer lines. With Jenson we came to questions about the nature of space-time itself; his suggestions, while not all to be accepted, were found to be of such revisionary calibre as to inspire similar effort toward a truly Trinitarian rationale for the relation between God and world. Of particular interest was the crucial appearance of the Spirit in Jenson's theology. Now God is no longer separated from time by his own ontological aversion to it but is rather its three "poles." In this respect, Jenson imbibes the spirit of Philoponus: whatever we want to say about space and time must *follow* from our confession of the gospel. Yet "confession" is operative here. Jenson's fidelity to Luther, coupled with his particular affinity for Hegel, brings him to conclusions similar in consequence to Zizioulas's theology and to that of Cyril behind them. His absolute rejection of a *logos asarkos* on the other hand, while a first in this study, brings the problematic dogmum around to its equally problematic corollary: If Jesus *is*—unqualifiedly—the Son, then what significance is left in the particular historical contingencies of his human life? If the "economic" Trinity *is*—unqualifiedly—the "immanent" Trinity, what theological weight remains in the economy?

These were questions forefront in the latest of Colin Gunton's works, and his consequent commitment to the divine economy made him an ideal final subject. In this respect Gunton allowed us to both extend our path across our modern theological terrain and to recapitulate many of the ones left unfollowed at our start with Irenaeus. In Gunton's thought, we had the possibilities and problems raised by the other seven, and an attempt to hold the whole thing together with Irenaeus' "two hands." For Gunton, theology begins in the recognition of Jesus's full humanity—the incarnate Son is a particular man enabled by the Spirit to fully obey the Father. And the placement of the Spirit here is the crux. For Gunton, everything to be said about God and creation starts from how this particular man somehow accomplished everything the Gospel says he did, and that "somehow" is the Spirit. The doctrine of the Trinity is operative at the first stages and throughout Gunton's theology. Indeed, the stated objective in the majority of his work is the finding in theology about the Trinity ways with which to imagine and explain precisely what this whole project is about: how God is both other than the world and related to it in a way that compromises neither of these. And although Gunton did indeed locate this question in deliberately christological terms, his application of what some have called a "heavy pneumatology"[1] meant he could reject as unnecessary many of the traditional apparati for understanding the relation of the two natures of Christ. Theology about the communication of attributes was an *alternative* to pneumatology for Gunton; it was a

---

1. A passing quip I once overheard from one of Gunton's nearest theological friends, John Webster.

conceptual device that compounded a needless conundrum at a point in theology where the personal activity of the Spirit is both more reflective of the divine economy and, coincidentally, more theologically robust. But Gunton's fidelity to the divine economy coupled with his penchant for particularity led him to a lately made change of course in his doctrine of God. Whereas he had long imagined the triune communion to be the final locus of divine unity, the idea that the Father—a particular person—somehow causes the being of the Son and the Spirit replaced this earlier view. This is an item of a doctrine of God that invoked some criticism in my treatments of Zizioulas and Jenson, but the Spirit once again opened in Gunton's theology some routes not available to those two.

~

And so we finished with theology about the Spirit, and in particular with the way including the Spirit in the christological economy opened new space for conceptualizing the God-world relation in Christ. But what does all this do for thinking about mediation? At the very least, it is an attempt to think about creation in terms set by the Christian confession and so by its theology about the Trinity. If Christ is who the church says he is then certain ideas follow, and others do not, and although most of the work in these pages has been about the ontological implications of routes not to be taken, we now come to certain trajectories which offer possibilities for the way ahead.

Having tracked the variations of Gnostic monism—some tending toward dualism, others less so—I can now say that couching Trinitarian theology between dualism on the one hand and monism on the other is to forfeit the enterprise before it begins. With Irenaeus I noted that the duality of God and world is often neglected as guilty by association with Gnostic dualism. But such a judgment has left Christian thought with a false agenda: dualism and monism are not opposite extremes, but the two poles internal to *one and the same* alternative to the mediated duality of God and the world. And if this is the case then any attempt to find a middle ground between these poles will be, in effect, a search for the centre of the one ontological opposite to the gospel. To affirm the incarnation is not to deny the opposition of matter and goodness (or union and conjunction, or humanity and divinity, or substance and personhood, or time and eternity, or cause and communion, or transcendence and immanence, or of any of the other dualisms that haunt the oft-swept rooms of Christian theology); it is rather to deny the *conceivability* of these oppositions.

I return to the work by Pannenberg that began this whole project:

> Christian theology can even maintain . . . that only the trinitarian God, who, in his infiniteness, not only transcends the world but is also infinite within it, can be conceived in a consistently monotheistic fashion. Every doctrine of God which simply sets God over against the world as transcendent actually thinks of God as a correlate to the world and as limited by his position *vis-à-vis* the world.[2]

So what is it about the doctrine of the Trinity that makes such a conception possible? In short, it is the way that it allows the Church to proclaim a theology that has it both ways. With both of God's hands holding the world to and apart from him, there is the possibility of a relation that does not dissolve into monism and an otherness that does not dissolve into dualism. Thus one of the crucial effects of this study has been an awareness of the ontological sameness of monism and dualism. In this respect, single-handed christologies and their consequent theologies of mediation require a choice between relation and otherness—the one "hand" able only to either distinguish or to unite, but not both. In Alexandria and its later manifestations this meant a theology in which God's immanence was dogma and his distinction from the world either a temporary problem or a theoretical mystery. In Antioch and its later manifestations the choice was for a theology in which God's transcendence was dogma and his relation to the world either superficial or inexplicable. The choice between these two theologies is also observable along the timeline of broader Western thought; Enlightenment deism preferring a transcendence of God over the world, and the response of our own era choosing instead either atheistic or pantheistic immanence. But, to repeat, the differences between these choices are relative. Both find their ontological terms within the one alternative to the story about how God mediates his own being and that of the world through the way the Spirit enables Jesus to be an obedient human.

∼

In sum, the Spirit enables the incarnate Son to be fully human and this "enabling" is the possibility of christological mediation. Yet we could take

---

2. Pannenberg, "Problems of a Trinitarian Doctrine of God," 256.

this line of thought even further than Gunton finally did: it cannot be just the Spirit who mediates between the humanity of the Son and the Father, for this would be to drop one "hand" at the most crucial juncture in Christian theology. If all of creation is mediated to the Father through the Son by the Spirit then we ought, I think, extend that insight even to the humanity of this Son. The danger here is of course a kind of naïve docetism, or perhaps a somewhat more complex Nestorianism, but neither need apply: the "humanity" of the Son is not a "thing"; it must not be reified. Here Zizioulas can make his crucial contribution. Although he himself identified only one "constitutive *schesis*" in the being of Jesus—the "triune" one—why not double this to include also Christ's human relations? This would suggest that the "hypostatic" union is not about the compatibility of two otherwise incommensurable entities, but that it is rather about the way in which the Son can be held by the Spirit in relation to the Father as the Only-begotten while simultaneously being held—indeed "enabled"—by the same Spirit in relation to everything else as the obedient man Jesus Christ. In this respect the confession about the conception of Jesus by the Holy Spirit need not refer merely to a punctilliar event lodged between two points in the linear past, but rather to some kind of pneumatologically mediated perpetual event. Christ's double *homoousion* on these terms is not a "con-substance-iality" but an on-going simultaneity of being-in-relation. Maybe instead of a dual-substance Christ somehow moving spatially through an intersection of time and eternity we have a dual-*schesis* Christ moving quite plainly through space-time.

I will come back to how this supposedly spatio-temporal Christ can also be eternal, but for now we should notice that such a concept allows us to say that Christ is a particular person for the same reasons everyone else is: he is recognizable by other persons as the one with whom they have particular relations, and this relational "recognition" is ontologically causative. His humanity consists of being recognized by the Father, the Spirit, and creatures as Jesus, and his divinity is his recognition by at least the Father and the Spirit as the eternal Son.

The value of this logic extends even into the discussion about the difference between God and everything else. Without constitutive relations the tradition has been left to recur to *a priori* beliefs about what it *must* mean to be divine and setting those attributes in contrast with what it *must* mean to be created. The result, as we have seen, has been a long prevalence of things like divine immutability, timelessness, substantial differences, and the rest. And, more to the point of our present concern, such a discussion has meant the concretization of a conundrum over the relation of the two natures of Christ: how on earth can this one be both immutable and mutable, timeless and temporal, one substance and another? And this brings us to what Jenson has gathered from others in our study: substance in Christology is indeed the problem when it comes to understanding God's relation to time, but it is not problematic *as such*, rather only so when it *precedes* relationality. Christ cannot be simultaneously two things—Philoponus' achievements notwithstanding—but he can be simultaneously in two different forms of relation. If substantiality has a place in Christian theology at all, it cannot be as the *ground* of Creator-creation otherness but only its result.

Along this line even the old chestnut about divine immutability might be sustainable. The Son's identity does not change when he begins a new set of creaturely relations since the newness marked by the incarnation does not alter the way his being is realized in the triune communion, it only expands the number of possible personal relations and so opens the triune life to creatures other than this Creator.

One of the primary effects of this study has been the realization that whenever we resort to Christ's divinity to identify him within humanity as a whole we risk losing that which makes this identification significant, namely his authentic humanity. But when the particular relations the Son enjoys with the Father and the Spirit are instead the basis of his identity, the uniqueness of Jesus need not be propped up by recourse to his divinity (and thus a submerging in it of his humanity), but due simply to the particular way the Spirit holds him in relation to other persons, to the Father and to the rest of humanity. In this respect Jesus is not unique among humans because he is divine, but simply because he is human, and all humans are unique. The same point in the other direction would similarly support Christ's triune particularity: he is not unique among the triune Persons because he is a creature—as Stancaro's anti-Arian logic would require—rather, he is divine, and all divine persons are unique. The universal significance of Jesus, therefore, is due neither to his possession of "generic" humanity nor to an effect attributable only to his "transcendent" divinity, but to the way the Spirit mediates his relation to any other human person to whom this Spirit introduces him. The saving relation between the Christian and Jesus is thus one according to the same form as any other human relation, it is one that is opened and enabled by the self-effacing, transcendent Spirit.

Such theology perhaps warrants a final dip into the problem of a *logos asarkos*. The paradox at its centre arises from an apparent tautology: the past reality of a non-creatured Son would appear to be a necessary corollary to the confession about the *ex nihilo* origin of creation. Leaving aside for the moment the implicitly linear notion of time in this, it is clear that matter was not co-eternal with God prior to creation, and that the Son was. The result of such logic has meant the presence in the Christian tradition of a figure with at least as much theological significance as Jesus but one which may or may not actually *be* this Jesus.

But on the terms just sketched, the change from a *logos asarkos* to a *logos ensarkos* is not one of identity—nor indeed one of single subjectivity—but rather one about the new relations God opens to himself when he creates something. And it is the close aligning of theology about the reality of a universe alongside God and that of the creaturely relations of Jesus started within it at the incarnation which brings together the often polarized doctrines of creation and redemption. Indeed the proximity here of creation and redemption suggests the question about what God was doing before the creation of the world is the same one (perhaps even deserving the same answer!) as the question about the identity of the Son before the incarnation. In this respect the dilemma over a *logos asarkos* is not solved but it is perhaps mitigated.

A final flurry of speculation will get us back to the nature of time.

Who walked in the pre-Fall garden? Who spoke with Abraham and wrestled with Jacob? Who endured Nebuchadnezzar's furnace? Quite simply, this must have been Jesus. That God has tensed himself in history and yet remains the creative centre of the time before and after this finite event at least means that the pre-incarnate theophanies are somehow ontologically continuous with the Jesus still to come. Yet how can this be? How could Jesus, so to speak, precede himself? One rather speculative suggestion presents itself:

To begin, we to need to follow Irenaeus and confess that consummated humanity is somehow *more* creaturely than the backwards version we now witness and experience. From here we could go on to say that the resurrected Christ was not just the Image of God but had become the consummated Image of God; humanity with all of its fully realized, eschatological attributes. This could mean the new body of Jesus was not less material than his mortal version, but more so; that he was somehow more intensely physical after his resurrection so that maybe he was able to pass through closed doors not because he was immaterial but because those doors and walls were somehow *less* material than he. From here we could further imagine that the consummation of his tensed constitution had similarly radical implications for his temporality. When we understand the resurrection of Jesus as the consummation of his humanity and his ascension as his consequent going ahead to the consummation of space-time—his hiddenness in the future—it is conceivable that to be a eschatological human entails not a Hellenic escape from time but an affirmative *intensification* of one's temporality. This could allow for the possibility of what we somewhat awkwardly refer to as *time-travel*. It would mean that Jesus was not able to go ahead to the future by virtue of a divinizing return to an atemporal Godhead, but as a feature of the new rules of his consummated *humanity*. If this is allowable, it opens the conceptually acrobatic possibility of his appearance in the pre-incarnational past as the consummated Jesus he was after his resurrection.

And so what is space-time on such a model? Whatever it be, theoretical physics should neither displace our theology nor run a dualizing second narrative. If we are approaching truth then knowledge from different premises should start to converge.

Maybe contemporary illustrations of the so-called "Big-Bang" are right. Maybe time is best sketched on neither a line nor a circle but along with space as a kind of *cone*. There need not be anything especially "meta" about physics on this model, but it is perhaps possible to be theological about it: if Jesus was in the beginning with God—if all things were created by and through *Jesus*—maybe the ontological singularity at the base of the cone is whatever happened at the start of it all in Mary's womb?

BIBLIOGRAPHY

Adams, Marilyn McCord. *William Ockham*. 2 vols. Notre Dame: University of Notre Dame Press, 1987.
Althaus, Paul. *The Theology of Martin Luther*. Translated by Robert Schultz. Philadelphia: Fortress, 1966.
Balthasar, Hans Urs von. *The Scandal of the Incarnation: Irenaeus against the Heresies*. Translated by John Saward. San Francisco: Ignatius, 1990.
Barnes, Michel Rene. "Augustine in Contemporary Trinitarian Theology." *Theological Studies* 56 (1995) 237–50.
———. "De Regnon Reconsidered." *Augustinian Studies* 26 (1995) 51–79.
Barth, Karl. *Church Dogmatics*. 2/1: *The Doctrine of God*. Translated by T. H. L. Parker et al. Edited by G. W. Bromiley and T. F. Torrance. Edinburgh: T. & T. Clark, 1957.
Battles, Ford Lewis. "Calculus Fidei." In *Calvinus Ecclesiae Doctor*, edited by Wilhelm Neusner, 85–110. Kampen: Kok, 1978.
———. "God Was Accommodating Himself to Human Capacity." In *Readings in Calvin's Theology*, edited by Donald McKim, 21–42. Grand Rapids: Baker, 1984.
Berdyaev, Nikolai. *The Russian Idea*. Translated by R. M. French. New York: Lindisfarne, 1992.
Boersma, Hans. "Irenaeus, Derrida, and Hospitality: On the Eschatological Overcoming of Violence." *Modern Theology* 19, no. 2 (2003) 163–80.
Booth, Edward G. T. "John Philoponus: Christian and Aristotelian Conversion." *Studia Patristica* 17, no. 1 (1982) 407–11.
Brecht, M. *Martin Luther: Sein Weg Zur Reformation 1483–1521*. Stuttgart: Calwer, 1981.
Buckley, Michael. *At the Origins of Modern Atheism*. New Haven: Yale University Press, 1987.
Butin, Philip Walker. *Revelation, Redemption and Response*. New York: Oxford University Press, 1995.
Calvin, John. *Institutes of the Christian Religion*. Translated by F. L. Battles. Edited by J. T. McNeill. Library of Christian Classics 20. Philadelphia: Westminster, 1960.
———. *Ionannis Calvini Opera quae supersunt Omnia*. Edited by Wilhelm Baum, Edward Cunitz, and Edward Reuss. 59 vols. *Corpus Reformatorum* [CR], vols. 29–87. Brunswick, CA: Schwetchke & Son, 1863–1900.
———. *Ioannis Calvini Opera Selecta*. Edited by Peter Barth, Wilhelm Niesel, and Doris Scheuner. 5 vols. Munich: Kaiser, 1926–1952.

———. *New Testament Commentaries*. 12 vols. Edited by David Torrance and Thomas F. Torrance. Grand Rapids: Eerdmans, 1959.
Canlis, Julie. "Being Made Human: The Significance of Creation for Irenaeus' Doctrine of Participation." *Scottish Journal of Theology* 58, no. 4 (2005) 434–54.
Carlson, Arnold. "Luther and the Doctrine of the Holy Spirit." *Lutheran Quarterly* 11 (1959) 135–46.
Chadwick, Henry. *The Church in Ancient Society. From Galilee to Gregory the Great.* Oxford History of the Christian Church. Oxford: Oxford University Press, 2001.
———. "Eucharist and Christology in the Nestorian Controversy." *Journal of Theological Studies* 11 (1951) 145–64.
———. "Philoponus the Christian Theologian." In *Philoponus and the Rejection of Aristotelian Science*, edited by Richard Sorabji, 41–56. London: Duckworth, 1987.
Congar, Yves. "Considerations and Reflections on the Christology of Luther." In *Dialogue between Christians: Catholic Contributions to Ecumenism*, 372–406. London: Chapman, 1966.
Cross, Richard. "Alloiosis in the Christology of Zwingli." *Journal of Theological Studies* 47 (1996) 105–22.
———. "On Generic and Derivation Views of God's Trinitarian Substance." *Scottish Journal of Theology* 56, no. 4 (2003) 464–80.
Cumin, Paul. "Looking for Personal Space in the Theology of John Zizioulas." *International Journal of Systematic Theology* 8, no. 4 (2006) 356–70.
———. "Robert Jenson and the Spirit of it All, Or You (Sometimes) Wonder Where Everything Else Went." *Scottish Journal of Theology* 60, no. 2 (2007) 161–79.
———. "The Taste of Cake: Relation and Otherness with Colin Gunton and the Strong Second Hand of God." In *The Theology of Colin Gunton*, edited by Lincoln Harvey, 65–85. London: T. & T. Clark, 2010.
Dalferth, Ingolf. "The Visible and the Invisible: Luther's Legacy of a Theological Theology." In *England and Germany: Studies in Theological Diplomacy*, edited by S. W. Sykes, 25, 15–44. Frankfurt: Lang, 1982.
Documents of the Christian Church. 3rd edited by Edited by Henry Bettenson and Chris Maunder. Oxford: Oxford University Press, 1999.
Dorner, Issac Augustus. *History of the Development of the Doctrine of the Person of Christ*. Translated by D. W. Simon. Edinburgh: T. & T. Clark, 1866.
Dostoevsky, Fyodor. *Demons*. Translated by Richard Pevear and Larissa Volokhovsky. London: Vintage, 1994.
Drews, Paul. *Die Disputationen Dr. Martin Luther*. Göttingen: Vandenhoeck & Ruprecht, 1895.
Driver, G. R., and L. Hodgson, editors. *The Bazaar of Heracleides*. Oxford: Oxford University Press, 1925.
Edmondson, Stephen. *Calvin's Christology*. Cambridge: University Press, 2004.
Farrow, Douglas. "St Irenaeus of Lyons: The Church and the World." *Pro Ecclesia* 4 (1995) 333–55.
Gebremedhin, Ezra. *Life-Giving Blessing: An Inquiry into the Eucharistic Doctrine of Cyril of Alexandria*. Uppsala: Borgströms, 1977.
Gilson, Etienne. *A History of Christian Philosophy in the Middle Ages*. London: Sheed & Ward, 1978.
Gogarten, Friedrich. *Der Mensch Zwischen Gott Und Welt*. Stuttgart: Vorwerk, 1956.

Gould, Graham. "Cyril of Alexandria and the Formula of Reunion." *The Downside Review* 106, no. 365 (1998) 235–52.
Grant, Robert M. *Irenaeus of Lyons*. Early Church Fathers. London: Routledge, 1997.
Greer, Rowan A. "The Dog and the Mushrooms: Irenaeus's View of the Valentinians Assessed." In *The Rediscovery of Gnosticism*, edited by Bentley Layton, 1:146–71. Leiden: Brill, 1980.
Grillmeier, Aloys. *Christ in Christian Tradition*. Vol. 1, *From the Apostolic Age to Chalcedon (451)*. Part 1, *The Birth of Christology*. Translated by John Bowden. 2nd rev. edited by Atlanta: Knox, 1975.
Grillmeir, Aloys, and Theresia Hainthaler. *Christ in Christian Tradition*. Vol. 2, *From the Council of Chalcedon (451) to Gregory the Great*. Part 4, *The Church of Alexandria with Nubia and Ethiopia after 451*. Translated by O. C. Dean Jr. London: Mowbray, 1996.
Gunton, Colin. "And in One Lord, Jesus Christ . . . Begotten, Not Made." In *Nicene Christianity: The Future for a New Ecumenism*, edited by Christopher Seitz, 35–48. Grand Rapids: Brazos, 2001.
———. *A Brief Theology of Revelation*. Edinburgh: T. & T. Clark, 1995.
———. *A Christian Dogmatic Theology*. Vol. 1, *The Triune God: A Doctrine of the Trinity as Though Jesus Makes a Difference*. Unpublished typescript. 2003.
———. "Creation and Mediation in the Theology of Robert W. Jenson: An Encounter and a Convergence." In *Trinity, Time and Church. A Response to the Theology of Robert W. Jenson*, edited by Colin Gunton, 80–93. Grand Rapids: Eerdmans, 2000.
———. *Father, Son and Holy Spirit: Essays toward a Fully Trinitarian Theology*. London: T. & T. Clark, 2003.
———. "God, Grace and Freedom." In *God and Freedom. Essays in Historical and Systematic Theology*, edited by Colin Gunton, 119–33. Edinburgh: T. & T. Clark, 1995.
———. "Immanence and Otherness: Divine Sovereignty and Human Freedom in the Theology of Robert W. Jenson." *Dialog* 30, no. 1 (1991) 17–26.
———. *The One, the Three and the Many: God, Creation and the Culture of Modernity*. Cambridge: Cambridge University Press, 1993.
———. "Persons and Particularity." Unpublished typescript. 2003.
———. *The Promise of Trinitarian Theology*. 2nd edited by Edinburgh: T.& T. Clark, 1997.
———. Review of *Systematic Theology, Volume 1: The Triune God* by Robert Jenson. *Pro Ecclesia* 8, no. 3 (1999) 364–65.
———. "The Spirit in the Trinity." In *The Forgotten Trinity. A Selection of Papers Presented to the B.C.C. Study Commission on Trinitarian Doctrine Today*, edited by Alasdair Heron, 3, 123–35. London: British Council of Churches, 1991.
———. *The Triune Creator: A Historical and Systematic Study*. Edinburgh Studies in Constructive Theology. Edinburgh: Edinburgh University Press, 1998.
———. "Two Dogmas Revisited: Edward Irvings' Christology." *Scottish Journal of Theology* 41 (1988) 359–67.
Gunton, Colin, and Robert Jenson. "The Logos Ensarkos and Reason." Unpublished typescript. January 2003.
Haardt, Robert. *Gnosis. Character and Testimony*. Translated by J. F. Hendry. Leiden: Brill, 1971.

Haas, Frans A. J. de. *John Philoponus' New Definition of Prime Matter: Aspects of Its Background in Neoplatonic and the Ancient Commentary Tradition.* Leiden: Brill, 1996.

Hardy, Daniel. "Coleridge on the Trinity." *Anglican Theological Review* 69, no. 1 (1987) 145–55.

Hart, Trevor. "Irenaeus, Recapitulation and Physical Redemption." In *Christ in Our Place: The Humanity of God in Christ for the Reconciliation of the World. Essays Presented to Professor James Torrance*, edited by T. A. Hart and D. P. Thimell. Exeter: Paternoster, 1989.

Hayes, Zachary. *The Hidden Center: Spirituality and Speculative Christology in St. Bonaventure.* New York: Franciscan Institute, 1992.

Helm, Paul. *Eternal God: A Study of God without Time.* Oxford: Oxford University Press, 1988.

———. *John Calvin's Ideas.* Oxford: University Press, 2005.

Helmer, Christine. *The Trinity and Martin Luther. A Study on the Relationship between Genre, Language and the Trinity in Luther's Works (1523–1546).* Mainz: Von Zabern, 1999.

Huck, F. "Die Entwicklung Der Christologie Luthers Von Der Psalmen- Zur Roemervorlesung." *Theol. Stud. Krit.* 102, Lutherana VI (1930) 61–152.

Irenaeus: Against Heresies. Translated by A. Roberts and J. Donaldson. *Ante-Nicene Fathers [ANF]*, edited by A. Roberts and J. Donaldson, 1:315–567. Grand Rapids: Eerdmans, 1880. Reprint, Peabody, MA: Hendrickson, 1996.

Jenson, Robert. "The Body of God's Presence: A Trinitarian Theory." In *Creation, Christ and Culture. Studies in Honor of T.F. Torrance*, edited by Richard McKinney, 82–91. Edinburgh: T. & T. Clark, 1976.

———. "Cosmic Spirit." In *Christian Dogmatics*, edited by Carl Braaten and Robert Jenson, 165–78. Philadelphia: Fortress, 1984.

———. "Creator and Creature." *International Journal of Systematic Theology* 4, no. 2 (2002) 217–21.

———. "For Us . . . He Was Made Man." In *Nicene Christianity*, edited by Christopher Seitz, 75–86. Grand Rapids: Eerdmans, 2002.

———. *God after God: The God of the Past and the God of the Future, Seen in the Work of Karl Barth.* New York: Bobbs-Merrill, 1969.

———. "The Great Transformation." In *The Last Things. Biblical and Theological Perspectives on Eschatology*, edited by Carl Braaten and Robert Jenson, 33–42. Grand Rapids: Eerdmans, 2002.

———. "Jesus in the Trinity." *Pro Ecclesia* 8, no. 3 (1999) 308–318.

———. "Jesus in the Trinity: Wolfhart Pannenberg's Christology and Doctrine of the Trinity." In *The Theology of Wolfhart Pannenberg*, edited by Carl E. Braaten and Philip Clayton, 189–206. Minneapolis: Augsburg, 1988.

———. "Pneumatological Soteriology." In *Christian Dogmatics*, edited by Robert Jenson and Carl Braaten, 2:124–142. Philadelphia: Fortress, 1984.

———. *Systematic Theology.* 2 vols. New York: Oxford University Press, 1997–1999.

———. "Theosis." *Dialog* 32 (1993) 108–12.

———. *The Triune Identity. God According to the Gospel.* Philadelphia: Fortress, 1982.

———. "You Wonder Where the Spirit Went." *Pro Ecclesia* 2, no. 3 (1993) 296–304.

Jonas, Hans. *The Gnostic Religion: The Message of the Alien God and the Beginnings of Christianity.* Boston: Beacon Hill, 1958.

Juntunen, Sammeli. "Luther and Metaphysics: What Is the Structure of Being According to Luther?" In *Union with Christ. The New Finnish Interpretation of Luther*, edited by Robert Jenson and Carl Braaten, 129–60. Grand Rapids: Eerdmans, 1998.

Kahler, E. *Die Religion in Geschichte und Gegenwart*. Vol. 3. 3rd edition Tübingen, 1956–1965.

Keating, Daniel. "Divinization in Cyril: The Appropriation of Divine Life." In *The Theology of St. Cyril of Alexandria: A Critical Appreciation*, edited by Thomas Weinandy and Daniel Keating, 149–86. London: T. & T. Clark, 2003.

———. *Theosis*. London: T. & T. Clark, 2005.

Kelly, J. N. D. *Early Christian Doctrines*. 5th rev. edition London: Continuum, 2003.

Kolb, Robert. "Luther on the Theology of the Cross." *Lutheran Quarterly* 16, no. 4 (2003) 443–67.

Landgraf, A. M. *Dogmengeschichte Der Frühscholastick*. Vol. 2/2. Regensburg: Puster, 1952–1965.

Lang, Uwe Michael. *John Philoponus and the Controversies over Chalcedon in the Sixth Century: A Study and Translation of the Arbiter*. Spicilegium Sacrum Lovaniense 47. Etudes Et Documents. Leuven: Peeters, 2001.

Lienhard, Marc. "La Doctrine Du Saint-Esprit Chez Luther." *Verbum Caro* 19, no. 76 (1965) 11–38.

———. *Luther: Witness to Jesus Christ: Stages and Themes of the Reformer's Christology*. Philadelphia: Augsburg, 1982.

Lloyd, A. C. *The Anatomy of Neoplatonism*. Oxford: Oxford University Press, 1990.

Logan, Alistair H. B. *Gnostic Truth and Christian Heresy: A Study in the History of Gnosticism*. Edinburgh: T. & T. Clark, 1996.

Lohr, Winrich. "Gnostic Determinism Reconsidered." *Vigilae Christianae* 46 (1992) 381–90.

Lohse, Bernhard. *Martin Luther's Theology: Its Historical and Systematic Development*. Translated by Roy Harrisville. Reprint, Edinburgh: T. & T. Clark, 2000.

Loofs, F. *Nestoriana: Die Fragmente Des Nestorius*. Halle: Niemeyer, 1905.

Loux, Michael, editor. *William of Ockham's Summa Logicae*. Vol. 1. Notre Dame: University of Notre Dame Press, 1974.

Luther, Martin. "Auslegung D. Martin Luthers Uber Das Sechste, Siebende Und Achte Capitel Des Evangelisten Joannis." In *Luthers Werke: Kritische Gesamtausgabe*, 33. Weimar: Böhlaus, 1883 -.

———. "The Disputation Concerning the Passage: 'the Word Was Made Flesh' (John 1:14) of 1539." In *Luther's Works*, edited by Martin Lehmann, 38:239 ff. Philadelphia: Fortress, 1971.

———. "Die Disputation de Divinitate et Humanite Christi." In *Werke: Kritische Gesammtausgabe*, 39/2:92–121. Weimar: Böhlaus, 1883 -.

———. "Die Disputation de Sententia: Verbum Caro Factum Est (Joh. 1,14) 1539." In *Luthers Werke: Kritische Gesamtausgabe*, 39/2:3–33. Weimar: Böhlaus, 1883-.

———. *Disputation on the Divinity and Humanity of Christ (1540)*. Translated by Christopher B. Brown. http://www.iclnet.org/pub/resources/text/wittenberg/luther/luther-divinity.txt.

———. "Sermons on the Gospel of St. John Chapters 6–8." *Luther's Works*, edited by Jaroslav Pelikan, 23. St. Louis: Concordia, 1959.

MacCoull, L. S. B. "A New Look at the Career of John Philoponus." *Journal of Early Christian Studies* 3, no. 1 (1995) 47–60.

MacKenzie, Iain M. *Irenaeus's Demonstration of the Apostolic Preaching: A Theological Commentary and Translation*. Aldershot: Ashgate, 2002.
Macquarrie, John. *Christology Revisited* by London: SCM, 1998.
Macro, A. D., and Helen S. Lang. "Introduction." In *On the Eternity of the World: De Aeternitate Mundi. Proclus*, 1–35. Berkeley: University of California Press, 2001.
Mannermaa, Tuomo. *Christ Present in Faith: Luther's View of Justification*. Translated by Kirsi Stjerna. Minneapolis: Fortress, 2005.
Martin, H. "Jean Philopon et La Controverse Tritheite du 6 Siecle." *Studia Patristica* 5 (1962) 519-25.
May, Gerhard. *Creatio Ex Nihilo. The Doctrine of "Creation out of Nothing" in Early Christian Thought*. Translated by A. S. Worrall. Edinburgh: T. & T. Clark, 1994.
McCormack, Bruce L. "For Us and for Our Salvation: Incarnation and Atonement in the Reformed Tradition." *Studies in Reformed Theology and History* 1, no. 2 (1993) 1–38.
McFarland, Thomas. *Coleridge and the Pantheist Tradition*. Oxford: Clarendon, 1969.
McGrath, Alister. *A Life of John Calvin: A Study in the Shaping of Western Culture*. Grand Rapids: Baker, 1990.
McGuckin, John. Introduction to *Cyril of Alexandria: On the Unity of Christ*, edited by John McGuckin. Crestwood, NY: St. Vladimir's Seminary Press, 2000.
———. *Saint Cyril of Alexandria and the Christological Controversy: Its History, Theology and Texts*. Crestwood, NY: St. Vladimir's Seminary Press, 2004.
McGuckin, John, editor. *Cyril of Alexandria: On the Unity of Christ*. Crestwood, NY: St. Vladimir's Seminary Press, 2000.
McKeena, John E. "The 7th Chapter of the Arbiter by John Philoponus." *Quodlibet* 1, no. 3 (1999). Online: http://www.quodlibet.net/articles/mckenna-arbiter.shtml.
Meijering, E. P. *God, Being, History: Studies in Patristic Philosophy*. Oxford: North-Holland, 1975.
Minns, Dennis. *Irenaeus*. London: Chapman, 1994.
Mozley, John. *The Impassibility of God: A Survey of Christian Thought*. Cambridge: Cambridge University Press, 1926.
Mühlenberg, Ekkehard. "Dogma Und Lehre Im Abenland." In *Handbuch Der Dogmen- Und Theologiegeschichte*, by Carl Andresen et al., 1:45–476. Göttingen: Vandenhoeck & Ruprecht, 1982.
Muller, Richard A. *Christ and the Decree: Christology and Predestination in Reformed Theology from Calvin to Perkins*. Durham, NC: Labyrinth, 1986.
Ngien, Dennis. "Chalcedonian Christology and Beyond: Luther's Understanding of the Communicatio Idiomatum." 45 (2004) 54–68.
Niesel, Wilhelm. *The Theology of John Calvin*. Translated by Harold Knight. London: Lutterworth, 1956.
Norris, Richard A. *God and World in Early Christian Theology: A Study in Justin Martyr, Irenaeus, Tertullian and Origen*. London: Black, 1966.
———. "The Transcendence and Freedom of God: Irenaeus, the Greek Tradition and Gnosticism." In *Early Christian Literature and the Classical Intellectual Tradition*, 87–100. Paris: Beauchesne, 1979.
Oberman, Heiko. *The Harvest of Medieval Theology: Gabriel Biel and Late Medieval Nominalism*. Grand Rapids: Eerdmans, 1963.
———. *Luther: Man between God and the Devil*. Translated by Eileen Walliser-Schwarzbart. New York: Doubleday, 1992.

Osborn, Eric. *Irenaeus of Lyons*. Cambridge: Cambridge University Press, 2001.

Pannenberg, Wolfhart. "Problems of a Trinitarian Doctrine of God." *Dialog* 26 (1987) 250–57.

———. *Systematic Theology*. 3 vols. Translated by Geoffrey W. Bromiley. Grand Rapids: Eerdmans, 1991.

Pearson, Birger, editor. *Nag Hammadi Codex VII*. Edited by J. M. Robinson and H. J. Klimkeit. The Coptic Gnostic Library 30. Leiden: Brill, 1996.

Philoponus, John. *Against Aristotle on the Eternity of the World*. Translated by Christian Wildberg. London: Duckworth, 1987.

———. *Arbiter*. In *John Philoponus and the Controversies over Chalcedon in the Sixth Century: A Study and Translation of the Arbiter*, by Uwe Michael Lang, 171–216. Spicilegium Sacrum Lovaniense 47. Etudes Et Documents. Leuven: Peeters, 2001.

———. *Corollaries on Place and Void*. Translated by David Furley. In *Place, Void, and Eternity*, 13–73. Ithaca, NY: Cornell University Press, 1991.

———. *De Aeterntate Mundi Contra Proclum*. Edited by Hugo Rabe. Leipzig: Teubneri, 1899.

———. *De Opificio Mundi Joannis Philoponi Libri VII*. Edited by Gualterus Reichardt. Leipzig: Teubneri, 1897.

Placher, William C. *Unapologetic Theology*. Louisville: Westminster John Knox, 1989.

Prenter, Regin. *Spiritus Creator*. Philadelphia: Muhlenberg, 1953.

Prestige, G. L. *Fathers and Heretics: Six Studies in Dogmatic Faith. The 1940 Bampton Lectures*. London: SPCK, 1958.

Rahner, Karl. *The Trinity*. New York: Herder & Herder, 1970.

Reynders, Bruno. *Lexique Camparé du Texte Grec et des Versions Latine, Armenienne et Syriaque de L'adversus Haereses de Saint Irenee*. 2 vols. CSCO 141–42. Louvain: Durbecq, 1954.

Robinson, J. Armitage. "The Doctrine of the Holy Spirit in Justin and Irenaeus." In *St. Irenaeus—the Demonstration of the Apostolic Preaching*, edited by W. J. Simpson and W. K Clarke. London: SPCK, 1920.

Rudolph, Kurt. *Gnosis: The Nature and History of an Ancient Religion*. Translated by Robert Wilson. Edinburgh: T. & T. Clark, 1983.

Russel, Norman. *Cyril of Alexandria*. Early Church Fathers. London: Routledge, 2000.

Sartre, Jean-Paul. *Existentialism and Humanism*. Translated by Philip Mairet. London: Methuen, 1973.

Schmitt, Charles. "Philoponus' Commentary on Aristotle's *Physics* in the Sixteenth Century." In *Philoponus and the Rejection of Aristotelian Science*, edited by Richard Sorabji, 210–27. London: Duckworth, 1987.

Schoedel, William R. "Enclosing, Not Enclosed: The Early Christian Doctrine of God." In *Early Christian Literature and the Classical Intellectual Tradition*, 75–86. Paris: Beauchesne, 1979.

———. "Gnostic Monism and the Gospel of Truth." In *Rediscovery of Gnosticism*, 379–90. Leiden: Brill, 1980.

———. "Topological Theology and Some Monistic Trends in Gnosticism." In *Essays on the Nag Hammadi Texts in Honor of Alexander Bohlig*, edited by M. Krause, 88–108. Leiden: Brill, 1972.

Schwarz, Reinhard. "Gott Ist Mensch. Zur Lehre von Person Christi Bei den Ockhamisten und Bei Luther." *Zeitschrift für Theologie und Kirche* 63, no. 1 (1966) 289–351.

Schweizer, Alexander. *Die Glaubenslehre der Evangelischreformierten Kirche.* Zurich: Orell, Füssli, 1847.

Schwöbel, Christoph. "The Triune God of Grace: The Doctrine of the Trinity in the Theology of the Reformers." In *The Christian Understanding of God Today,* edited by James M. Byrne, 49-64. Dublin: Columba, 1993.

Scott, Alan. *Origen and the Life of the Stars.* Oxford: Clarendon, 1991.

Sellers, R. V. *Two Ancient Christologies: A Study in the Christological Thought of the Schools of Alexandria and Antioch in the Early History of Christian Doctrine.* London: SPCK, 1954.

Siddals, Ruth. "Logic and Christology in Cyril of Alexandria." *Journal of Theological Studies* 38, no. 2 (1987) 341-67.

Simplicius. *Against Philoponus on the Eternity of the World.* Translated by Christian Wildberg. In *Place, Void and Eternity,* 105-28. Ithaca, NY: Cornell University Press, 1991.

Siorvanes, Lucas. *Proclus: Neo-Platonic Philosophy and Science.* New Haven: Yale University Press, 1996.

Smail, Thomas. "The Holy Trinity and the Resurrection of Jesus." In *Different Gospels,* edited by Andrew Walker, 63-96. London: Hodder & Stoughton, 1988.

Sorabji, Richard. "General Introduction." In *Philoponus against Aristotle on the Eternity of the World.* London: Duckworth, 1987.

―――. *Matter, Space and Motion. Theories in Antiquity and Their Sequel.* Ithaca, NY: Cornell University Press, 1988.

Sorabji, Richard, editor. *Philoponus and the Rejection of Aristotelian Science.* London: Duckworth, 1987.

Starowieyski, M. "Le Titre *Theotokos* avant le Conicle d'Ephese." *Studia Patristica* 19 (1989) 236-42.

Steiger, Johann Anselm. "The Communicatio Idiomatum as the Axle and Motor of Luther's Theology." Translated by Carolyn Schneider. *Lutheran Quarterly* 14, no. 2 (2000) 125-58.

Strohl, H. *Luther Jusqu'en.* Paris: P. U. F., 1962.

Studer, Basil. *Trinity and Incarnation: The Faith of the Early Church.* Translated by Matthias Westerhoff. Edited by Andrew Louth. Edinburgh: T. & T. Clark, 1993.

Tanner, Kathryn. "Jesus Christ." In *The Cambridge Companion to Christian Doctrine,* edited by Colin Gunton, 245-72. Cambridge: University Press, 1997.

Tolpingrud, Mitchell. "Luther's Disputation Concerning the Deity and Humanity of Christ." *Lutheran Quarterly* 10 (1996) 151-78.

Torrance, Alan J. *Persons in Communion: Trinitarian Description and Human Participation.* Edinburgh: T. & T. Clark, 1996.

Torrance, T. F. *The Hermeneutics of John Calvin.* Edinburgh: Scottish Academic, 1988.

―――. *Space, Time and Incarnation.* Edinburgh: T. & T. Clark, 1997.

―――. *Transformation and Convergence in the Frame of Knowledge.* Belfast: Christian Journals, 1984.

Turcescu, Lucian. "'Person' Versus 'Individual,' and Other Modern Misreadings of Gregory of Nyssa." *Modern Theology* 18, no. 4 (2002) 527-39.

Turner, H. E. W. "Nestorius Reconsidered." *Studia Patristica* 13 (1975) 306-21.

Tylenda, Joseph. "Calvin's Understanding of the Communication of Properties." In *Calvin and Calvinism,* edited by Richard Gamble, 8:54-65. New York: Garland, 1992.

———. "Christ the Mediator: Calvin Versus Stancaro." *Calvin Theological Journal* 8 (1972) 5–16.

———. "The Controversy on Christ the Mediator: Calvin's Second Reply to Stancaro." *Calvin Theological Journal* 8 (1972) 131–57.

Van Buren, Paul. *Christ in Our Place: The Substitutionary Character of Calvin's Doctrine of Reconciliation*. Edinburgh: Oliver & Boyd, 1957.

VanDenBroek, Roelof. *Studies in Gnosticism and Alexandrian Christianity*. Edited by J. M. Robinson and H. J. Klimkeit. Nag Hammadi and Manichaean Studies. Leiden: Brill, 1996.

Verrychken, Koenraad. "The Development of Philoponus' Thought and Its Chronology." In *Aristotle Transformed*, edited by Richard Sorabji, 233–74. London: Duckworth.

Volf, Miroslav. *After Our Likeness: The Church as the Image of the Trinity*. Grand Rapids: Eerdmans, 1998.

Weinandy, Thomas. "Cyril and the Mystery of the Incarnation." In *The Theology of Cyril of Alexandria: A Critical Appreciation*, edited by Thomas Weinandy and Daniel Keating, 23–54. London: T. & T. Clark, 2003.

———. *Does God Suffer?* Edinburgh: T. & T. Clark, 2000.

Welch, Lawrence. *Christology and Eucharist in the Early Thought of Cyril of Alexandria*. San Francisco: Catholic Scholars, 1994.

White, Graham. *Luther as Nominalist: A Study on the Logical Methods Used in Martin Luther's Disputations in the Light of Their Medieval Background*. Helsinki: Luther-Agricola Society, 1994.

Wickham, Lionel. *Cyril of Alexandria: Select Letters*. Oxford Early Christian Texts. Oxford: Clarendon, 1983.

Wildberg, Christian. *John Philoponus' Criticism of Aristotle's Theory of Aether*. Berlin: de Gruyter, 1988.

Williams, Michael Allen. *Rethinking "Gnosticism": An Argument for Dismantling a Dubious Category*. Princeton: Princeton University Press, 1996.

Willis, E. David. *Calvin's Catholic Christology: The Function of the So-Called Extra Calvinisticum in Calvin's Theology*. Studies in Medieval and Reformation Thought. Leiden: Brill, 1966.

Wyatt, Peter. *Jesus Christ and Creation in the Theology of John Calvin*. Allison Park, PA: Pickwick, 1996.

Yeago, David. "The Bread of Life: Patristic Christology and Evangelical Soteriology in Martin Luther's Sermons on John 6." *St. Vladimir's Theological Quarterly* 39, no. 3 (1995) 257–79.

Young, Frances. "*Theotokos*: Mary and the Pattern of Fall and Redemption in the Theology of Cyril of Alexandria." In *The Theology of St Cyril of Alexandria: A Critical Appreciation*, edited by Thomas Weinandy and Daniel Keating, 55–74. London: T. & T. Clark, 2003.

Žižek, Slavoj. *The Puppet and the Dwarf. The Perverse Core of Christianity*. Cambridge: MIT Press, 2003.

Zizioulas, John D. *Being as Communion: Studies in Personhood and the Church*. Crestwood, NY: St. Vladimir's Seminary Press, 1985.

———. "The Doctrine of God the Trinity Today: Suggestions for an Ecumenical Study." In *The Forgotten Trinity*, edited by Alistair Heron. London: British Council of Churches, 1989.

———. "The Doctrine of the Holy Trinity: The Significance of the Cappadocian Contribution." In *Trinitarian Theology Today: Essays on Divine Being and Act*, edited by Christoph Schwöbel, 44–60. Edinburgh: T. & T. Clark, 1995.

———. *Eucharist, Bishop, Church: The Unity of the Church in the Divine Eucharist and the Bishop during the First Three Centuries*. Translated by Elizabeth Theoktritoff. Brookline, MA: Holy Cross Orthodox, 2001.

———. "The Father as Cause: A Response to Alan J. Torrance." King's Research Institute in Systematic Theology, King's College London, 1997. Typescript manuscript.

———. "Human Capacity and Human Incapacity: A Theological Exploration of Personhood." *Scottish Journal of Theology* 28, no. 5 (1975) 401–48.

———. "On Being a Person. Towards an Ontology of Personhood." In *Persons Divine and Human*, edited by Colin E. Gunton and Christoph Schwöbel, 33–46. Edinburgh: T. & T. Clark, 1991.

———. "Preserving God's Creation: Three Lectures on Theology and Ecology (2)." *King's Theological Review* 12, no. 2 (1989) 41–45.

———. "Preserving God's Creation: Three Lectures on Theology and Ecology (3)." *King's Theological Review* 13 (1990) 1–5.

———. "The Teaching of the 2nd Ecumenical Council on the Holy Spirit in Historical and Ecumenical Perspective." In *Credo in Spiritum Sanctum. Pisteuo Eis to Pneuma to 'Agion. Atti Del Congresso Teologico Internazionale Di Pneumatologia in Occasione Del 1600 Anniversario Del I Concilio Di Constantinopoli E Del 1550 Anniversario Del Concilio Di Efeso. Roma, 22–26 Marzo 1982*, edited by R. P. Jose Saraiva Martins, 1:29–54. Vatican City: Libreria Editrice Vaticana, 1982.

www.ingramcontent.com/pod-product-compliance
Lightning Source LLC
Chambersburg PA
CBHW062020220426
43662CB00010B/1410